Going Coastal New York City

A Guide to the Waterfront

New York Bight

❝ When it's not serving as a mere footstool for the skyline, the New York waterfront shown to the world through movies is a place of intrigue, romantic and dark. But it can be so much more. It is our place to turn away from crowds – of people and of thoughts – to face a vast openness. In every borough there are quiet fringes that gently nurture patience, waiting for the sunset, a tug on the fishing line, or for the tide to roll in. And the coastal environment is not just to be gazed upon, but to be touched – let saltwater buoy you to the weightless liberation of swimming; let marsh and dune grasses prickle your calves as you shore walk; fill your palm with the delightfully alien textures of seaweed; feel the heave of a wave as you dig your paddle in, lifting your kayak over the crest. Be amazed, anew, at New York City. ❞

Erik Baard

Going Coastal
New York City

A Guide to the Waterfront

Barbara La Rocco

Library of Congress Control Number: 2003091437

ISBN 0-9729803-0-X

Concept & Writing: Barbara La Rocco
Maps: Zhennya Slootskin
Research: Zhennya Slootskin, N. Jessica Ortiz Patacsil, Jeffrey E. Pearson
Editorial Interns: Amy Shields, Kristen DeMarco
Design: Barbara La Rocco, Zhennya Slootskin
Cover Art & Illustrations: Patricia Redding Scanlon (pg. 1, 123, 263)
Beachcombing Illustration: Peggy Kochanoff (pg. 134, 135)
Photos: Jim Crowley (pg. 33, 205) nylighthousephotos.com; Dave Frieder (pg. 149)
davefrieder.com; Etienne Frossard (pg. 52, 125) etiennemf@att.net; Bridget Gorman
(pg. 228); Don Riepe (pg. 129, 133, 141, 222, 237, 248, 253) alsnyc.org; Benjamin
Swett (pg. 3) benjaminswett.com; Noble Maritime Collection (pg. 103); South Street
Seaport Museum (pg. 77, 173)
Maps Sources: Bronx River map (pg. 42) designed by George Colbert. Map provided
for use in this publication by Parnership for Parks, a joint program of City Parks
Foundation and NYC Dept. of Parks & Recreation; Pelham Bay Park map (pg. 46)
provided by City of New York/Parks & Recreation, Van Cortland & Pelham Bay Parks

For promotional sales or sponsorship, call 718-243-9056, email
info@goingcoastal.org or visit www.goingcoastal.org. Copies of this book may
be ordered directly from the publisher.

The sales from this book support the programs of Going Coastal, Inc., a public
benefit corporation that has as its object to promote the responsible use and public
enjoyment of coastal resources.

Published by Going Coastal, Inc.
First printing: March 2004

Printed in the U.S.A.

Acknowledgements

This book is made possible by funding from Furthermore: a program of the J. M. Kaplan Fund, support provided by the Fund for the City of New York and fiscal sponsorship by the New York Chapter of the American Littoral Society.

Going Coastal, Inc. wishes to express our grateful appreciation and acknowledge the waterfront enthusiasts who cooperated in our research and generously contributed narratives, illustrations and photographs for this book: Cy Adler of Shorewalkers; Erik Baard writer; "Wildman" Steve Brill; Norman Brouwer of South Street Seaport Museum; Noah Budnick of Transportation Alternatives; Ann Buttenwieser waterfront planner and author; Arthur Cholakis; Carter Craft of Metropolitan Waterfront Alliance; Jim Crowley author; Brian Cudahy author; Carlotta DeFillo of Staten Island Historical Society; Diana diZerega Wall of NY Unearthed; Barbara Dolensek of City Island Historical Society; Cathy Drew of The River Project; Jim Driscoll of the Queens Historical Society; Owen Foote of Gowanus Canal Dredgers; Marcia Fowle of NYC Audubon Society; Dave Frieder renowned bridge photographer; Etienne Frossard photographer; Tim Hollon of Circle Line; Bob Huszar; Teddy Jefferson & Mark Heath of Swim the Apple; Alex Karinsky of Gotham Surfers; Jason Kempin photographer; Peggy Kochanoff illustrator & author; William Kornblum author; Capt. Brendan McCarthy; Roger Meyer of NY Outrigger; Barbara Newman of the NY Aquarium; Noble Maritime Collection; Vincent Paparo of NY Rowing Assn.; Robert Pirani of Regional Plan Assn.; Marcia Reiss historian and author; Don Riepe Guardian of Jamaica Bay, NY Chapter of American Littoral Society; Theodore W. Scull of the World Ship Society NY Chapter; David Sharps of the Waterfront Museum; Louie Shreiner of Northeast Aquanauts; Paul Sieswerda of the NY Aquarium; Richard Stepler of South Street Seaport Museum; Sparkman & Stephens Yacht Builders; Benjamin Swett photographer; Prof. Lloyd Ultan of the Bronx Historical Society; John Waldman of Hudson River Foundation; and T. K. Wallace of Manhattan Sailing Club.

Special thank you also to the following individuals and organizations who supported our efforts: Brooklyn Bridge Park Coalition; The Battery Conservancy; Downtown Alliance; Gateway National Park; Hudson River Park Trust; National Park Service; Natural Resources Group of NYC Parks & Recreation Dept.; NYS Office of Parks, Recreation and Historic Preservation; Dana Litvack of Partnership for Parks; Stroock & Stroock & Lavan LLP; Leslie R. Morris, Judith Siegel Lief and Elizabeth M. Ryan, and assistance from Nilus Mattize, a volunteer of The McGraw-Hill Companies Writers to the Rescue Program.

About this Book

Going Coastal ™ New York City is the first in a series of coastal guidebooks published by Going Coastal, Inc. The guide is designed to make the coast more accessible and meet the needs of anyone interested in water-based activities in the City of New York.

The guide is organized in three parts:

Go Coastal - A circumferential tour of the five boroughs featuring the waterfront sights, parks and cultural attractions. It provides practical details about each location and is illustrated throughout with representational maps designed to facilitate the reader's orientation.

Get Wet - An easy to use alphabetical guide to recreational, sports and cultural activities available in the waters that surround New York City. Each feature is introduced by distinguished residents who share their knowledge and personal experiences of the New York waterfront. Throughout the section, notable nautical New Yorkers are highlighted in brief biographies. The maps in this section show where a particular attraction is situated.

Dive In - Information for the reader's convenience on how to get involved in waterfront stewardship. We describe the natural, public and working aspects of the city's waterfront and how to go about obtaining more information.

Contents

Go Coastal

Get Wet

Dive In

Key to Symbols

- Mass Transit
- Ferry/Water Taxi
- Greenway/Bike Paths
- Marina/Yacht Club
- Waterfront Restaurant
- Scenic View
- Under Construction

Go
Coastal

Manhattan

Waterfront History

By Norman J. Brouwer

T he growth of the Port of New York was one of the major American success stories of the industrial age. After almost two centuries of fairly equal status with the ports of Boston, Philadelphia and Charleston, New York rose in the second quarter of the 19th century to where it was handling more trade than all of these ports combined. It would remain the busiest port in North America until 1989. Around 1912 New York became the busiest port in the world, a position it held for over half a century.

The East River side of Manhattan was favored during the sailing ship era because of its shelter from prevailing westerly winds, and from ice coming down the Hudson. From 1715 to 1815 this shoreline was steadily moved out into the River through landfill, allowing the laying out of a succession of waterfront streets, first Water Street, then Front Street, and finally, South Street. In the process, the slips indenting the shore were filled in. The locations of two of them are still indicated by the wide streets near the South Street Historic District, which still bear the names Peck Slip and Burling Slip.

One of New York's unique advantages as a seaport was its access to the interior of the continent, which served as an ever-expanding hinterland supplying commodities for export and providing a growing market for imports. The Hudson River, navigable for almost 150 miles, passes through the Appalachian Mountains in the highlands around West Point. In the mid-1820s this avenue for commerce was linked, by construction of the Erie Canal, not only with the rich farmlands of central New York State but, through the Great Lakes, with much of the interior of the continent.

In 1846 New York saw the launching of the *Rainbow*, the world's first clipper ship, at the Smith & Dimon Shipyard on the east side of Manhattan. High profits to be made in the Chinese tea trade were the initial stimulus, but the discovery of gold in California just two years later created an even greater demand for these ships. The clippers were the largest sailing vessels of the period, and were designed to be the fastest. Their sharp, graceful hulls and towering rigs made them the most beautiful sailing ships the world had ever seen. The clipper ship era was brief. Sailing vessels, built for carrying capacity rather than speed, would continue to be seen at piers along South Street well into the early years of the 20th century, but the center of activity in the Port was now shifting to the west side of Manhattan.

In 1807, Robert Fulton inaugurated the first steamboat service on the Hudson with his *North River*. It was not until the 1830s that steam engines became sufficiently economical in their use of fuel to be practical for coastwise and transoceanic trade. The earliest ocean steamships were wooden-hulled side-wheelers, the majority produced by East River shipyards, until iron construction came into favor in the early 1870s. New York shipbuilding remained very

View from the Battery

© 2000 Benjamin Swett

active through the Civil War, during which a Greenpoint builder produced the revolutionary warship *USS Monitor*, designed by John Ericsson, with engines produced by the Delamater Iron Works located on the west side of Manhattan. After the war New York shipyards went into decline.

The first major pier on the Hudson River side of Manhattan was built at the foot of Albany St. in 1797. After regular transatlantic service was established in 1838, the lower west side developed rapidly to become New York's steamship waterfront. By the 1850s, the Collins Line, the most successful American flag transatlantic company prior to the Civil War, was operating out of a pier at the foot of Canal St. Steamship companies favored covered piers with better protection for cargo from the weather and theft. During the 1890s construction had begun on a series of large piers with two-storey sheds, south of West 23rd St. The "Chelsea Piers" and the Ambrose Channel dredged at the entrance to the Port during the same years, made it possible for New York to accommodate the first giant liners of the 20th century, such as the White Star Line's *Olympic*, and Cunard Line's *Lusitania* and *Mauritania*. The *Olympic's* sistership *Titanic* was bound for one of these piers when she was lost in 1912.

In the early 1930s, even larger piers were built between West 48th St. and West 52nd St., to accommodate the liners *Normandie*, *Queen Mary* and *Queen Elizabeth*. These were the piers modernized in the 1970s to create the current Passenger Ship Terminal. Most west side piers were built with "head houses" at the street that extended to meet their neighbors on either side, effectively blocking any view of the River from inland.

In the second half of the 20th century, new systems for the transportation of goods brought dramatic changes to the Port. Containerization of cargo was introduced around 1960, utilizing standardized forty-foot units easily transferred between road, rail, water and even air transportation systems. Once it came into general use, the old Port facilities consisting of covered piers and warehouses, by then in need of major rebuilding, had become obsolete. Terminals designed to handle containers were built in Staten Island, Brooklyn, south New Jersey, and on adjoining Newark Bay at Elizabethport. These facilities kept the Port of New York one of the most active in the Country, though this activity is not apparent in the historic heart of the Port, Manhattan Island, where most of the old piers and ferry terminals have now either been converted to modern uses or replaced by shoreline promenades and parks.§

Norman Brouwer is the Curator of Ships and Marine Historian at South Street Seaport. He is author of *International Historical Register of Historic Ships* and co-author of *Mariner's Fancy: The Whaleman's Art of Scrimshaw* with Nina Helman.

Go Coastal:
Manhattan

New York is a port city that has prospered from its enormous natural harbor since its founding days. Manhattan has 28.5 miles of water frontage bound by Upper New York Bay and the Hudson, Harlem and East rivers. In recent years, new waterfront parks and public spaces have opened along much of its shore.

New York Harbor

New York Harbor is one of the world's best natural harbors and the city's chief asset. The harbor is part of the NY/NJ Harbor Estuary, where seawater is diluted with freshwater from rivers and streams. New York is the only eastern city that has a functioning estuary. The brackish waters of the harbor are an extremely productive eco-system that is home to all kinds of animals, birds, plants, and aquatic life. An arm of the Atlantic Ocean, the harbor is tidal with a range of five to six feet. At ebb tide, there is a tidal current of one to two knots. The greatest natural depth is less than 30 feet, deepest at the Narrows. Channels have been dredged to 45 feet. The harbor is divided into Lower New York Bay and Upper New York Bay, separated by a two-mile strait at the Narrows. The threshold is marked on the north by Rockaway Point and Sandy Hook, NJ on the south. It is located at the apex of the New York Bight, a natural bend in the coast that forms a large embayment from Montauk down the Jersey shore. The Lower Bay is lined with parks, marshland and barrier beaches. The Upper Bay, at the confluence of the Hudson and East Rivers, links Manhattan with the other boroughs and New Jersey. The harbor is surrounded by the most populated coastal region in the United States and the sixth largest city in the world. The entire North American continent forms its hinterland. The harbor takes in the Hudson, Harlem, East, Hackensack, Passaic and Raritan rivers; Jamaica, Gravesend, Flushing, Newark, and Raritan bays; Newtown Creek, Arthur Kill, and Kill Van Kull. Many islands dot the harbor and its inland waterways. Harbor waters are used for moving freight, transportation, waste disposal, commercial fishing and recreation.

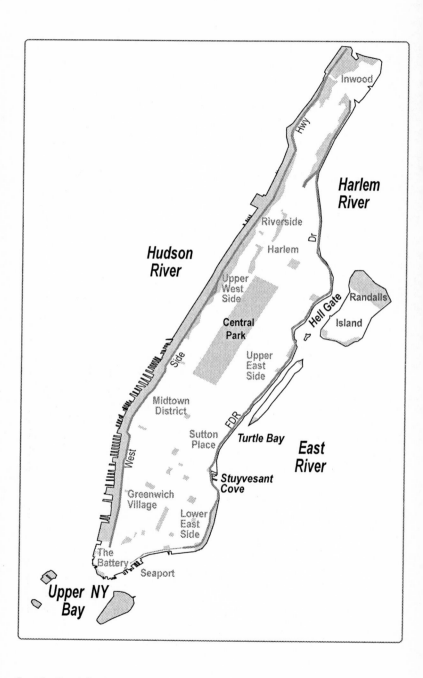

Statue of Liberty Ferry Boats depart the Battery every 20 minutes. Visitors pay for ferry transit only, admission to Liberty and Ellis Islands is free. 212-269-5755; **Governors Island Ferry** departs the Battery Maritime Bldg. Slip 7. 212-514-8296. Private vessels are not permitted to dock at the islands.

View of the Statue of Liberty and Robbins Reef Lighthouse from the Staten Island Ferry.

Statue of Liberty National Monument Liberty Island. 27.5 acres. A gift from the people of France and the first sight to greet ships arriving in New York Harbor since 1886. *Liberty Enlightening the World* was erected atop star-shaped Fort Wood and is a functioning lighthouse. Only the grounds are currently open to the public. Educational programs, historic site, lighthouse, museum, refreshments, restrooms, tours and vista. 212-363-3200 nps.gov/stli

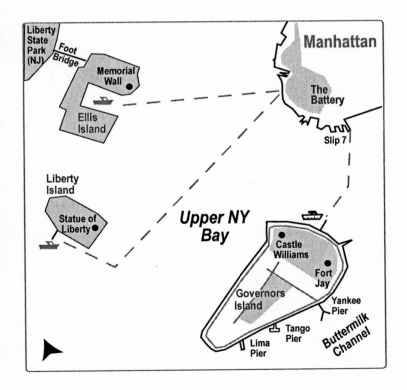

Ellis Island Immigration Museum
Ellis Island. 28 acres. Two in five
Americans can trace their ancestry
to Ellis Island. It was the gateway for
about 12 million immigrants between
1892 and 1954. Educational programs,
historic site, museum, picnic area,
refreshments, restrooms, tours and
vista. 212-363-3206 ellisisland.com

**Governors Island National
Monument** 172 acres. Just 800 yards
off the Battery, Governors Island
has been reserved for military use
since 1755. The island was returned
to New York State in 2003 by the
federal government for the token
price of $1. Landmark forts Castle
William and Fort Jay are part of the
22 acre national monument area on
the north shore. An additional 42
acres encompass the historic district.
Portions of the island will be open to
the public as parkland and used by
City University of NY. Seasonal ferry
and tours of the historic district are
offered by the National Park Service.
Historic site, tours and vista.
212-514-8302 nps.gov/gois or rpa.org

Harbor Park Harbor sites that
embody New York as a port city in
maritime trade and immigration have
been designated a New York State
Urban Cultural Park. Sites include:
Liberty and Ellis Islands, Battery
Park, Pier A, the South Street Seaport
District, the Empire-Fulton Ferry
State Park in Brooklyn and Snug
Harbor on Staten Island.

The Battery

People have been tampering with the
size and shape of The Battery since
the Dutch colony took root on the
prow of Manhattan Island. Castle
Clinton was originally built on a
reef 100 yards off shore until Battery
Park was extended by landfill in
the 1850s to incorporate the old
fort. The Battery is named for a row
of canons that are now mounted
northeast of the former Customs
House, at the foot of Broadway. The
surrounding area contains many
of the most interesting reminders
of the city's rich maritime heritage.
The Customs House is now home
to the Museum of the American
Indian. The maritime past of the
temple-like building is revealed
in ceiling murals of harbor scenes,
created by Reginald Marsh. The post
office at 25 Broadway was built in
1921 for the Cunard Line. Murals in
the building's main hall hint at its
former opulence and seafaring past.
The signs above the doorways to the
Citibank Building at 1 Broadway
designate 'First Class' and 'Cabin
Class' entrances, a leftover from
when it was the United States Lines
Building.

 Subway 4, 5 to Bowling
Green; N, R to South Ferry

 A continuous loop around
Manhattan offers 17 miles of
waterfront greenway, with only a
few on-street segments. A divided

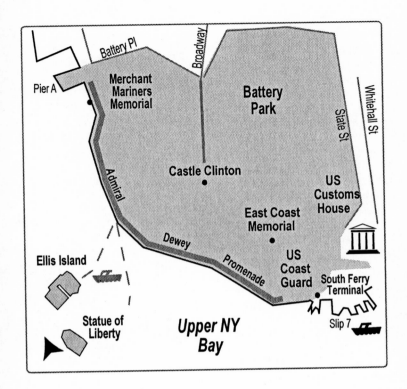

ped/bike path connects Hudson and East River esplanades at the Battery.

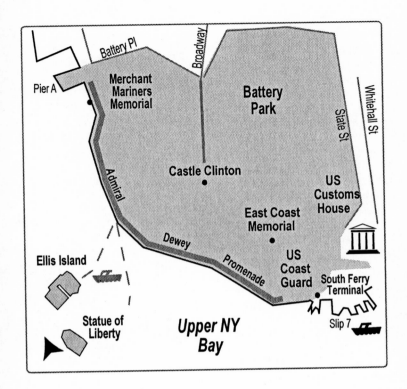 Whitehall Terminal Staten Island Ferry. The free ferry to Staten Island is the city's most visited tourist attraction. Destroyed by fire in 1991, the new glass and steel terminal incorporates "green" design and features harbor views. 718-727-2508

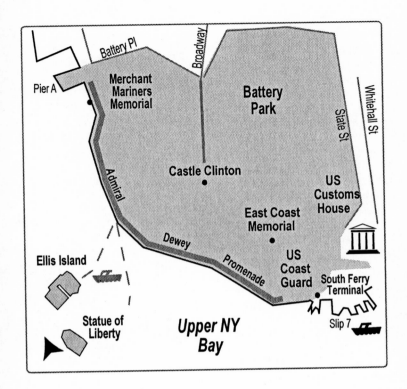 American Park at The Battery, Rise Bar

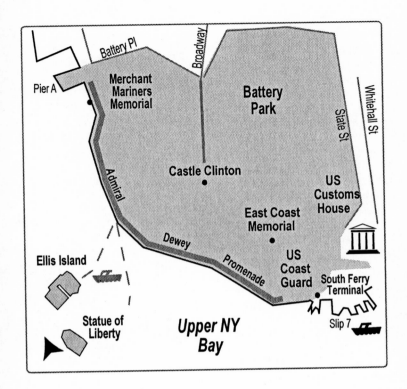 Free tours of historic downtown are conducted by the Downtown Alliance. 212-606-4064

Battery Maritime Building
Foot of Whitehall St. 1909 landmark beaux-arts style terminal used by the Governor's Island ferry. Future plans may include a floating hotel, conference center or catering hall. ✖

U.S. Coast Guard Site The proposed removal of the USCG Bldg. will add two acres of waterfront access. ✖

Battery Park 23 acres. One of the city's most visited, historic and magnificent vistas. 21 monuments and memorials, many commemorating maritime events, grace the storied lawns and 24 garden beds designed by landscape architect Piet Oudolf. Biking, ferry landing, fishing, historic site, playground, promenade, refreshment, restrooms and vista. 212-344-3491 thebattery.org

Castle Clinton National Monument The round fort has served as harbor defense, immigration depot, the city's first aquarium, and a performance space (Castle Garden 1824–1855). Now used for a popular summer concert series, a National Park Service visitors center and the ticket office for the Statue of Liberty Ferry. The site is being transformed back to a performance space. A roof and second tier will be added. Educational programs, events, historic site, museum, tours and vista. 212-344-7220 nps.gov/castleclinton

Battery Park Points of Interest:

American Merchant Mariner's Memorial The sculpture depicts four men and a lifeboat: two sailors look out to sea and a third is reaching down to grasp the outstretched hand of a drowning seaman, who is only visible at low tide. The names of 6,700 merchant seamen lost in WWI and WWII are encapsulated there.

Aquatic Carousel The ride and nearby water spray are a reminder of when NY Aquarium was sited at the Battery. ✖

East Coast Memorial A bronze eagle perched in the midst of eight granite tablets that record the names

of the 4,601 American servicemen who died in the Atlantic during WWII.

The Seawall Called "The River That Flows Two Ways," incorporates a narrative about The Battery and the Hudson River on 37 cast-iron panels.

The 'Sphere' Designed by Fritz Koenig as a symbol of peace, it stood in the plaza of the World Trade Center for 30 years and was damaged and salvaged after the 9/11 attacks.

Pier A The oldest covered pier in Manhattan and a city landmark, built in 1886 to house the Department of Docks. The pier later served as a fireboat station. The clock tower, erected in 1919 as a WWI memorial, tolls hours by ship's bells. Administration of the pier may be transferred to Battery Park City to facilitate redevelopment and public access. Historic site and vista. ✖

Hudson River

The world's largest tidal river originates 315 miles north of New York City at Lake Tear of the Clouds in the highest peaks of the Adirondack Mountains. The Indians called the Hudson "the river that flows two ways," because fresh water flows from the mountains to the ocean, as saltwater floods upstream with each incoming tide. The highest freshwater flows are in spring and fall from snow melt and rain. From New York Harbor to Troy it is not a true river but a "drowned valley." This is because the land that the river flows through was once at a higher elevation, but sank allowing water to enter the valley. The river has cut a gorge in the ocean floor to the continental slope. The Hudson Canyon flows 120 miles out to sea before plunging into an abyss believed to be 9,000 feet deep, which is the predominant underwater feature of the Eastern Seaboard. Commercial seamen refer to the lower Hudson below the George Washington Bridge as the North River because it was the northern reach of the Dutch territory. The Hudson River's straight, deep channel has played a vital role in commerce. The width of the river is about 1.5 miles. The lower Hudson has a natural depth of about 16 feet and is continuously dredged to 45' depth to maintain shipping channels. It is a federal navigation waterway and a no discharge zone for its entire length.

The Hudson supports populations of protected Atlantic and shortnose sturgeon and more than 100 species of fish. Shad and stripers journey up the river to spawn each year. A license is not required to fish in the Hudson, only in its tributaries. The Hudson River is the nation's largest federal Superfund site, covering 200 miles. Polychlorinated biphenyls (PCBs) dumped by General Electric contaminated both the Upper and Lower Hudson and small amounts continue to seep into the river from bedrock beneath the old plants, which GE is slated to remedy. Because of the pollution, fish caught in the Hudson may be harmful for humans to eat.

Battery Park City

Battery Park City has picturesque esplanades, parks, athletic fields, residential towers, the World Financial Center and one of the nation's top high schools. The 92-acre neighborhood was artificially created from the excavation of the World Trade Center in the 1970s. The shoreline corresponds to pier-end limits established by the Army Corps of Engineers in the 1860s. Battery Park City is a "green" community, from the naturalistic edge of South Cove to the ecologically friendly anchorage system at North Cove Marina. The nation's first "green" high-rise is in Battery Park City: the luxury residential tower consumes less energy and conserves more water than traditional buildings.

Subway 4, 5 Bowling Green; 2, 3, or 1, 9 to Chambers St; N, R to South Ferry or Rector St.

Hudson River Greenway runs 13-miles from Battery Park to Fort Washington Park.

World Financial Center, North Cove

North Cove Marina, North Cove YC, Manhattan YC

Gigino's, Hudson River Club, Grill Room, Steamer's Landing

Panorama of Upper New York Bay and Liberty from the lush green lawns of Wagner Park.

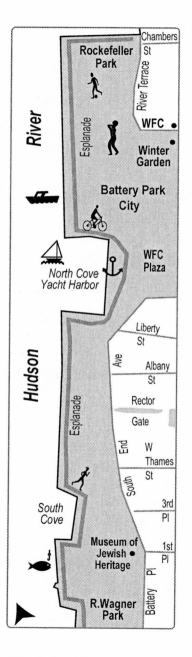

Battery Park City 30 acres. A 1.2 mile waterfront esplanade links a collection of distinctive parks and gardens. Ball fields, biking, blading, educational programs, esplanade, events, excursion boats, fishing, picnic areas, playgrounds, refreshments, restrooms, sailing school, tennis, volleyball and vista. 212-267-9700 bpcparks.org

Battery Park City Points of Interest:

Museum of Jewish Heritage
18 First Pl. A living memorial to the holocaust, offering harbor views from the third floor. 212-509-6130

The Real World Tom Otterness' miniature bronze figures playing amid piles of giant pennies.

Irish Hunger Memorial An authentic fieldstone cottage dismantled in Ireland and reconstructed on-site.

Skyscraper Museum 212-968-1961

Hudson River Park

A long stretch of greenways, piers and esplanades to enjoy concerts, films, kayaking, boating and other public events. The park and pier reconstruction is taking place in stages with interim paths and piers used until final uses are determined.

Subway 1, 9 Houston/ Varick; Christopher St.; A, C, E, L W 4th St.; C, E Spring St. A, C, E to 14th St.; C, E to 23rd St.

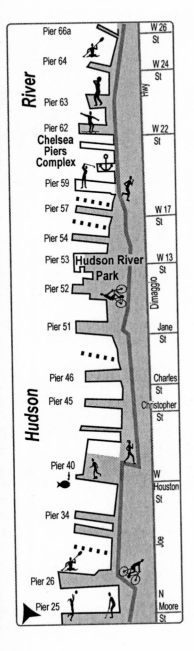

Separate bike/ped. paths from North Moore to 59th St. RiverBikes rental and repair kiosks are located at Piers 25, 63 & 84.

NY Water Taxi: Pier 63, Pier 45, & Christopher St. ✖

Pier 40 Mooring Field, Surfside 3 Marina, Pier 63

Filli Ponte, Pier 25 Snack Shack, Chelsea Brewery, Pier 63 Bar

Relax on the elevated deck at the end of Pier 25 and enjoy views of the river and harbor.

Hudson River Park North Moore to 59th St. 550 acres. Five miles of waterfront comprising 13 pier parks extending up to 1,000 feet into the Hudson River. Piers 32, 49, 58, and 72 are piling fields that provide fish and wildlife habitat. Pier 40, Gansvoort Peninsula, Piers 64 and 66 are slated to be transformed for recreational use. 212-791-2530 HudsonRiverPark.org

Pier 25 North Moore St. A town dock hosting youth programs and the historic steamboat *Yankee*. The pier is slated to be rebuilt and a mooring field added on the south side. Biking, educational programs, fishing, floating dock, historic ship, mini-golf, movies, picnic area, playground, port-a-lets, refreshment, sand volleyball, table tennis and vista. 212-732-7467 manhattanyouth.org ✖

Pier 26 Hubert St. Free kayaking and youth sailing programs at the

Downtown Boathouse. River Project is an education and research center that studies the Hudson. This pier will be rebuilt to its original length. Boat storage, educational programs, ecology center, fishing, floating dock, habitat, paddling, port-a-lets, rowing, sailing and vista. ✖

Pier 34 Two slim piers that extend to the Holland Tunnel vents and escape tower. Only one is open to the public with benches for enjoying the view. A skate park, batting cages and trapeze school operate seasonally just south of the piers. Biking, blading, fishing and vista.

Pier 40 W Houston St. 15.5 acres. Formerly a passenger ship dock built in 1962 for the Holland America Line, it is the largest pier in the park. The pier has a wide public promenade, rooftop soccer field and parking lot. It is home to Floating the Apple rowing, NY kayaking, excursion boats, indoor recreational facilities and a large parking garage. The future use of the public areas will include an historic ships pier for the *Clearwater* and *Lilac*. Ball fields, barbecue grills, batting cages, biking, blading, boat building, educational programs, esplanade, excursion boats, fishing, davit launch crane, mooring field, paddling, parking, playground, picnic area, rec center, restrooms, rowing and vista. 212-989-3764 pier40.org ✖

Pier 42 Morton St. The pier will be rebuilt with public areas and a skate park. ✖

Pier 45 Christopher St. A fountain marks the head of the popular pier with open sun deck, grass lawn, seating areas and shade structures. Biking, blading, picnic area, sunbathing and vista.

Pier 46 Charles St. An Astroturf lawn and a pile field off the western-half of the pier. Refreshment, restrooms, sunbathing and vista.

Pier 49 A viewing balcony looks out on the pile field, which serves as a fish nursery. Habitat and vista.

Pier 51 Jane St. A nautically-themed children's play area. Floating dock, playground, water spray and vista.

Pier 52 & 53 Gansevoort Peninsula W 12th St. Herman Melville worked as a customs inspector near the piers named for his grandfather Peter Gansevoort. The 8.5 acre parcel is the site of an old incinerator, salt storage and sanitation truck parking and Manhattan's last active waterfront fire company, Marine Co. #1. Relocation of city sanitation operations will open the site for park usage. ✖

Pier 54 W 13th St. A steel arch marks the entry of the former Cunard White Star Line docks—where the *Carpathia* landed survivors of the *Titanic*. Biking, blading, concerts, fishing, historic site, movies and vista. ✖

Pier 56 W 14th St. The pier will be rebuilt for public use as park of the park. ✖

Pier 57 W 15th St. The oldest

unaltered pier on the waterfront, it is the former Grace Lines port and is architecturally significant because it is a floating pier supported by three hollow concrete boxes. A Bus Depot recently vacated the pier, and future uses are under consideration. ✖

Piers 59–61 Chelsea Piers W 17th to 22nd St. 30 acres. Originally designed by Warren and Wetmore, architects of Grand Central Station, the piers were built to accommodate large luxury liners. The *Lusitania* departed from the piers to England in May 1915, when she was torpedoed by a German U-boat, an event that sparked America's entry into WWI. Today, a sports complex occupies four piers offering public recreation and waterside access. It contains a golf club, ice rink, bowling alley, gymnastics center, health club, marina and waterfront catering spaces. A public esplanade wraps around the perimeter of each pier, which provide berths to excursion boats, private yachts and the Tug *Pegasus*. Biking, blading, bowling, esplanade, events, excursion boats, golf, historic ships, ice skating, marina, refreshments, restrooms, sailing school, water taxi landing and vista. 212-336-6099 chelseapiers.com

Piers 62–64 Chelsea Waterside Park W 22nd to 24th St. 2.5 acres. The park includes Basketball City, the skate park and the triangular park east of the roadway. Ball fields, basketball, biking, blading, dog run,

picnic area, playground, RiverBikes, skate park, and water taxi stop. 212-924-5433

Pier 63 Maritime W 23rd St. Not really a pier, but a Lackawana Railroad Barge moored behind Basketball City, that offers public access and an outdoor bar and grill. It is home to the *Frying Pan, John J. Harvey* and other historic ships, as well as Manhattan Kayaking and NY Outrigger. Events, hand launch, historic ships, paddling, refreshment, restrooms and vista. 212-989-6363

Pier 64 W 24th St. A park pier that will be rebuilt for public use. ✖

Pier 66A Float Bridge W 26th St. A restored wooden B & O Railroad Float Bridge that was active from 1954 to 1973, transferring railroad cars to barges. It is on the State & National Register of Historic Places. Downtown Boathouse conducts free public kayaking on summer weekends. Historic site, paddling and vista.

Pier 66 W 26th St. The pier will be rebuilt to house community boating programs. ✖

Midtown Maritime District

The midtown waterfront is a 33-block stretch of commercial piers that is home port to commuter ferries, sightseeing boats, yacht charters, ocean liners and dinner cruises. Pier sheds, heliport, tow pound and parking garages obstruct water views. Pier 84 offers the best riverside access.

Otherwise, access is limited to the NY Waterway waiting area and the upper parking deck of Circle Line pier. West side development of the nearby Hudson Yards may include expansion of the Jacob Javits Convention Center and an 86,000 seat stadium.

Subway A, C, E then west via M50 Bus line. NY Waterway operates free shuttle buses to midtown locations and on the west side waterfront. To catch a ride, hail one of the red, white and blue buses.

The Hudson River Park Greenway continues through the midtown area. The district has heavy bus, taxi and limo traffic crossing the bikeway.

Piers 78, 79 & 84; Clinton Cove Park ✗

Cruise ship arrivals and departures from aboard the NY Waterway ferry to Weehawken, N.J.

Pier 76 W. 36th St. The NYPD tow pound is home to a large population of feral cats. About half the pier will be incorporated into the park.

Pier 78 W 38th St. NY Waterway Terminal and bus garage. Refreshments, restrooms and vista. 800-53-FERRY nywaterway.com

Pier 79 A new 5-slip ferry terminal built for multiple operators around the Lincoln Tunnel vent piers will include public viewing areas. ✗

Piers 81 & 83 W 41st to 43rd St. World

Yacht and Circle Line piers. Excursion boats, parking, refreshments, restrooms and vista.

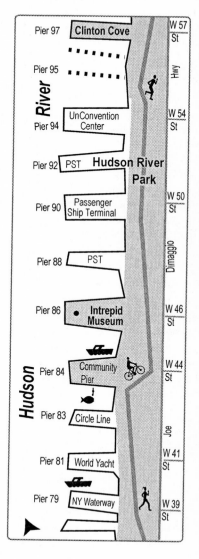

Pier 84 W 44th St. Large open public space featuring shaded seating, environmental programs and a community branch of the Botanical Gardens. Biking, boathouse, educational programs, events, fishing, habitat, davit launch, Floating the Apple rowing, picnic area, playground, refreshments, restrooms, RiverBikes, water taxi stop and vista.

Pier 86 Intrepid Museum W 46th St. Sea-air-space museum aboard one of the most battle-tested ships in U.S. history, alongside the *Growler* submarine and, the newest addition, a British Airways Concorde jet. Biking, educational programs, events, historic ships, museum, refreshments, restrooms, tours and vista.
212-245-0072 intrepidmuseum.com

Piers 88, 90 & 92 Passenger Ship Terminal W 48th to W 52nd St. Port o' call to the world's longest ocean liners at five berths. Carnival cruise ships are the port's largest regular users, their Cunard Line *Queen Mary II* arrives April 2004. The Show Piers are three glass enclosed exhibit spaces situated above each of the passenger ship piers.
212-246-5450 nypst.com

Pier 94 The UnConvention Center Accommodates mid-sized trade shows. Renovations include public areas. ⚒

Piers 95, 96 & 97 Clinton Cove Park W 55th to 57th St. A large community park, boardwalk and small boat dock, when the Sanitation Dept. relocates. ⚒

Riverside

The Upper Westside provides excellent waterside access. Riverside South connects Hudson River Park with Riverside Park, and has a fishing pier and waterfront path. The park is part of Donald Trump's 16 building residential development on the former site of the Penn Central Rail yards. To the north, Riverside Park's gorgeous views, well-kept gardens and urban marina are the community's greatest asset. Riverside has waterfront playgrounds, bike paths, and tennis courts (96th St.). Henry Hudson Drive weaves through Riverside Park narrowing waterside access to footpaths in some areas. One of the last segments of this evolving shoreline is the Harlem on the Hudson's redevelopment. It was once a lively waterfront where Day Liners ferried people up the Hudson. The area begins just south of the Fairway Market parking lot and will serve as a link between Riverside Park and the service road at Riverbank State Park.

By Subway 1, 2, 3 to 72nd & Broadway; 1, 2 to W 79th St. or 86th St.; 1 to 137th or 145th St.

The path extends from W 69th to W 72nd through Riverside Park South to Riverside Park (detour 83rd to 91st Sts.). It runs adjacent to the river at Cherry Walk from 100th to 125th Sts. The path detours to 12th Ave. from 125th to 135th then to Riverbank Park service road.

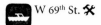 W 69th St. ✗

🚤 79th St. Boat Basin, Dyckman Marina

☕ O'Neal's at Riverside South, Boat Basin Café, Tubby Hook Café, Terrace in the Sky

👁 Riverside Drive run on a bluff above the Hudson River and offers one of the most scenic waterview drives in the city.

Riverside South W 59th to 72nd St. 21.5 acres. A 715-foot recreational pier and public esplanade. Basketball, biking, dog run, esplanade, fishing, handball, historic site, refreshment, soccer and vista. 212-496-0226

69th St. Float Bridge The 90 year old float bridge No. 4 of the NY Railroad at the foot of W 69th St., is to be restored as a small ferry landing. At 63rd St., the rusted ruins of lighterage Piers C and D are picturesque "accidental artwork" that will probably be demolished as part of park construction. Ferry landing, historic site and vista. ✗

Riverside Park W 72nd to 155th St. 323 acres. 4 miles of landscaped waterfront park and gardens. Ball fields, biking, birding, dog runs, esplanade, fishing, habitat, hand launch, historic site, marina, playgrounds, refreshments, restrooms, tennis, skate boarding, soccer, volleyball and vista. 212-408-0264 riversideparkfund.org

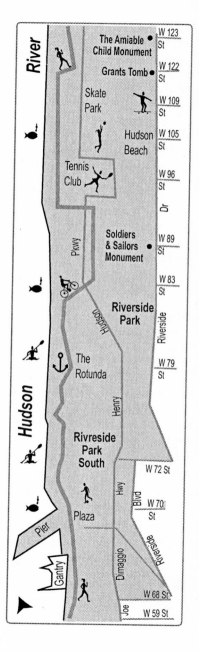

Riverside Park Points of Interest:

79th St. Boat Basin 110 slip marina and visitor dock. A-Dock is a 370-foot-long pier open for public strolls and kayak launching.

Soldiers & Sailors' Monument W 89th St. Corinthian columns encircle the temple-like landmark installed in 1902 to commemorate Union soldiers and sailors who served in the Civil War.

Grant's Tomb W 122nd St. The nation's largest mausoleum and final resting place for Ulysses S. Grant and his wife, Julia. nps.gov/gegr

The Amiable Child Monument W 123rd St. The private grave of St. Clair Pollock, a 5-year-old boy who fell to his death from the surrounding rocks in 1797. When the city bought the property, they agreed to maintain the child's grave.

Harlem Piers St. Clair Place, 125th St. to W 133rd St. A three-year revitalization effort begun in 2004 will transform the four block strip on the river, including the Fairway parking lot, to create a wharf, three piers for fishing and boat landings and an esplanade. ✗

Riverbank State Park 679 Riverside Dr. W 137th to 144th St. 28 acres. The only state park in Manhattan, Riverbank is a large recreation and sports complex located on the roof of the North River Sewage Treatment Plant. The park rises 70 feet above the Hudson River and was inspired by

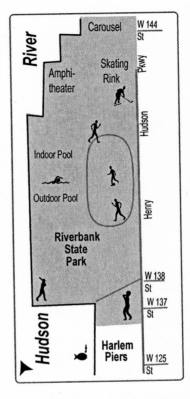

Japanese urban roof gardens. The Totally Kid Carousel features 36 whimsical sculpted animals by artist Milo Mottola, which were created from art by local children. The best access to the park is from Riverside Drive. There is a stairwell from the service road up to the park. Amphitheater, ball fields, basketball, events, handball, indoor pool, picnic area, promenade, restrooms, refreshments, soccer, tennis, track, skating and vista. No bikes or pets permitted in state parks. 212-694-3600 nysparks.com/parks

Upper Manhattan

In northern Manhattan, the land rises high above the shore making it difficult to access the water. The highest elevation on Manhattan Island is 265 feet above sea level located upland at 184th St. in Bennett Park. There are numerous places on the hillside to enjoy views of the Hudson River and the Palisades. The city's hilliest park is Inwood Hill Park, located where the Hudson and Harlem Rivers meet and where Peter Minuet's bargain purchase of Manhattan took place under a tulip tree.

 Subway A to 181st or 190th or 207th St.

 The greenway extends from 145th St to George Washington Bridge. The path is lit through Fort Washington Park (access 155th, 158th & 181st Sts) and follows Henry Hudson Pkwy. from 181st St to Dyckman St.

View of Little Red Lighthouse and George Washington Bridge from Riverbank State Park.

Fort Washington Park
W 158 to Dyckman St. 145 acres. Under the George Washington Bridge, sloping lawns edged by an outcrop of boulders on

Jeffrey's Hook support a lighthouse. The best access to the park is along the shore from Riverside Park. Ball fields, basketball, fishing, lighthouse, playground, historical site, restrooms, tennis, tours, urban ranger programs and vista.

Little Red Lighthouse 178th St. Made famous by the children's book *The Little Red Lighthouse and the Great Gray Bridge,* the Jeffrey's Hook Light has stood on the banks of the Hudson River since 1921. It is accessible from the shore directly under the bridge or from W 181st St. and Lafayette Pl.

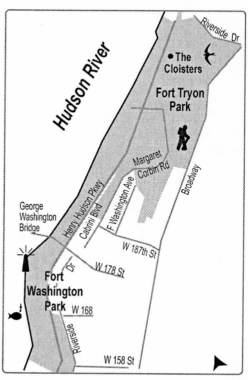

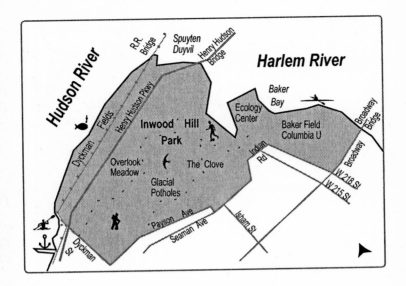

Fort Tryon Park Riverside Dr. W 192 to Dyckman St. 67 acres. The former Billing's estate was a gift to the city from John D. Rockefeller Jr.'s. He also purchased the land across the river to provide an unspoiled view of the Palisades from the park. Birding, hiking, historic site, museum, refreshments, restrooms and vista.

The Cloisters The monastery houses the Metropolitan Art Museum's medieval art collection. 212-923-3700

Dyckman Fields Dyckman St. Level playing fields located between the active rail line and the river. Ball fields, barbecuing, biking, blading, fishing, hand launch, marina, refreshment and vista.

Inwood Hill Park 218th & Indian Rd. 196 acres. Trails lead to Indian cave shelters, glacial rock formations, woodlands and Manhattan Island's last remaining salt marsh. Ball fields, biking, birding, ecology center, fishing, habitat, hiking, historic site, restrooms, train-spotting and vista. Forever Wild Area. 212-408-0264

Harlem River

The Harlem River is an 7.5-mile-long tidal strait that separates Manhattan from the mainland of the Bronx. It connects the Hudson and East rivers and is crossed by 14 bridges. The passage to the Hudson had initially run through the turbulent Spuyten Duyvil Creek, which snaked in an S-shape around Marble Hill. The Harlem River Ship Canal was cut to straighten the waterway and create a shortcut between the Long Island Sound, the Hudson River and ports north of New York City. The new route partitioned Marble Hill to the Bronx side of the passage. The neighborhood remains a postal and voting district of Manhattan, though it is physically in the Bronx. Columbia's Crew can be seen practising early mornings on the 2,000 meter rowing course between the Henry Hudson Bridge and Sherman Creek. A new boathouse is being built on the banks of Sherman Creek, which has the last remaining natural shoreline in Manhattan. Harlem River Drive blocks access to the waterfront and cuts Highbridge Park off from the riverside.

Subway A to 207th St. (last stop); 1 to 215th St.; 1, 9 to Dyckman St., 168th St. or 181st St.; Bus M35 Bus to Randall's Island.

The Henry Hudson Bridge bike/ped. path is on the west side of the bridge. The Harlem River Speedway runs for two miles from Dyckman to 163rd St. and is accessed at Dyckman St. or W 155[th]St. Ped/bike access to Randall's Island is at 103rd St. footbridge or footpath on the Triborough Bridge.

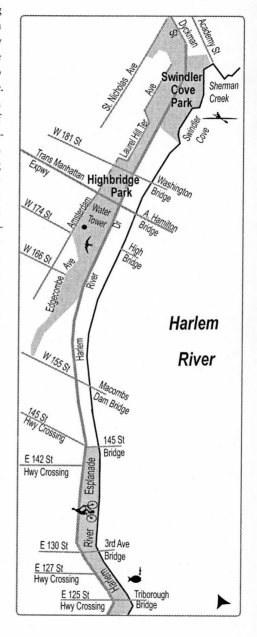

Watch the Railroad Swing Bridge at Spuyten Duyvil open for Circle Line boats from Inwood Hill Park. View of the Harlem River from the base of High Bridge Water Tower.

Baker Field Athletic Complex

218th St. 26 acres. The 60' by 60' blue "C," first painted on the Bronx rock-face by the crew team in 1952, is across the river from the Baker Field sport's grounds, where Lou Gehrig once played ball. Crew is the oldest sport at Columbia, dating to 1872. The Class of 1929 Boathouse is named for the last class to win the national rowing championships. On race days, free shuttle buses transport spectators from the boathouse to the finish line at Sherman Creek. 212-854-CREW columbia.edu/cu/crew

Swindler Cove Park

Sherman Creek E Dyckman St. & 10th Ave. nyrp.org 5 acres. Enter through the oars on the aluminum gateway to restored wetlands and a children's garden. Bette Midler's NY Restoration Project has built a two-story $10 million floating boathouse that will be administered by NY Rowing. Birding, educational programs, fishing, habitat, launch, restrooms, rowing and vista. nyrowing.org

Highbridge Park

E 155th St. to Dyckman St. 119 acres. A 2.5-mile stretch of upland park situated 200 feet above the Harlem River. Ball fields, basketball, bird watching,

historic site, pool, playground, restrooms and vistas. 212-927-2400

High Bridge & Water Tower

174th St. The bridge and tower were once part of the Croton Aqueduct, which carried water into Manhattan. The footbridge is the city's oldest interborough crossing, connecting Highbridge Park with a small park in the Bronx. The urban rangers offer occasional tours of the water tower and there is interest in reopening the bridge, which has been closed since the 1970s. High Bridge is part of the Old Croton Aqueduct Trail and a link in the East Coast Greenway system, a trail from Maine to Florida.

Harlem River Esplanade

E 145th to 125th St. 20 acres. An apron park to be completed in phases as part of road and bridge repair projects. Pedestrian access to the waterfront exists at E 142nd, E 127th and E 125th Sts. Biking, blading, esplanade, fishing, picnic area and vista. ✖

Randall's & Ward's Island

272 acres. The islands were joined by landfill at Sunken Meadow. A boardwalk over Little Hell Gate Cove and the waterfront path on the western shore allows access to the island's natural areas. Ball fields, barbecuing, biking, birding, blading, cricket, educational programs, fishing, habitat, horseback riding, golf, picnic areas, restrooms, tennis, track and vista. (Amphitheater and water park.✖) 212-830-7721 risf.org

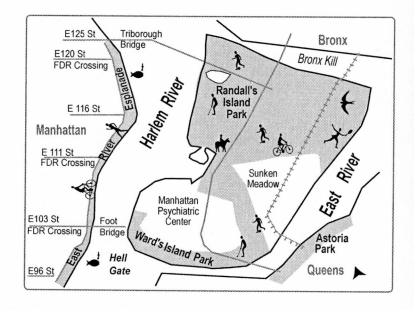

East River

A 14-mile-long tidal strait that runs through the center of the City of New York, the East River connects New York Harbor with the Long Island Sound and links four of the city's five boroughs. The river is a major transportation route with main channel depths of 35 to 40 feet and a mean tidal range of 4 to 5 feet. FDR Drive flanks the river for 9.5 miles, from the Triborough Bridge to the Battery. The roadway is bound by waterfront and upland parks. Much of FDR Drive is built on landfill. The section from 30th Street to 23rd Street is constructed on rubble from bombed British cities, which arrived

as ballast in warships during WWII. Sea termites are threatening the wooden pilings that support parts of the drive and the bulkhead along in East River Park. FDR Drive blocks the shoreline along much of the East River. Reconstruction of the drive will result in improved waterside public access.

Hell Gate

Hell Gate is Dutch meaning "bright passage." It is where the East River receives the Long Island Sound tide from the east and the ocean tide from the south, which causes strong currents and frequent whirlpools. The largest planned explosion prior to the atom bomb was ignited in the Hell Gate to destroy a nine acre obstacle to navigation known as Flood Rock.

 Subway 4, 5, or 6 to 86th or 125th St.

 A bike/ped. path extends from 125th to 63rd St. through Carl Schurz Park (stairs) and Bobby Wagner Walk, and connects with pedestrian bridge to Randall's Island at 103rd St. All East River crossings have bike access.

 90th St. Pier

 Club Gustavino

 View of Hell Gate and Roosevelt Island Lighthouse from Gracie Mansion on Horn's Hook.

Mill Rock Island 96th St. 2.5 acres. The tiny island 1,000 feet from shore is not open to the public. It is an avian habitat and occasional pit stop for kayakers on the river.

Bobby Wagner Walk 125th to 63rd St. A 3-mile-long trail, built in 1939 as part of FDR construction There are pedestrian overpasses to the waterside at intervals along the esplanade. The narrow passage from E 90th to E 80th St. is called John Finley Walk. Biking, blading, fishing, ferry landing, pier and vista.

107th Street Pier Covered fishing pier. Biking, fishing and vista.

Carl Schurz Park East End Ave. from 90th to 83th St. 15 acres. At Horn's Hook, the park is named after the soldier, statesman, and journalist Carl Schurz (1829–1906). Basketball, biking, esplanade, ferry landing, fishing, historic site, playground, restrooms, tours and vista.

Gracie Mansion 96th St. Built in 1799 as the country home of shipping magnate Archibald Gracie, it has been the official mayoral residence since 1942. Tours by appt. 212-570-4751

Roosevelt Island

Roosevelt is a 2-mile-long city-owned island of 8,500 residents fringed on the western shore by a esplanade and parks that overlook Manhattan. The East River splits around the island. Most boats navigate the swift waters of the west channel because the east channel has only 40 feet of clearance. Ball fields, barbecuing, basketball, biking, esplanade, fishing, gardens, picnic areas, historic sites, lighthouse, restrooms, tennis and vista.

 Subway F to Roosevelt Island Station; 59th St. **By Tram:** The only commuter cable car in North America. The tram runs every 7.5 minutes during rush hour and on the quarter hour all other times.

 Pathways run along much of the island's waterfront.

 Rooftop Restaurant

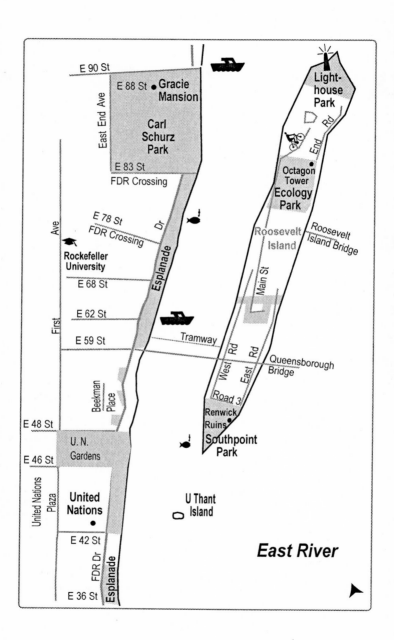

E 90 St

E 88 St • Gracie Mansion

Light-house Park

East End Ave

Carl Schurz Park

E 83 St

FDR Crossing

Rd

End

Octagon Tower

Ecology Park

E 78 St

FDR Crossing

Dr

Roosevelt Island

Roosevelt Island Bridge

Ave

Esplanade

Rockefeller University

E 68 St

Main St

First

E 62 St

E 59 St

Tramway

West Rd

East Rd

Queensborough Bridge

Beekman Place

Road 3

Renwick Ruins

E 48 St

Southpoint Park

U. N. Gardens

E 46 St

United Nations Plaza

United Nations •

U Thant Island

East River

E 42 St

FDR Dr

Esplanade

E 36 St

The best view of the Macy's Fourth of July Fireworks is from the Roosevelt Island esplanade.

Lighthouse Park On the northern tip of the island, the lighthouse was built in 1872 by convicts using local quarried stone, and was designed by architect James Renwick Jr., who also designed St. Patrick's Cathedral. Biking, esplanade, fishing, historic site, lighthouse, picnic area and vista.

Ecology (Octagon) Park 15 acres. Centered by the massive octagonal ruin of America's first municipal insane asylum (1839). Ball fields, barbecue grills, historic site, picnic area, tennis and vista.

Southpoint Park A new park on the southern tip of the Roosevelt Island by the Renwick Ruins, which is the remains of the 1856 smallpox hospital designed by James Renwick Jr. Biking, fishing, habitat, historic site, picnic area and vista.

Turtle Bay

Edgar Allen Poe wrote of pleasant days rowing in the little bay, named for the abundance of turtles that once populated it. Diplomatic residences, world-renowned hospitals and medical centers line the elevated shore, filling almost ten blocks. The neighborhoods of Sutton Place and Beekman Place are wealthy enclaves rising on a bluff above the East River. The area features several pocket parks along the seawall, including Sutton Place Park (57th St.) Sutton Promontory (59th to 53rd St.) and Riverview Terrace (E 58th St). The slender profile of the UN General Assembly building and the adjacent gardens reach out over FDR Drive to the water's edge. The entire United Nation's complex sits in international territory, atop land once occupied by slaughterhouses. Con Edison's waterside steam plant, located on nine acres between 35th and 41st St., will be replaced by residential towers that may include a public esplanade.

 Subway 6 to 59th St.

 FDR Drive interrupts the waterside path below 54th St. to 37th St. when riders must travel inland on 1st Ave.

 E 62nd St. ✗

Top of Beekman Tower, UN Delegates Dining Room

East River Pavilion E 60th St. A small park built on top of a former waste transfer station. A large sculpture called East River Roundabout hangs above the park. Biking, blading, dog run, fishing and vista. 212-755-3288

Detmold Park West of FDR Dr. E 51st to 49th St. A footbridge leads to a short waterside esplanade. Dog run, gardens, playground and vista.

MacArthur Park West of FDR Dr. E 48th to 49th St. Named for

General MacArthur, the park offers unobstructed river views. Playground, restrooms, water spray and vista.

U.N. Plaza E 42nd to 46th St. An elevated promenade and public sculpture garden overlooking the East River. Historic site, refreshments, restrooms, tours and vista.

Glick Park E 38th to 36th St. Riverside seating area. Esplanade and vista.

U Thant Island (Belmont Island) The island, adjacent to the U.N., is leased to followers of Sri Chimnoy who have installed a large metal arch as tribute to U Thant, the UN secretary-general from 1961–1971.

Stuyvesant Cove

Waterside Plaza is built on a platform over the East River. The isolated residential complex contains a public shoreside plaza, seaplane mooring, and marina and is home to the UN International School. The Water Club restaurant is permanently moored north of the plaza. A narrow park hugs Stuyvesant Cove where a tiny sand beach has formed on top of pier pilings and debris dumped off docks once occupied by a cement plant.

East River Park was created as part the highway construction for the FDR. The opening scene of *Moby Dick* takes place in a shanty town in Corlear's Hook, the place where the East River curves south in the Lower East Side. The waterfront was the busiest shipbuilding center in the nation, with 30 yards in operation in 1832. The *America* schooner yacht, for which the America's Cup is named, was built on this shore. The area was also the city's red light district.

 Subway F to 34th, 23rd or 14th St.

 The East River Bikeway follows a service road past Waterside Plaza to Stuyvesant Cove, where it narrows. The path runs uninterrupted to South Street Seaport.

 E 34th St; E 23rd St. �֍

 NY Skyport Marina

 The Water Club

Waterside Plaza E 28th to 25th St. An open riverfront plaza amid the four residential towers elevated over the East River and walkway around the marina. Excursion boats, fishing, marina, parking, playground, picnic area and vista.

Stuyvesant Cove Park E 23rd to 18th St. 2 acres. Landscaped with gardens, benches and shade areas. A "green" building that relies on water and solar power is being built to house the community environmental center. Biking, birding, ecology center, educational programs, fishing, habitat and vista. 212-673-7507 stuyvesantcove.org ✖

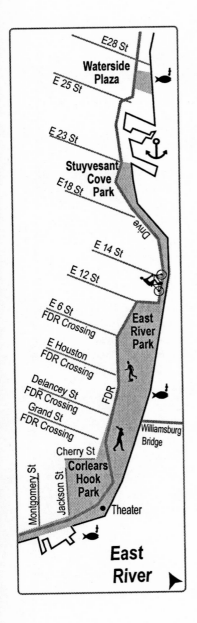

East River Park (John Lindsey Park) E 12th to Montgomery St. 57 acres. A wide waterfront esplanade surrounding playing fields. Corlear's Hook Amphitheater was the original home of Joseph Papp's "Shakespeare in the Park." The often neglected park and landmark theater were restored in one week's time as part of the TV show "Challenge America," with activist, Erin Brockovich. The waterside path is closed for bulkhead repair. Ball fields, basketball, biking, events, fishing, barbecuing, historic site, picnic area, playground, restrooms, tennis, track, volleyball and vista.

Piers 42–35 Jackson St. One of the last places ships brought cargo into Manhattan. The Fruit (Pier 41) and Banana (Pier 36) piers are currently used for parking municipal vehicles. Reuse proposals calls for a portion of the piers to be developed as public recreational space. ✗

Seaport District

The South Street Historic District is an area of restored 19th century buildings that is one of the city's top tourist attractions, encompassing 11 blocks from Pearl Street east to South Street and Peck Slip south to Burling Slip. The Titanic Memorial Lighthouse, at the corner of Pearl and Water Streets, marks the entrance to the district. The Schermerhorn Row section is Manhattan's oldest block

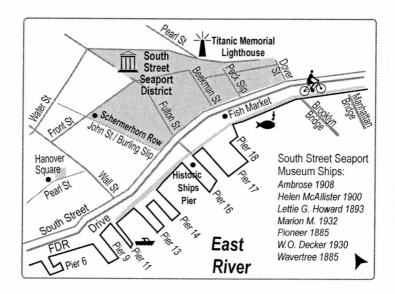

and the first in the country to be lit by electricity. Thomas Edison's first power plant was located at 40 Fulton Street. Herman Melville sent Ahab to sea on this block. Schermerhorn Row has undergone extensive interior renovation of the upper floors to prepare for the museum's permanent exhibit "World Port New York." This was the site of the Fulton Ferry Hotel, recalled in Joseph Mitchell's collection of short stories *Up in the Old Hotel*. The "Historic Front Street" project is a commercial development of will renovate eleven 19th century buildings on Front Street and Pecks Slip in the Seaport District. The FDR Drive viaduct overshadows the Seaport District and obstructs sightlines. Suggestions to open

views and improve access include tearing down the viaduct south of the Brooklyn Bridge or converting the northbound lanes into a public esplanade.

Subway 2, 3, 4, 5, J, Z or M to Fulton St.; A, C to Broadway-Nassau. The walls of Fulton St. Station are decorated with tiles depicting New York Harbor scenes and historic ships.

The waterfront sidewalk widens into separate bike/ped paths and extends south past Pier 11 ferry landing and around Whitehall Terminal construction to Battery Park path and the westside.

 Pier 11/Wall St.

Paris Café, Carmine's, South Street Seaport eateries

View of the East River and Upper Bay from the foot-path of the Brooklyn Bridge.

Under the Bridges A landscaped path and sitting area below the Manhattan and Brooklyn bridges overlooks a small beach, where fishermen cast from the shore and kayakers beach for a rest. A series of interpretive signs mounted along the path enlighten about the maritime history of the area.

Fulton Fish Market 200 Water St. Fishmongers sell about a million pounds of fish a night at the nation's oldest wholesale fish market. It will relocate to a new modern facility in Hunts Point in the Bronx by 2005. Operates 2 a.m. to 8 a.m. The Seaport schedules tours. 212-406-4985

Pier 17 Pavilion A shopping mall and food court with views of the East River and Brooklyn Bridge. Biking, events, excursion boats, refreshments, restrooms and vista. 212-SEA-PORT southstreetseaport.com

South St. Seaport Museum 207 Front St. Recreates and chronicles the history of the Port of New York in storied ships and in galleries housed in restored buildings throughout the landmark district. Educational programs, historic site, tours and vista. 212-748-8600 southstseaport.org

Pier 16 Historic Ship's Pier South Street Seaport Museum. The largest private collection of historic vessels in the nation. Vessels are open for tours and some for sailings. Boat building, boat modeling, educational programs, events, excursion boats, historic site, museum, refreshments, restrooms, tours and vista.

Piers 9, 13 & 14 Pier deterioration forced the closing of the tennis club and a plan to build a branch of the Guggenheim Museum fell through. The piers will likely be demolished.

Pier 11/Wall St. The pier & esplanade is a major commuter ferry terminal with an open deck and seating area. Biking, ferry landing, picnic area, refreshments, restrooms and vista.

55 Water St. Plaza West of FDR. The elevated public plaza facing the East River is wedged between the towers of the city's largest office structure. A proposed makeover to better connect the site with the waterfront is in development. Vista. 55water.com

Pier 6 Downtown Heliport. A skyport operated by the Port Authority that offers helicopter sightseeing rides and passenger transit. 212-943-5959

The Bronx

Waterfront History

By Professor Lloyd Ultan

Although The Bronx is the only one of New York City's five boroughs that is part of the mainland, it is surrounded on three sides by water. It is not surprising, therefore, that its waterfront has played an important part in its growth and development.

The first use of Bronx waters was for transportation and commerce. Until the advent of railroads, water transportation was the easiest and cheapest form of travel. Colonial settlers built docks from their waterfront property to moor boats and ships to exchange goods with New York City at the tip of Manhattan. The town of Westchester maintained a dock on Westchester Creek where boats came up the East River from New York twice weekly to exchange goods. A similar dock served the town of Eastchester on the Hutchinson River where New York boats arrived weekly via Long Island Sound. Stone was quarried on the manor of Fordham and shipped by boat along the Harlem and East Rivers. Benjamin Palmer envisioned City Island as the great entrepot for the entire Long Island Sound region. Gouverneur Morris gave directions to potential visitors to sail up the East River past today's Randalls Island to his home. Similarly, Elizabeth Colden DeLancey instructed her father, Cadwallader Colden, to come by boat along the East River into the Bronx River to the dock she and her husband, Peter DeLancey, maintained at West Farms.

In the nineteenth century, Jordan L. Mott built the Mott Haven Canal off the Harlem River for commercial shipping, and his own dock was located there on the river beside his iron foundry. Gouverneur Morris II promoted Port Morris as a commercial landing as well. As the only Bronx deep water port, oil tankers unloaded their cargo into pipelines there in the twentieth century. The Harlem River Ship Canal was cut through Spuyten Duyvil to allow deep-draft ships to travel between the Hudson and East Rivers. Nineteenth century passenger steamboats plied the Harlem and East Rivers docking at Landing Road in Fordham, Morris Dock (now Morris Heights), Highbridge and Mott Haven to carry commuters to Wall St. Today, passenger ferries dock at Yankee Stadium. Soon, fishing boats will land at the new fish market in Hunts Point.

In the nineteenth century, however, the use of the Bronx waterfront also was seen for recreation and amusement. Gouverneur Morris enjoyed casting for fish off Stony Island (now Port Morris), and fishing for bass with his friends in a boat in the Harlem River. The opening of High Bridge in 1849 attracted tourists to cross it for the spectacular view. This led to an amusement park opening just below the span. Hotels opened to serve guests. Other amusement parks later

Stepping Stone Lighthouse   © 2002 Jim Crowley

opened along the East River at Oak Point and Soundview. Wealthy men established yacht clubs on the Harlem in Highbridge, on the Hudson in Riverdale, along the East River in Port Morris and on Long Island Sound on City Island. A state-mandated commission purchased Pelham Bay Park in 1888 to be "the Newport of the masses," where anyone could fish, bathe, and sail without joining a posh yacht club. In 1937, the new Orchard Beach was added to the recreational facilities of this shorefront park. Today, there are plans to build a major golf course in Soundview Park with its waterfront views. Plans are also being generated to create recreational sites along the Hudson, Harlem and East River waterfronts in The Bronx.

Thus, the Bronx waterfront is still used for travel, commerce and recreation. It is a major factor in the borough's history.§

Lloyd Ultan, The Bronx County Historian, is a professor of history at the Edward Williams College of Fairleigh Dickinson University in Hackensack, NJ and a Centennial Historian of New York City. He is the author of articles and books on Bronx and American history, including *The Beautiful Bronx*, *The Bronx In The Frontier Era*, *Presidents of the United States*, *Legacy of the Revolution: The Story of the Valentine- Varian House* and co- author of the *Life in The Bronx* book series.

Go Coastal:
The Bronx

The Bronx is the only borough that is not an island. It is a peninsula with 80 miles of shoreline, bound on the west by the Hudson and Harlem Rivers, on the south by the Bronx Kill and East River, and on the east by the Long Island Sound. The Hudson shore presents stunning views, but little access. Waterfront neighborhoods throughout the Bronx are almost completely cut off from the water, but this is changing. Community efforts have been successful in opening new access and improving existing parkland all along the water's edge.

Hudson River

The Hudson River edges three miles of shore in the northwest corner of the Bronx. Riverdale and its attractive parkland sit on a high-forested bluff above the Hudson commanding superb views of the river and the New Jersey Palisades. New York Central Railroad built their Hudson Line along the shore in the 1860s, effectively separating the community from the water. The only legal access points are at the Riverdale Yacht Club and St. Vincent's Point, which are not open to public use. Renovation of the rail line includes plans to recover access to the waterfront at the Metro North Stations in Riverdale and Spuyten Duyvil. The state is restoring natural wetlands on the coast and may install platforms for fishing and wildlife observation.

The Hudson River meets the Harlem River at Spuyten Duyvil, a Dutch name meaning "in spite of the devil." Legend states the creek's name stems from the tragic fate of a brave trumpeter who swam across the turbulent creek, "in spite of the devil," to warn colonists of an English attack. He drowned sounding the trumpet to his last breath.

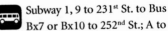 Subway 1, 9 to 231st St. to Bus Bx7 or Bx10 to 252nd St.; A to 207 St. and Bx7 Bus to 252nd St.; MTA Metro North to Riverdale Station

 Metro North Riverdale Station, 254th St. A Metro North Lifetime Bike Permit is $5. 212-499-4386. The Hudson River Greenway Plan calls for a bicycle and pedestrian trail offering continuous access along the entire length of the Hudson River.

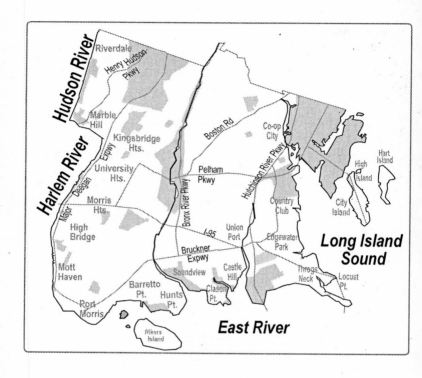

 Riverdale Yacht Club

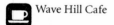 Wave Hill Cafe

The view from a window seat on the southbound Metro-North Hudson Line, when the train hits the bend at Spuyten Duyvil, includes the train itself posed against the city and river.

Riverdale Park Palisades Ave. between 232nd & 254th St. 97 acres, A long narrow park containing deep ravines and thick native forest, archeological sites and the oldest extant dock on the Hudson River—19th century Dodge Dock. Birding, habitat, hiking, historic site and vista. Forever Wild Area.

Wave Hill 675 W 252nd St. 28 acres. Beautiful public gardens and magnificent views across the Hudson to the Palisades. The historic mansion and country estate was built in 1843 and deeded to the city in 1960. Thomas Huxley and Charles Darwin once visited the grounds and famous former residents include Teddy Roosevelt, Mark Twain and Toscanini.

Birding, habitat, hiking, historic site, educational programs, environmental center, events, refreshments, restrooms and vista. 718-549-3200 wavehill.org

Henry Hudson Park Independence Ave. at W 227th St. 9 acres. On the hill above where Henry Hudson put in the Dutch vessel *Half Moon* in 1609. Nearby Halve Maen Overlook offers views of the river and Palisades. Baseball, basketball, habitat, handball, historic site, playground and vista.

Spuyten Duyvil Shorefront Park between Edsall Ave. & Spuyten Duyvil Metro-North Station. 6.5 acres. In the shadow of the Henry Hudson Bridge, the park encompasses a freshwater pond. Birding, fishing, habitat and vista.

Harlem River

The city's early passion for rowing was nurtured on the flat waters of the Harlem River in the 1800s. Rival clubs built boathouses along the riverside and recreational rowers crowded the water. On summer weekends, hundreds pulled on the river and more watched the activity from the grand promenade on High Bridge. The first female crew rowed down the Harlem in the 1930s. The river is a 7.5-mile-long tidal strait between the Hudson River and East River. The digging of the Harlem River Ship Canal in 1895 straightened the river to make

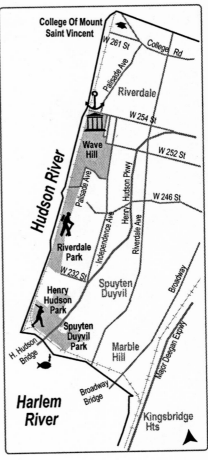

it a commercial waterway, which cut 14 miles off the route around Manhattan from the Long Island Sound. Water depths vary from 12 to 26 feet and the river ranges from 400 to 620 feet wide, widest at the High Bridge. The ornamental 30-foot lighthouse atop H. W. Wilson Company has been a highly visible marker on the river bank since 1929.

Subway 1, 9 to 225th St. Marble Hill; 4 to 138th St. Grand Concourse; 161st St. to Yankee Stadium

Most of the Harlem River crossings have bike paths. Roberto Clemente State Park has a dedicated bike trail.

Yankee Stadium Landing: NY Waterway and Seastreak offer ferry service from N.J. and Manhattan during baseball season.

Bronx Community College Hall of Fame at University Ave. & W 181st St. rises above the waterfront of University Heights overlooking river and city skyline.

Regatta Park W Fordham Rd. extending from W 225th St. to Roberto Clemente State Park. The park will provide one mile of riverside access. It is in the early planning stages. ⚒

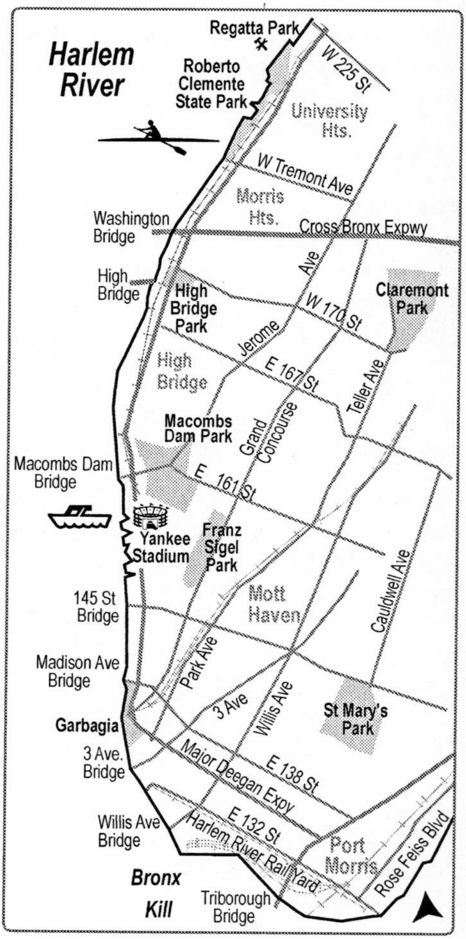

Roberto Clemente State Park W Tremont Ave. & Mattewson Rd. 25 acres. One of the most widely used parks in the city, named for the famed baseball player from Puerto Rico A boathouse for the Empire State Rowing Association and several local collegiate crews is planned. Esplanade, ball fields, basketball, biking, hand launch, picnic area, playground, pool, restrooms, rowing and vista. No pets are permitted in State Parks. 718-299-8750

High Bridge Park University Ave. at W 170th St. 1 acre. A green space at the Bronx foot of High Bridge on a bluff overlooking the river, where the

Old Croton Aqueduct water pipes are carried over the Harlem River. Vista.

Yankee Village 162nd St. A proposed redevelopment plan for Yankee Stadium and the Bronx Terminal Market envisions a waterfront esplanade and park with increased ferry service. ✂

Garbagia south end of Park Ave. east of the Railroad Bridge. 7.5 acres. A waste prevention park that features whimsical sculptures made from trash.

Bronx Kill

At low tide, it is possible to wade across rocks in the shallow water of the Bronx Kill between the south shore of the Bronx and Randall's Island. The shore is dominated by the 96-acre Harlem Rails Yards, which hamper water access.

East River

The Bronx shore of the East River is a truly urban waterfront extending for six miles from the Harlem River to the Long Island Sound. The river is the site of the worst maritime disaster in NYC history, when on June 15, 1904 the steamboat *General Slocum* burst into flames while carrying German immigrant families from the Lower East Side upriver to their annual church picnic. The boat was poorly equipped for the emergency and beached on North Brother Island. Over 1,021 lives were lost, mostly women and children. The Captain, who lost his sight in the fire, was blamed for the tragedy and sent up the river to Sing Sing Prison. There is a memorial to the *General Slocum* victims in Tompkins Square Park. The river is also the site of a two-century-old treasure hunt to locate the British frigate *HMS Hussar*. The ship was carrying the payroll for the British navy and about 50 American war prisoners when it sank off the Bronx shore on November 25, 1780. The fortune was never recovered. Divers search the waters off Port Morris in the latest salvage attempt. Hunts Point Terminal Market, the world's largest food distribution facility, is located on the South Bronx riverbank. Many of the waterway's former industrial sites are scheduled to be converted to parks.

Bay of Brothers

North Brother is a 13-acre city-owned island that was once home to Mary Mallon, the typhoid carrying cook who was held there in quarantine without trial and against her will for 26 years. Typhoid Mary died on the island in 1938. Today, there are several abandoned buildings, including a crumbling lighthouse and TB sanatorium. The island is now part of the Harbor Heron Complex, a protected area for wading birds. South Brother Island shares seven acres with a bird sanctuary and private owner. The islands together are one of seven designated "important bird areas" in the city.

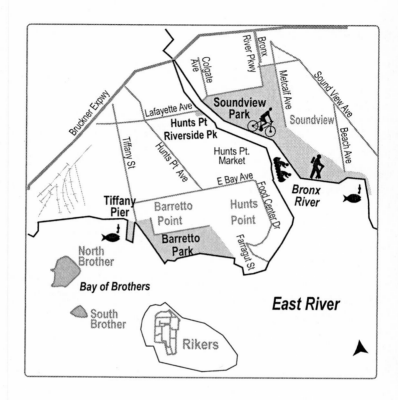

Rikers Island is the world's largest penal colony. Ten jails in all, it sits 1,000 feet off the coast of Hunts Point. About 16,000 men and women are interned for short stays in Rikers' jails and prison barges moored nearby. There is no docking or anchoring allowed near the island.

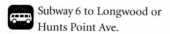 Subway 6 to Longwood or Hunts Point Ave.

Tiffany St. Pier looks out on the ruins of the lighthouse on North Brother Island.

Tiffany St. Pier Foot of Tiffany St. The 410-foot pier is constructed entirely of recycled plastic. It is the biggest all plastic structure built in the country. And, dreaded marine wood borers won't damage it. The pier replaces one built in 1995 that was melted by lightning. Fishing, picnic area and vista.

Barretto Point Park Barretto St. & Viele Ave. 5 acres. An abandoned brownfield being transformed to a waterside park. Amphitheater, ball courts, picnic area and vista. ✖

Bronx River

The Bronx River travels through a 23-mile verdant corridor from Kensico Dam in Westchester and flows through 8 miles of the Bronx. The Mohegan Indians called it Aquehung, which means the "River of High Bluffs." The river changes from saltwater to the only freshwater river within city limits just north of East 180th St. Despite years of neglect, life in the river is thriving. The Bronx River runs through native forest, botanical gardens, the zoo, and the industrial South Bronx before emptying into the East River. More than 75 bridges span the river, which runs from 15 feet wide to 2,000 feet across at its mouth. It has four waterfalls, which canoes must portage around. As the river flows south the shoreline becomes less accessible. There are proposals to demolish the Sheridan Expressway in order to create a 28-acre riverfront park and link in the Bronx River Greenway. A state license is required to fish the Bronx River. The best way to experience the river is by canoe. Each spring, the annual Bronx River Flotilla paddles through the gardens and zoo, normally restricted areas. Canoe tours of the river below the zoo are conducted seasonally by the Bronx River Alliance and The Point. (See Paddling)

 Subway 2 to Pelham Pkwy. Station or Bronx Park East Station. Free trolley transport weekends and Holidays to Bronx Park cultural sites.

 The Bronx River Greenway is an 11.5 mile off-street trail that follows the river from Kensico Dam to Bronx Park and links to the Pelham Bay Pkwy. North path. The greenway below Bronx Park to Soundview is in place. Within Soundview Park a 1.3-mile off-road path extends around the lagoons, beginning at Lafayette St. to the O'Brien St. entrance. ✗

 Snuff Mill in the New York Botanical Gardens

👁 Waterfalls cascading just inside the Bronxdale gate of the zoo.

Muskrat Cove 238th St. Paved path edging the river. Biking, habitat, hiking and vista.

Shoelace Park 233rd St. to Gun Hill Rd. A 2-mile narrow park to where the river oxbows as it reaches Gun Hill Rd. and runs under the historic Duncomb Bridges. Birding, fishing, habitat, hand launch (canoe put-in at 219th St.), hiking, biking, picnic area, playgrounds, restrooms and vista.

Bronx Park Bronx Park East & Brady Ave., Gun Hill Rd. to E 180th St. 720 acres. The path winds through the public Bronx River Forest to waterfalls that are only accessible with admission to the Botanical Gardens or Bronx Zoo. Ball fields, birding, fishing, habitat, handball, hand launch, hiking, historic site, parking, playground,

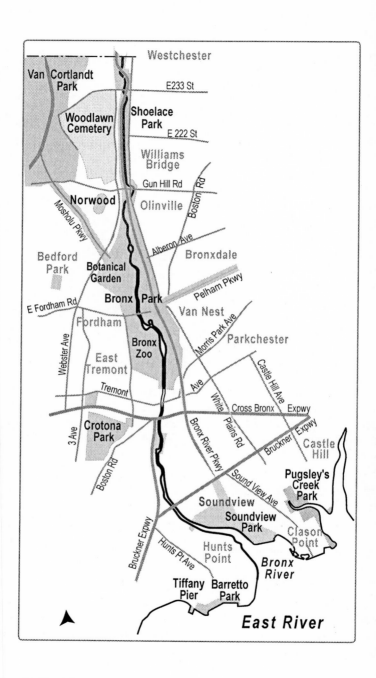

picnic area, restrooms and vista.
Forever Wild Area. 718-430-1890

New York Botanical Gardens
200th St. & Kazimiroff Blvd. 250 acres.
The first Botanical Garden in the U.S.
on the former Lorillard Estate. Follow
the Snuff Mill Trail along the river to a
waterfall that once powered the restored
tobacco Snuff Mill, which is now a
restaurant. 718-817-8700 nybg.org

Bronx Zoo Fordham Rd. & Bronx
River Pkwy. The bison pasture fronts
the river at a double waterfall. "Bronx
River Walk" is a public nature trail the
zoo plans to be built along the river.
718-367-1010 wcs.org

West Farms Park East 180th St.
3 acres. The park's waterfall was originally built as a dam to power a mill.
Barbecuing, garden, hand launch,
picnic area and vista.

Starlight Park 174th to 172nd St.
Complete reconstruction of the park
will include a boathouse and water
access. Ball fields, basketball, floating
dock, habitat, restrooms and vista. ✗

Cement Plant Park Edgewater Rd. 10
acres. An abandoned plant that will
be transformed to parkland. ✗

Garrison End of Garrison Ave.
1 acre. On the rivers west side, the lot
will become a sculpture garden. ✗

Hunts Point Riverside Park Foot of
Lafayette Ave. at Edgewater Rd. The
best river access, the parcel is slated to
be rehabilitated to a lush green park.

Amphitheater, educational programs,
fishing, floating dock, paddling, playground, picnic area and vista. ✗

Soundview Park & Lagoons
Lafayette Ave. 156 acres. 24 acres of
lagoons. Restored tidal wetlands and
a meadow. Ball fields, biking, birding, esplanade, fishing, habitat, hiking,
track and vista.

Westchester Creek

Westchester Creek is a 2.5-mile tributary of the upper East River. The creek
is shallow with depths averaging from
one to five feet and widths ranging
from 175 to 600 feet, where it meets
Pugsley's Creek. Landscaped public
esplanades run along housing developments at Shorehaven (Soundview)
and Castle Hill Estates (Castle Hill
Ave.). The Bronx YMCA occupies a
waterfront site on the western banks
at the entrance to Westchester Creek.

 Subway 6 to E 177th St. then
Bx36 Bus to Clason Point.

 Soundview Greenway is an 8-
mile path from Soundview Park
to Ferry Point Park that will utilize
new esplanades through residential
projects. ✗

 Metro Marine Sales

 Soundview Park offers views
of the Manhattan skyline, and
Throgs Neck and Whitestone bridges.

Clason Point Park Sound View Ave. 4.25 acres. The neglected park on tip of Clason Point was the site of a large Indian settlement. Fishing, hand launch, habitat and vista.

Castle Hill Park Foot of Castle Hill Ave. 4 acres. At Castle Hill Neck, an undeveloped park overlooking the East River and Whitestone Bridge. To be rebuilt with a new fishing pier. 🛠

Pugsley's Creek Park Foot of Sound View Ave. 4 acres. Nature trails and freshwater wetlands. Ball fields, birding, fishing, habitat and hand launch.

Ferry Point Park Beneath the Whitestone Bridge at Schley & Emerson Ave. 414 acres. About half of the parkland on the former landfill is being transformed into an 18-hole luxury golf course, designed by Jack Nicklaus. The city's first new course in 35 years is slated to open in 2005. Ball fields, basketball, birding, biking, esplanade, fishing, golf, habitat, hiking, picnic area, restrooms and vista. 🛠

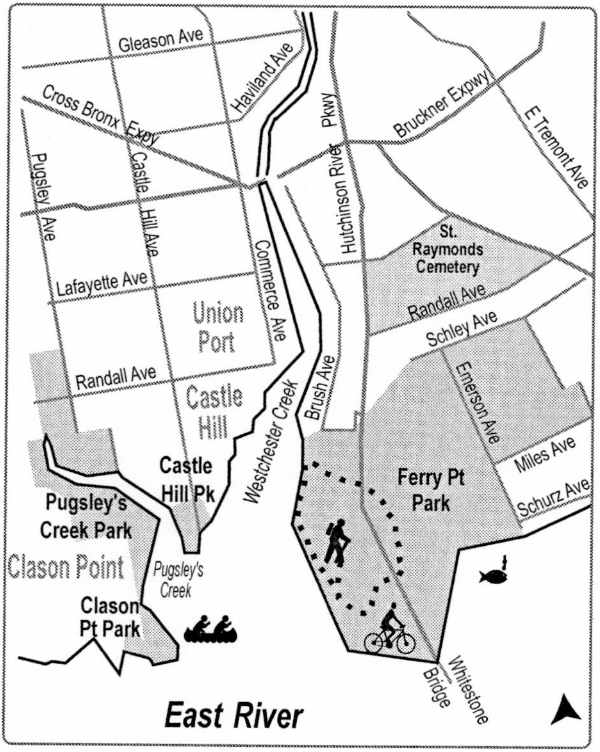

Long Island Sound

The Bronx coast of Long Island Sound is the largest recreational boating area in New York City. The Sound is an estuary that provides feeding, breeding and nesting for a diversity of plants and wildlife. The entrance to the Long Island Sound is marked by the Throg's Neck Bridge. The Maritime Academy is based on the outer end of Throg's Neck, at historic Fort Schuyler. The shore is confined to member-only access at private beach clubs and former summer colonies, such as Edgewater and Silver Beach, which have converted to cooperative ownership.

 Subway 6 to Westchester Sq., then Bx40 Bus to campus gate.

 QBx1 bike-on-bus shuttle over the Whitestone Bridge.

 Hammond Cove, Barrons Boatyard, Fenton Marine, Locust Point Yacht Club

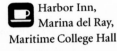 Harbor Inn, Marina del Ray, Maritime College Hall

 SUNY Maritime campus offers panoramic views of the Long Island Sound.

SUNY Maritime College 6 Pennyfield Ave. The nation's first maritime college is located at former Fort Schuyler, which was an active military installation until 1932. Biking, fishing (by permit), historic site, museum, parking, picnic area, refreshment, restrooms and vista. 718-409-7200 sunymaritime.edu

Maritime Industry Museum Collections of maritime industry artifacts. 718-409-7218

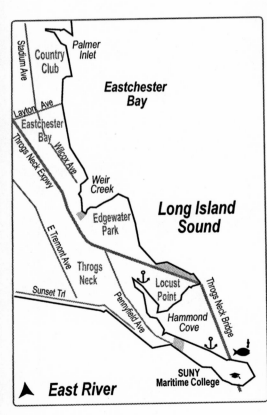

Eastchester Bay & Hutchinson River

Eastchester Bay is a mile-long water body between City Island and Throg's Neck. The salt marsh that fringes the coast acts as a nursery for aquatic life and habitat for shorebirds. It is a largely inaccessible residential coast. A new waterfront development at the former Sunrise Marina property is taking full advantage of location to include boat slips and a full-service marina for homeowners. Pelham Bay Park, the largest city park, dominates the northeastern shore of Eastches-

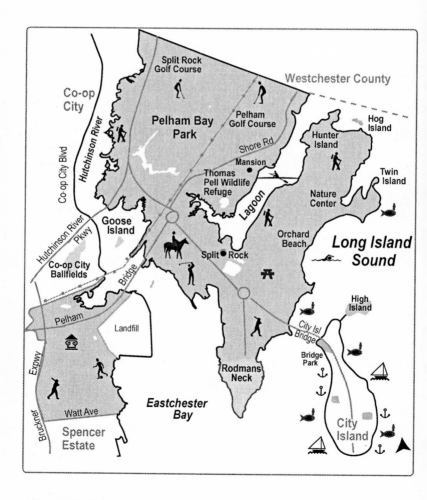

ter Bay, between the Hutchinson River and Long Island Sound. From the time the city took control of the land in 1888, community groups have successfully ensured that the parkland preserves its natural beauty and remains public space. A present day initiative is reclaiming Palmer's Inlet for public use.

The Hutchinson River flows five miles from its headwaters in Westchester County to Eastchester Bay parallel to the landscaped Hutchinson River Parkway. It is named for religious exile Ann Hutchinson, who established a settlement on the north bank in 1642 and where she met her tragic end in an Indian massacre a year later. The towers of Co-op City rise on the spot where Ann's cottage once stood. The riverside is inaccessible at the 330-acre site residential site. On the Pelham Bay Park side of the river, trails pass salt marsh and offers views of wading birds on Goose Island, which sits in the middle of Goose Creek.

Subway 6 to Pelham Bay (last stop). Bus Bx5; Bx12 or NY Express Bus to Pelham Bay station.

Pelham Bay Park and City Island are accessible from the west via Pelham Pkwy. Greenway. From the south: Hutchinson River Greenway, an overgrown trail that extends from the Whitestone Bridge to the Merritt Pkwy. in Connecticut is ripe for rehabilitation.

Ampere YC, Bronxonia YC, Stepping Stone YC

View of crew teams sculling on the Pelham Bay Lagoon from the Siwanoy Trail.

Veteran's Memorial Park Throg's Neck Expwy. 9.25 acres. On Weir Creek. Ball fields, biking and vista.

Pelham Bay Park 2,766 acres. The park contains a sandy beach, two protected sanctuaries, vast expanses of salt marsh, and hundreds of acres of woodland. Ball fields, barbecuing, basketball, beach, birding, biking, canoeing, golf, fishing, habitat, handball, hand launch, hiking, historic site, horseback riding, nature center, paddling, picnic areas, refreshment, restrooms, rock climbing, rowing, sun bathing, swimming, tennis, track, volleyball and vista. Forever Wild Area. 718-430-1890

Pelham Bay Park Points of Interest:

Orchard Beach. 115 acres. A mile-long man-made beach, built in the 1930s on landfill that covered Pelham Bay. Sand was barged from the beaches of Rockaway. Barbecuing, basketball, beach, boardwalk, handball, playgrounds, picnic area, parking, promenade, refreshments, restrooms, showers, swimming, volleyball and vista. 718-885-2275

Orchard Beach Nature Center Urban park ranger programs including nature study and seasonal canoe trips in the lagoon. 718-885-3466

Hunter Island Marine Zoology & Geology Sanctuary 125 acres. Kazimiroff Nature Trail loops through the sanctuary. The most southerly extension of the rocky New England coastline marked by huge glacial boulders. The lagoon is used as a rowing basin by intercollegiate teams. Birding, fishing, habitat, hand launch, hiking, nature center, rock climbing and vista.

Thomas Pell Wildlife Refuge 489 acres. Split Rock Trail through Goose Creek Marsh. Birding, historic site, horse-back riding, golf, habitat, hiking, nature trails and vistas.

Bartow-Pell Mansion & Museum 895 Shore Rd. Landmark 19th century federal-style mansion, open to the public. 718-885-1461

Pelham Bit Stables 9 Shore Rd. Trail rides ($25/hr) and lessons on waterfront bridle paths through marshes and forest. 718-885-0551

Split Rock & Pelham Bay Golf Courses 718-885-1258

City Island History

City Island is a small community at the edge of New York City located just beyond Pelham Bay Park in the Bronx and surrounded by the waters of western Long Island Sound and Eastchester Bay. With Execution Light to the northeast and Stepping Stone Lighthouse to the south, City Island has a rich nautical history, much of it preserved by the City Island Historical Society and Nautical Museum (cityislandmuseum.org).

Originally inhabited by the Siwanoy Indians, who lived during the summer on the plentiful clams, oysters and fish they found here, City Island was first established as an English settlement in 1685. The English crown granted Thomas Pell ownership of the island and parts of Westchester County, which lasted until 1749, when ownership passed to other individuals. During the 1700s, many of the island's residents were either oystermen or Hellgate pilots who helped navigate ships down the East River to New York Harbor. Ideally situated to service schooners traveling between New York and points north and south, the island became an important shipbuilding and yachting center during the nineteenth and twentieth centuries.

The two world wars brought about a conversion from yacht building to the construction of submarine chasers, tugboats, Vosper-style P.T. boards, landing craft, and minesweepers for the United States government. After World War II, yachting returned and with it the building of 12-meter sloops that successfully defended the America's Cup. Today the presence of yacht clubs, sailing schools, marinas, sailmakers, fishing and lobster boats, as well as marine supply, repair shops, and seafood restaurants, reflect City Island's role as a nautical community.

Submitted by Barbara Dolensek,
City Island Historical Society

City Island

City Island is a historic nautical village of Victorian homes, yacht clubs, marinas and seafood restaurants. No resident is more than two blocks from the water, yet there is little public waterfront. Fishing and sailing are chief recreations on the 1.5-mile-long island. A world-famous shipbuilding and yachting center that has produced five winning America's Cup sloops, City Island is designated as one of 17 New York State Historic Maritime Centers and the only one in the City. Many of the island's winning yachts return each spring for the annual blessing of the fleet celebration.

Public waterfront access on the 230-acre island is limited to a tiny esplanade located just over the City Island Bridge, a waterside cemetery and the City Island wetlands.

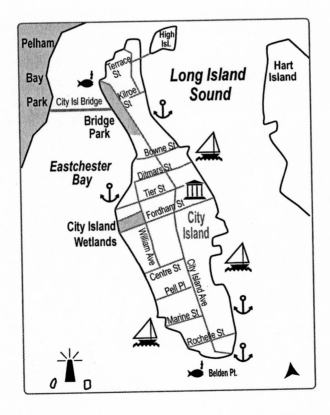

The waters around City Island contain shallow flats and reefs with abrupt drop-offs, which have been the cause of many shipwrecks. Some form small islands and are visible only at low tide. All of the islands in the surrounding waters have restricted access. A narrow footbridge leads from City Island to High Island, home to the WFAN and WCBS radio towers. Since 1869, almost 800,000 indigent dead have been buried three-deep at the city's potter's field on Hart Island. An artist's colony took up residence on Rat Island in the late 19th century. Hog Island was once claimed by a female squatter, who lived there until her death in 1930. Other nearby islands include: Big Town Island, Buck Rock Island, Chimney Sweep, Cuban Ledge, Green Flats and Rivers Island.

 Subway 6 to Pelham Bay Park to Bx29 Bus to City Island.

 City Island Bridge path links to Pelham Bay Park path.

 City Island Gas Dock, Consolidated Yachts, Evers Seaplane, Kirby Marine, Royal Marina, Sailmaker, Sunrise Marina, City Island YC, Harlem YC, Morris YC, Stuyvesant YC, NY Sailing Center, Sea Anchors, Minneford YC, Touring YC

 Johnny's Famous Reef, Tony's On the Pier, The Lobster Box, Anna's Harbor, Seashore Restaurant

 View of Stepping Stone Lighthouse amid squealing gulls from the large outdoor patio of Johnny's Famous Reef on Beldon Point.

Bridge Park City Island Ave. A waterfront esplanade and narrow lawn.

City Island Wetlands Bay St. 8 acres. The last remaining wetlands on the island. Habitat and vista.

Brooklyn

Waterfront History

By Marcia Reiss

Brooklyn began on its waterfront. It was here, along more than 100 miles bordering the turbulent East River, tranquil bays, ocean beaches and winding creeks, that Native Americans enjoyed an unimaginable bounty of fish and fertile soil for thousands of years. And it was here, four centuries ago, that the first European settlers established farms and villages, connected to Manhattan and the Old World by a lifeline of ferryboats and sailing ships.

Sailing through the Narrows and up the East River in the early 17th century, the Dutch had their eyes fixed not just on Manhattan, but also on Brooklyn. Soon after establishing the center of New Amsterdam in Lower Manhattan, they cut the first canal from the Red Hook peninsula to Gowanus Creek settled along Greenpoint's Newtown Creek, and started the first ferry route from Manhattan to the foot of today's Old Fulton St, the start of the old City of Brooklyn.

From Greenpoint to Red Hook, the waterfront was literally Brooklyn's cutting edge of development. It expanded with masses of landfill, reached into the waters with fingers of new piers and soared upwards with the towering masts of great ships. The new waterfront began to take shape after the War of 1812 when New York became the nation's leading port. The invention of the steamboat in 1815 and the opening of the Erie Canal in 1825 created an unprecedented demand for dock space. While shippers were already vying for space in crowded Lower Manhattan, Brooklyn's spacious waterfront had the clear advantage, particularly for bulk cargoes like grain, sugar and coffee. In 1850, the largest port facility in the nation, Red Hook's Atlantic Docks, was completed with room for 150 ships, huge grain silos and hundreds of warehouses. In these days before the construction of the Brooklyn Bridge, the grain terminals were the tallest structures on the city's horizon and dozens of them, filled with Midwestern grain from Erie Canal barges, lined the Brooklyn shore, ready for shipments abroad.

At the same time, Greenpoint became a burgeoning shipbuilding center. Great rafts of logs were towed from Canada down the St. Lawrence and Hudson rivers to Greenpoint where thousands of men and boys crafted them into graceful clipper ships, sloops, schooners, yachts, paddleboats and ferries. Greenpoint shipyards and ironworks turned out the largest and most famous vessels of the day, including the *USS Monitor*, the Union's first ironclad vessel. Hundreds of other warships were built and repaired in the Brooklyn Navy Yard. Opened in 1801, the navy yard grew over the next 150 years to become the zenith of Brooklyn's industrial might

The thriving port spurred the growth of an astounding number and diversity of industries. Some of the biggest companies in the world—Domino and Jack Frost Sugar, Corning Glass and Standard Oil—came to the Brooklyn waterfront in the 19th century. Although many were known by their Manhattan addresses, their massive operations were in Brooklyn where they could receive raw materials and ship finished products with ease. Hundreds of smaller manufacturers—Brillo, Benjamin Moore, Borax, Sterno, and Eskimo Pie—once operated in the neighborhood known today

Brooklyn Bridge & Empire Stores

© 2002 Etienne Frossard

as DUMBO. Breweries, printing plants, sugar and oil refineries had transformed Williamsburg from a farming village to a city in 1851, a time when it was nearly as large as the separate City of Brooklyn. In his 1856 poem, "Crossing Brooklyn Ferry," Walt Whitman described the "wild yellow and red light" of the refinery chimneys against the Brooklyn sky. These "black arts" also darkened and fouled the sky with smoke, soot and sulfuric fumes. Others, like Greenpoint's glass and porcelain factories, where Mary Todd Lincoln purchased tableware for the White House, produced works of great artistry.

For skilled craftsmen, manual laborers, and daring industrialists, the Brooklyn waterfront in the 19th and early 20th centuries was a place of virtually unlimited opportunities. But the waterfront was not only a place for work. Even when industry dominated the shoreline, boys swam in the East River by jumping off the piers. Those who could afford it traveled south to the glittering amusement parks of Coney Island, the grand hotels of Brighton and Manhattan Beach, the horseracing tracks of Sheepshead Bay and the great estates and resorts of Bay Ridge. Throughout the 19th century, these were the summer places to be.

Like other industrial centers in the northeast, Brooklyn changed dramatically in the 20th century, particularly after the Second World War when many manufacturing and shipping firms moved to other parts of the country. Yet the changes on the waterfront had begun much earlier. Ironically, they began to shift after the completion of the greatest structure on the waterfront—the Brooklyn Bridge. Once the bridge opened in 1883, it provided a quicker, safer, and more reliable river crossing than the ferries ever could. Although ferry service from the end of Fulton St. continued for several more decades, the area, once Brooklyn's commercial center, became a backwater as businesses moved inland. The pattern was repeated all along the waterfront as other bridges, elevated trains, subway lines, cars, trucks and airplanes made the old ferry landings and shipping piers all but obsolete.

While the old shipyards, warehouses and factories deteriorated, the waterfront and its haunting sense of history have continued to draw people and inspire new developments. Nearly half a millennium after the first European settlement, Brooklyn is rediscovering and reinventing itself on its waterfront. The revitalization of the old industrial neighborhoods from Greenpoint to Red Hook is a continuing expression of Whitman's joyous delight in experiencing the city at its edge. "Just as you feel when you look on the river and sky," the poet said in 1856, "so I felt."§

Marcia Reiss has been involved with the New York City waterfront as a journalist, city official, university professor and parks advocate. She is the author of *Brooklyn Then and Now* 2001; *New York Architecture in Detail* 2003, and a series of history guides to Brooklyn neighborhoods published by the Brooklyn Historical Society.

Go Coastal:
Brooklyn

Brooklyn is the second largest borough in size and the largest in population, the equivalent of the fourth largest city in the country. The borough is situated on the extreme western end of Long Island and is practically surrounded by water. About 80% of the waterfront acreage is publicly owned. The enormous diversity of the Brooklyn waterfront comprises the industrialized north shore, port facilities bounding the Upper Bay, the barrier beaches of the Atlantic Coast and the natural ecosystem of Jamaica Bay.

East River

The East River is not a true river, but a tidal strait that reaches from Upper New York Bay to the Long Island Sound. Early navigators called it the East River because it was the route used to travel east to Long Island and New England. It is a federal channel and part of the Intercoastal Waterway. The East River separates Manhattan and Brooklyn. It ranges from .5 to 3.5 miles wide with depths from 22 to over 100 feet deep. The river has two mouths and a hydraulic current where differences in the time and height of high water cause a strong flow of water from one end of the river to the other and back again. The tide may be ebbing on the East River while flooding on the Hudson and tidal currents are swifter here than the Hudson, running about four knots at the Brooklyn Bridge. Three great bridges link Brooklyn and Manhattan and are the defining feature of the Lower East River. A small natural cove survives on the shore between the Brooklyn and Manhattan bridges. North America's longest auto tunnel runs under the river from Brooklyn to the Battery. Brooklyn's north shore, Greenpoint and Williamsburg, are largely landlocked. Residents challenge debris filled abandoned lots and derelict piers to reach the water's edge. Crowds gather in make-shift parks to witness amazing views of the sun setting behind the midtown Manhattan skyline. Reclamation of the once heavily industrialized coast entails rezoning and revitalization that will eventually open close to 50 acres of waterfront space for public use. Further south, the city and state are transforming the Brooklyn Piers into a continuous waterfront park. An off-street greenway is planned to link the entire East River coast.

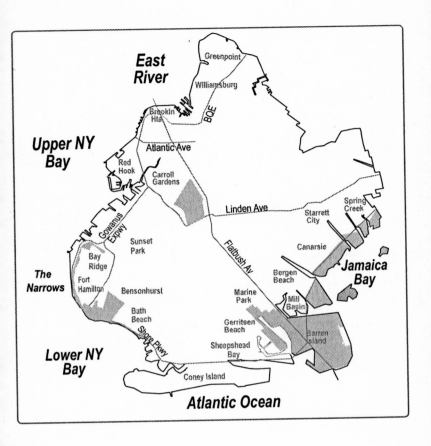

Newtown Creek

Newtown Creek flows west for about four miles to form a natural boundary between Brooklyn and Queens and empties into the East River. Its tributaries include: Dutch Kills, Whale Creek, Maspeth Creek and English Kills. The creek was once one of the country's busiest commercial waterways rivaling the Mississippi. It is today one of the most polluted waterbodies in New York Harbor, home to the city's largest waste treatment plant and the site of the largest oil spill in U.S. history—the 17 million gallon ExxonMobil underground spill. The cleanup will take years. To improve sightlines and access to the water, pocket parks are planned at street-ends along the creek and under bridges that cross it.

Subway G to Greenpoint Ave. at Manhattan Ave.

 Brooklyn Waterfront Greenway is a dedicated bike/ped. path that will extend from Greenpoint to Sunset Park. brooklyngreenway.org ✘

 Pulaski Bridge offers views of the Midtown Manhattan skyline and the East River looking out across Newtown Creek.

Newtown Creek Treatment Plant
Whale Creek. Greenpoint Ave. 53 acres. The wastewater facility is undergoing an upgrade that will include the creation of a public nature walk on the perimeter of the plant along the waterfront. ✘

Manhattan Avenue Street-end
The small park and overlook is one of the few places to access Newtown Creek. Boat building, boathouse, fishing, launch, paddling and vista.

Barge Park Manhattan Ave. at Franklin St. The park is located a few feet from the water, yet has no access. A former sludge tank near the site may be adapted for reuse as a community environmental center. Ball fields, playground and vista.

Java & Kent Street-ends A riverside esplanade will link the street-ends and lead to a new fishing pier. ✘

WNYC Site End of Greenpoint Ave. 1.2 acres. An undeveloped city park on the lot where the WNYC radio towers once stood. ✘

Bushwick Inlet

Bushwick Inlet separates Greenpoint from Williamsburg. Fuel-oil depots and gas plants line the southern shore of the inlet. The north shore was once home to Continental Iron Works, where the *USS Monitor* was built and launched on January 30, 1862. The ship's famed iron hull immediately made all other warships obsolete. A monument to the designer of the *Monitor*, John Ericsson, stands in nearby McGolrick Park.

 Subway M, Z Marcy Pl. or L to Bedford Ave.; G to Nassau Ave.

 Williamsburg Bridge paths connect to the Lower East Side.

 Giando on the Water

 Wallabout Channel is visible from Kent Ave. at Division Ave.

East River State Park Kent Ave. N 7th to N 9th St. 9 acres. A new public park developed by the State and NYU at the former Brooklyn Eastern District car-float terminal, vacant since 1983 when the terminal closed after almost 150 years of operation. Ball fields, fishing, picnic area, promenade and vista. ✘

Grand Ferry Park Kent Ave. at Grant St. .5 acre. The site of an old ferry landing and the birthplace of Pfizer Pharmaceuticals, this little park looks out on the "sweet" activity of the nearby Domino Sugar docks. Historic site, picnic area and vista.

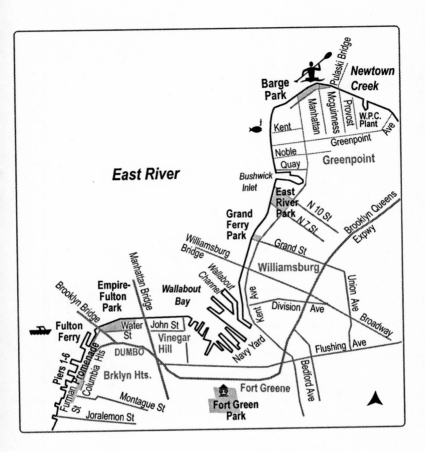

Wallabout Bay

Wallabout Bay, meaning "bay of foreigners," is named for the French speaking Walloons of South Belgium who settled the area. More soldiers perished aboard British prison ships moored in Wallabout Bay than in all of the battles of the American Revolution. In 1808, the remains of thousands of sailors were discovered in the muddy bottom of the bay during dredging to expand the Navy Yard. The remains are now interred in nearby Fort Greene Park (Hudson Ave. at Front St.) in a 149-foot Doric column memorial to the lost soldiers. The walled compound of the Brooklyn Navy Yard effectively blocks all sightlines to the water along the semi-circular cove. On the south shore of the bay, Vinegar Hill is a five-block neighborhood of wooden houses named for a famous battle of Irish independence. The shore affords limited water views and no access.

Brooklyn Navy Yard

Flushing & Cumberland Ave. 260 acres. Thomas Jefferson commissioned the Yard in 1801. Ships built in the yard include: Robert Fulton's steamboat *Clermont;* the *Maine,* which started the Spanish-American war; the *Arizona,* a casualty of Pearl Harbor and the *Iowa,* aboard which the Japanese surrendered. Frank Sinatra and Gene Kelly danced ashore there in the movie "On the Town." Purchased by the city in 1966, the campus-like complex operates as an industrial park that includes hundreds of small businesses, the world's largest exporter of shark fins, and a Hollywood-type movie studio. The old Navy Yard acreage is still somewhat intact and the Yard remains a leader in the ship repair industry. It has six dry docks and five piers, the oldest of which is a historic landmark built in the 1850s. The fleet of FDNY Marine Co. 6 is berthed there, including the Fireboat *Kevin C. Kane,* which made more runs than any fireboat in the world. There is no public access, but occasional tours are conducted by the Brooklyn Historical Society. A scale model of the 1942 Yard is on exhibit at the Maritime Museum in Fort Schuyler at SUNY Maritime College in the Bronx.

Fulton Ferry

The foot of Old Fulton Street marks where ferry service began between Brooklyn and Manhattan in 1642 with regular rowboat crossings. Robert Fulton launched steam service here with the *Nassau* in 1814. The surrounding neighborhood DUMBO, an acronym for "Down Under the Manhattan Bridge Overpass," is dominated by the immense granite blocks of the Manhattan Bridge Anchorage. The remains of a railroad that once carried supplies to factories along the waterfront still imprints the cobbled streets. The Gothic towers of the Brooklyn Bridge define the view and provide a high perch for Peregrine Falcons, which have taken up residence in the east tower. The anchorage of the Brooklyn Bridge contains catacomb-like vaults that anchor the cables holding up the bridge. It is now a performance and exhibit space. Some of the borough's oldest buildings stand in the shadow of the landmark bridges. The Empire Stores, a Civil War-era tobacco warehouse, frames Empire-Fulton Ferry State Park. The refurbished Fulton Ferry Landing pier is inscribed with lines from Whitman's poem "Crossing Brooklyn Ferry." It is a favored spot for wedding photos and sunset views. Walt Whitman edited the *Brooklyn Daily Eagle* from 1846 to 1848 in the nearby Eagle Warehouse at 28 Old Fulton St. and he set type for *Leaves of Grass* at a print shop at 70 Fulton St.

Subway A to High St.; F to York St.; G to Clinton; 1, 2 to Clark St; N, R to Court St.; 4, 5 to Borough Hall

 Manhattan and Brooklyn bridges both have bike/ped. access. Manhattan Bridge enter near Jay & High Sts. Enter the Brooklyn Bridge footpath at Boerum Place or by stairs at Cadman Plaza East.

 Fulton Ferry Landing

 Brooklyn Ice Cream Factory, Bubby's, Grimaldi's, Pete's Downtown, River Café

 Brooklyn Hts. Promenade provides dramatic views of the harbor and cityscape.

Brooklyn Bridge Park 67 acres. The expansive park will stretch from the Manhattan Bridge to Atlantic Ave. uniting existing city and state parks to create 1.3 miles of continuous public access. 718-802-0603 bbpc.net ✘

Main Street Lot & Playground
Plymouth at Washington St. 1.5 acres. The first segment of Brooklyn Bridge Park open to the public offers pathways through native vegetation, unique sitting areas from which to view the river and a landscape that slopes down to a small tidal cove between the Manhattan and Brooklyn bridges, where the shoreline has been reclaimed by nature. A nautical-themed playground occupies the inland edge of the park. Birding, habitat, launch, playground and vista.

Empire-Fulton Ferry State Park
26 New Dock St. 9 acres. A verdant ramble bound by a riverside boardwalk, natural cove and the historic Empire Stores. Birding, esplanade, events, habitat, historic site, picnic area, restrooms and vista. No pets, fishing or bikes are permitted in state parks. 718-858-4708

Fulton Ferry Landing Old Fulton & Furman Sts. Beautifully restored public pier at the site of the city's first ferry landing under the Brooklyn Bridge. Olga Bloom's Bargemusic (718-624-4061) is permanently docked on the southside of the pier. Historic site, picnic area, refreshment, restrooms, water taxi stop and vista.

Brooklyn Piers 1 to 6 Furman St. The piers will eventually be turned over to Brooklyn Bridge Park. They are currently still in commercial use except for Pier 4, which is a community garden. Future plans envision fishing piers, marinas, hotels and recreational facilities. ✘

Brooklyn Heights Promenade
Columbia Hts. Remsen St. to Orange St. The famed 1/3-mile-long walkway is one of Brooklyn's most popular attractions. It is located in the brownstone neighborhood of Brooklyn Heights, the site of a Revolutionary War fort and the city's first suburb. Built in 1950, the promenade is suspended 50 feet above the water, and projects over two tiers of highway and the piers. Playground and vista.

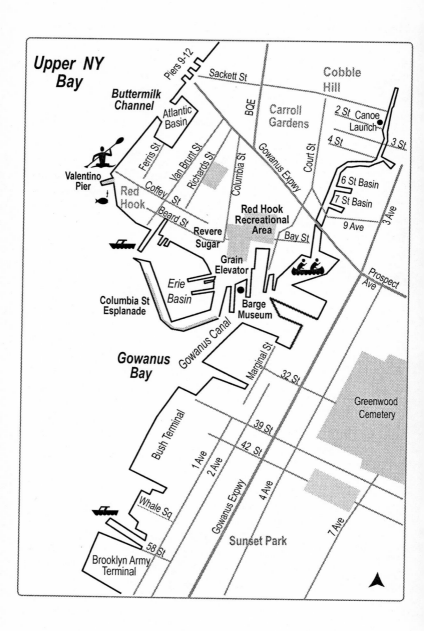

Upper NY Bay

Piers 9-12

Sackett St

Buttermilk Channel

BQE

Cobble Hill

Atlantic Basin

Carroll Gardens

2 St Canoe Launch

4 St

3 St

Ferris St

Van Brunt St

Richards St

Columbia St

Gowanus Expwy

Court St

Valentino Pier

Red Hook

Coffey St

6 St Basin

7 St Basin

Beard St

9 Ave

3 Ave

Revere Sugar

Red Hook Recreational Area

Bay St

Columbia St Esplanade

Erie Basin

Grain Elevator

Barge Museum

Prospect Ave

Gowanus Bay

Gowanus Canal

Marginal St

32 St

Greenwood Cemetery

Bush Terminal

39 St

42 St

1 Ave

2 Ave

4 Ave

Gowanus Expwy

7 Ave

Whale Sq

58 St

Sunset Park

Brooklyn Army Terminal

Upper New York Bay

The East River opens into the sheltered harbor of Upper New York Bay, which measures about 5.5 miles across. Port facilities mark the shore landscape and limit access to the water. The Brooklyn port is the closest shipping access from the open sea. An international fleet of container and cargo ships berth at piers in Red Hook and Sunset Park. Buttermilk Channel, Gowanus Bay and Erie Basin each contribute a coastline to the peninsula of Red Hook, named for its red clay soil and hook shape. Red Hook was home to a thriving shipping district for over 150 years before the change to containerization. South Brooklyn is reactivating terminals that had closed decades ago to accommodate increases in port traffic, and area residents are evaluating new uses for the industrial waterfront. Improvements to the port promise greater public access in the form of perimeter spaces and viewing areas around the piers in Red Hook and Sunset Park.

Buttermilk Channel

As the Brooklyn waterfront bends south, it fronts Buttermilk Channel. The channel is a half-mile-wide strait between Brooklyn and Governor's Island. Before being dredged for port traffic it was possible to cross the channel by foot at low tide. The name is supposed to have come from Dutch settlers who crossed the water to sell buttermilk on Governors Island.

 Subway F to Smith/Carroll St.

 Brooklyn Waterfront Greenway to run along Columbia and Van Brunt Streets. ✕

 Alma Restaurant

Mother Cabrini Park Foot of President St. A small park across from the port terminal providing views of the harbor and the working waterfront. Playground, picnic area, water spray and vista.

Brooklyn PA Marine Terminal & Red Hook Container Port 100 acres. Atlantic Ave. to Atlantic Basin. Piers 7 & 8: one of the few remaining port facilities where longshoremen still handle bulk cargo, the terminal is the highest U.S. point of entry for cocoa beans. It also has transient ship berthing. Piers 9 to 12: handle 65,000 containers a year. The contract with pier operator American Stevedore runs out in 2004 and new uses for the piers are under review.

Erie Basin

The Erie Basin was developed in the 1850s, when Red Hook was one of the busiest and most modern ports in the country. The southern terminus of the Erie Canal is the largest man-made harbor on the East Coast. It now serves as a moorage for barges, tugs and small ships. The city's last warehouse piers and walled shipyards dot the waterfront. Many interesting and historic properties that surround Erie Basin are slated to reinvent themselves in the future. Red Hook Stores, a 5-story brick warehouse at the foot of Van Brunt Street, will be developed as a Fairway supermarket. A big box Ikea Store is awaiting community approval to occupy New York Shipyard. Todd Shipyard, an operating dry dock since the Civil War when the *USS Monitor* was repaired there, is one of the largest waterfront parcels offered for sale on the entire East Coast. The old Revere Sugar Refinery, across the quay from the Beard St. Warehouses, is being marketed for sale as Sugar Bay Industrial Park. Trolley tracks have been laid from Beard St. to Pier 41 where they plan to one day operate restored trolleys, but funding shortfalls have put those plans on hold. The Brooklyn Clay Retort and Fire Brick Works at 76 Van Dyke Street is the first of the areas historic buildings to be designated a NYC landmark.

 Subway F, G to Smith/9th St. then Bus 77 to Van Dyke & Van Brunt St.; A, C, F to Jay St./Borough Hall then B61 Bus to the last stop.

Sunny's Bar

Valentino Pier offers spectacular sunset views that span the entire Upper Bay, from the Verrazano Bridge to the Statue of Liberty and Lower Manhattan.

Valentino Pier End of Coffey St. 2.2 acres. A popular fishing pier with seating areas, flanked by grass lawns and small pebble beach. Biking, hand launch, fishing and vista.

Conover Street Waterfront Park Foot of Conover St. A small garden park with seating area. Vista.

Beard Street Pier Van Brunt St. Civil War-era brick warehouses, privately restored to commercial space for artisans and small businesses, are homeport to NY Water Taxi, the Brooklyn Waterfront Artists Pier Show and a sunken lightship whose masts reach above the waterline. An esplanade on the western side of the quay is open to the public. Davit launch, esplanade, historic ship, historic site, rowing and vista.

Red Hook Recreation Area Bay St. 58 acres. The park is separated from the waterfront by industrial properties. Ball fields, basketball, biking, handball, picnic area, pool, playground, restrooms and vista. 718-722-3211

Columbia St. Esplanade Foot of Columbia St. The 500-foot wide pier extends the length of the Erie Basin breakwater with a biking lane and plenty of room to cast a fishing line into the bay. The Grain Elevator at the head of the pier, in use until 1965, is the largest one on the eastern seaboard. Biking, esplanade, fishing and vista.

Waterfront Museum Barge
Columbia St. Terminal. A restored 1914 Lehigh Valley Railroad Barge that features historic exhibits and seasonal events. The barge will relocate to Conover St. when the pier there is repaired. Educational programs, events, historic ship, an d museum. 718-624-4719 waterfrontmuseum.org

Gowanus Canal

Named for Chief Gowanee of the Canarsie Indian tribe, Gowanus Creek reportedly produced oysters the size of dinner plates. The canal was built in 1848 by widening the creek for barge transport and extends a 1.5 miles inland from Gowanus Bay. The petite commercial channel quickly became so polluted from industrial waste and dyes that it was branded Lavender Lake. Clean-up of the canal began when a pumping fan used to circulate clean water from the Upper Bay was fixed in 1999. The pump was installed in 1911 and had been out of order since the 1960s. Harbor seals have recently been sighted and oysters have been reintroduced to its waters. New pocket parks built where streets dead-end at the canal allow limited waterside access.

 Subway F, G to Smith/9th St.

 5 bridges with bike/ped. path across the canal at Union, Carroll, 3rd & 9th Sts & Hamilton Ave.

 Peer down the Gowanus Canal from one of the bridges.

2nd Street Launch A small street-end park and canoe launch maintained by the Gowanus Dredgers Canoe Club. Over 1,000 boats launch from the site each year. 718-443-0849

Carroll St. Bridge Built in 1888, it is the oldest retractile bridge in the country. It operates by rolling back on steel wheels along tracks.

The Pumping Station Union St. Landmark built in 1911, flushes 200 million gallons of water from Upper Bay through the canal each day.

Gowanus Bay

Gowanus Bay is bound by the industrialized Sunset Park waterfront, which extends from the mouth of Gowanus Canal to 66th St. This has traditionally been a working waterfront of docking ports, basins, dry docks and warehouses. It is home to the NYPD Harbor Unit, a federal prison and marine transfer station, as well as hundreds of small businesses. A container and automobile port is being reactivated at South Brooklyn Marine Terminal.

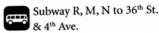 Subway R, M, N to 36th St. & 4th Ave.

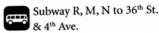 58th St. Pier

Sunset Park Waterfront Park From 44th to 50th St. 24 acres. A waterfront esplanade and public park. ✖

Brooklyn Army Terminal 1st Ave. & 55th St. Designed by Cass Gilbert and built in 1919, the terminal was the departure site for 80% of U.S. troops sent overseas in World War II. It closed in 1970. Reactivation of the terminal is part of port expansion plans.

Bush Terminal 2nd Ave. & 41st St. 100 acres. Built in 1890, the complex of piers and warehouses once housed 25 steamship lines and served as the model for industrial parks built nationwide. Today, the terminal operates as a light industry center for manufacturing firms.

The Narrows

Considered the gateway to New York Harbor, the Narrows strait connects Upper New York Bay and Lower New York Bay. The ridge above the Narrows has played an important strategic role in harbor defense since revolutionary times. While the history of the Brooklyn waterfront farther north is heavily influenced by shipping and industry, the neighborhood of Bay Ridge overlooking the Narrows was once home to some of New York's wealthiest citizens. The Verrazano Narrows Bridge spans the strait linking Fort Hamilton in Brooklyn and Fort Wadsworth in Staten Island. The Belt Parkway edges the waterfront of the Narrows and Lower Bay, beginning at Owl's Head Park. Miles of wide esplanade and linear parks run the entire length of the parkway, on the waterfront and upland margins. Under the Verrazano is Denyse Wharf, an 18th century remnant that now forms a small beach. The site is used as a marine lab by local high schools.

 Subway R to Bay Ridge Ave.

 Shore Pkwy. Greenway extends the entire Brooklyn shore, beginning at 69th St. Pier. The Verrazano Bridge has no access, except during the NY Marathon when runner's start the race on the bridge 295 feet above the water.

 Lai Yuen

Shore Road travels on a ridge above the Narrows and presents broad views of Lower NY Bay.

Owl's Head Park Shore Rd. 27 acres. Above the waterfront, the view is unmatched for watching ships transit the harbor. Biking, dog run, playground, skateboarding and vista.

Cannonball (John Paul Jones) Park 4th Ave. 5.5 acres. A 20" black Parrot cannon and cannonballs dominate the landscape against the backdrop of the bridge and Lower Bay. Vista.

69th St. Pier The pier extends 600 feet into the bay. It is a favorite spot for fishermen and strollers and marks the start of the shorefront greenway. Biking, fishing, picnic area and vista.

Narrows Botanical Gardens Shore Rd. 4.5 acres. Native plant garden. narrowsbg.org

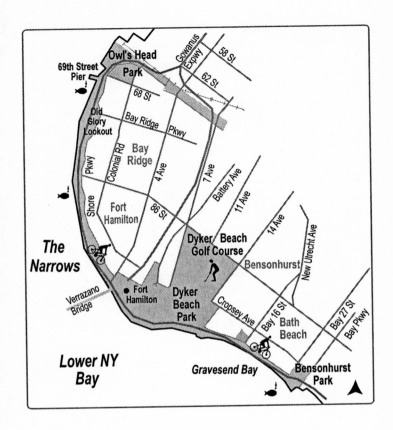

Fort Hamilton 8302 Colonial Rd. 155 acres. The Army's "Boots on the Ground in New York City." The campus offers stunning views and is home to the Army Corps of Engineers, North Atlantic Division. Built 1825, Andrew Jackson and Robert E. Lee served there and attended St. John's Church nearby, known as the church of generals. Within the campus, Colonel's Row, Fort Hamilton Community Club, Lee House and the Harbor Defense Museum are on the National Register of Historic Places. Fort Lafayette once stood on a reef opposite Fort Hamilton and is now used to anchor the tower of the Verrazano-Narrows Bridge. hamilton.army.mil

Harbor Defense Museum Bldg. 230, Sheridan Loop. A unique collection of coastal defense artifacts located right in the old fort. Admission and tours are by appointment. 718-630-4349 harbordefensemuseum.com

Lower New York Bay

Lower New York Bay encompasses the area below the Narrows to Breezy Point at the tip on Rockaway Peninsula. The Lower Bay is larger than the Upper Bay, measuring 100 square miles. Water depths are shallow ranging from 6 to 35 feet. Federal channels are dredged to 45 and 50 feet. The Brooklyn shore faces southward. On the waterfront, a series of artwork and educational panels known as "Waterwalk" illustrate the local aquatic environment. Lower New York Bay has several coves, inlets, creeks and inner bays, which have served as venues for ship wrecks, pirates and smugglers. The inlets of the Lower Bay protected the notorious rum-running boat *The Cigarette*, owned by Bay Ridge mobster Vannie Higgins. The namesake of today's powerboats was the fastest boat in New York waters during Prohibition, traveling at 50 mph.

Gravesend Bay

South of the Verrazano Bridge, the shore curves to form Gravesend Bay. It is the eastern boundary of Lower Bay and reaches three miles across. The relatively calm waters are a fish nursery bound by the neighborhoods of Dyker Heights, Bensonhurst and Bath Beach. As with Bay Ridge to the north, these coastal neighborhoods gained a reputation in the 19th century as seaside resorts. Today, Gravesend Bay is a destination for recreational boaters and fishermen.

 Subway M, W to 86th St. & Bay Pkwy. to B1 Bus.

 Shore Road Greenway waterfront trail parallels the Belt Pkwy. from Bay Ridge Ave. to Dreier-Offerman Park. At Bay Pkwy. cyclists must ride the slim shoulder of old Shore Pkwy. to the path over the Cropsey Ave. Bridge to Coney Island.

 Marine Basin Marina

Dyker Beach Park Shore Pkwy. at 86th St. 216.5 acres. The parkway bisects the park, restricting upland sections from the water. Ball fields, bocce, handball, golf, kite flying, playground, picnic area and vista.

 Dyker Golf Course 718-836-9722

Bath Beach Playground Shore Pkwy. & 17th Ave. Basketball, blading, bocce, handball, restrooms, softball and vista.

Bensonhurst Park 21st Ave. & Bay Pkwy. 17.5 acres. A shady sitting area and promenade adjacent to the tennis bubbles on the bay. Ball fields, basketball, bikeway, fishing, tennis, picnic tables and vista. 718-946-5048

Dreier-Offerman Park Shore Pkwy. & Bay 44th St. 110 acres. A wrought-iron gate opens to playing fields, a grass meadow and restored wetlands along the shore. A large part of the park is unimproved. Ball fields, basketball, biking, birding, blading, bocce, events, fishing, habitat, hiking, playground, picnic areas, restrooms and vista.

Coney Island Creek

Coney Island Creek is a tidal inlet about 1.5 miles long that originates at a storm drain near Shell Road and empties into Gravesend Bay. The creek once formed a channel with Sheepshead Bay, but was landfilled in 1910, re-shaping Coney Island into a peninsula. The brackish waters provide a nursery for killifish. Wetland restoration along the shore includes a nature trail alongside the Home Depot. the parks on Coney Island Creek are popular fishing grounds and sacred site to colorful baptism ceremonies.

 Subway W to Bay 50th St; Bus B74 to Mermaid Ave.

 Woroco Fuel Dock

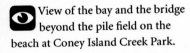 View of the bay and the bridge beyond the pile field on the beach at Coney Island Creek Park.

Kaiser Park Neptune Ave. at W 27th St. 26 acres. Open lawns encircled by a running track and grilling areas adjacent to the fishing pier. Baseball, barbecue grills, basketball, biking, birding, esplanade, fishing, habitat, playground, picnic area, pier, restrooms, tennis and vista.

Coney Island Creek Park Bayview Ave. 9.8 acres. Dunes and a beach popular with shorecasters and seiners tossing for smelt and mullet. Beach, birding, fishing, habitat and vista.

Atlantic Ocean

Coney Island is a barrier sandbar and the westernmost island in a chain of islands that extend along the southern shore of Long Island. It was named by Dutch settlers for the wild rabbits or "konijin" that populated the land. Sea Gate is a gated community on the western shore of the island. Behind the walls are 43 square blocks of about 900 homes and the Norton Point Lighthouse. Public access to Coney Island's beach begins at the start of Riegelmann's Boardwalk at W 37th St. Before 1923, beach-goers paid a fee to use changing rooms and access the water. Eighty feet wide, the famous boardwalk travels eastward for three miles through the carnival of Coney Island to the Russian cafes of Brighton Beach. The waters offshore are popular with local dive clubs because fish congregate at a pipe that draws fresh seawater to the aquarium's tanks and discovery of the Steel Pier and other remnants from Coney Island's peak amusement days.

 Subway F, Q & W to Stillwell /Coney Island; N to Brighton Beach and B1 Bus eastbound to Oriental Blvd. at Manhattan Beach.

 Ocean Pkwy. Greenway is the country's first designated bikeway/ It is five miles from Prospect Park to Coney Island.

 Nathan's, Ruby's Bar, Tatiana, Volna, Winter Garden, Moscow

View from one of the 16 swinging seats of 150-foot-high Deno's Wonder Wheel (W 12th St.).

Coney Island Beach & Boardwalk
W 37th St. to Seabreeze Walk. The birthplace of the roller coaster, hot dog and beach bathing. Summers crowds pack the midway games and fishing at Steeplechase Pier (W 17th St). Aquarium, basketball, beach, biking, fishing, handball, historic site, playgrounds, refreshments, restrooms, pier, scuba, sunbathing, swimming, volleyball and vista. 718-946-1350

Keyspan Stadium 1904 Surf Ave. Home field for NY Met's AAA-team, the Brooklyn Cyclones at the former Steeplechase Amusement Park. The restored Parachute Jump sits in a corner of the new ballpark. The landmark ride was the Lifesaver exhibit at the 1939 World's Fair and was relocated to Steeplechase. 718-449-8497

New York Aquarium (WCS)
W 8th St. & Surf Ave. The nation's oldest aquarium and Brooklyn's most popular attraction. Sculptor Toshio Sasaki's 332-foot-long wall "Symphony by the Sea" facing the beach. 718-265-FISH nyaquarium.com

Brighton Beach Seabreeze Walk to Corbin Pl. A wide sand beach with a distinctly Russian accent that is less crowded than neighboring beaches. Beach, biking, fishing, playground, restrooms, refreshments, shade pavilions, sunbathing, swimming, volleyball and vista.

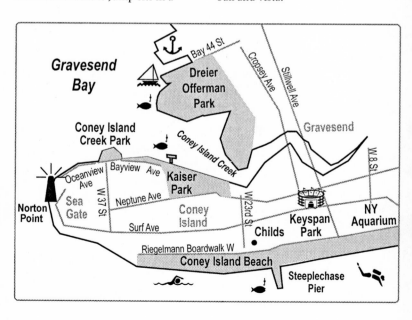

Manhattan Beach Oriental Blvd. 40 acres. A compact family beach with a boardwalk and esplanade looking out at Breezy Point across Rockaway Inlet. Baseball, basketball, barbecue grills, biking, esplanade, fishing, parking, playground, picnic area, restrooms, swimming, tennis and vista.

Kingsborough Community College 2001 Oriental Blvd. 72 acres. The site of a maritime training station during WWII that was given to the city in the 1960s. The school a degree in marine technology. A waterfront esplanade around the campus is open to the public weekdays and Saturdays. Seasonal concerts, educational programs, events, lighthouse, marina and vista. 718-368-4644 kbbc.cuny.edu

Sheepshead Bay

Sheepshead Bay is home to the city's fishing fleet and plenty of seafood restaurants. There are still a few narrow alleys of summer bungalows amid the boat clubs and eateries that line Emmons Avenue. The bay is an excellent natural anchorage protected from the Atlantic. Party boats are moored at piers that were originally built by the WPA. Boats offer half-day bay fishing and full-day ocean fishing. In the afternoon they sell the day's catch right off the boats. Austin Corbin, developer of the Manhattan Beach Hotel, built the wooden footbridge at 19th Street. At the time, it was feared undesirables would cross to the beachside resorts. Today, the bridge is

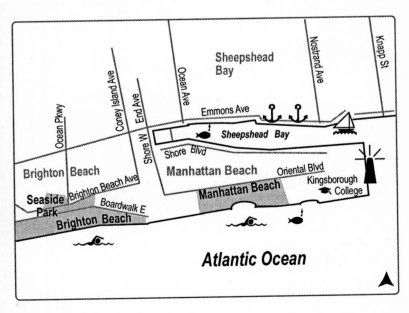

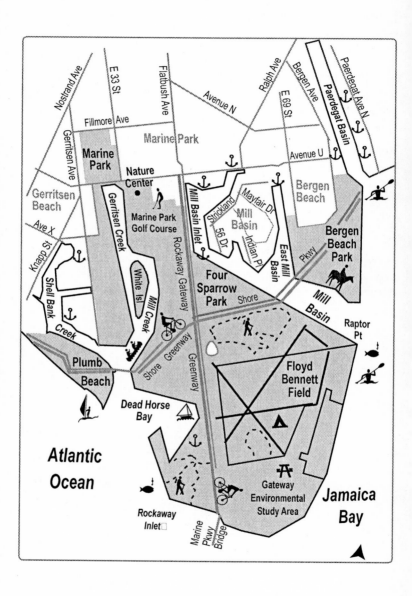

Marine Park

Nostrand Ave

E 33 St

Flatbush Ave

Avenue N

Ralph Ave

Bergen Ave

E 69 St

Paerdegat Ave N

Paerdegat Basin

Fillmore Ave

Gerritsen Ave

Marine Park

Marine Park

Avenue U

Bergen Beach

Nature Center

Gerritsen Beach

Gerritsen Creek

Marine Park Golf Course

Strickland

Mayfair Dr

Mill Basin

56 Dr

Indian Pl

East Mill Basin

Bergen Beach Park

Mill Basin Inlet

Ave X

Knapp St

White Isl

Mill Creek

Rockaway Gateway

Four Sparrow Park

Shore

Pkwy

Mill Basin

Raptor Pt

Shell Bank Creek

Plumb Beach

Shore

Greenway

Greenway

Dead Horse Bay

Floyd Bennett Field

Atlantic Ocean

Jamaica Bay

Gateway Environmental Study Area

Rockaway Inlet

Marine Pkwy Bridge

a popular spot for fishing and netting crabs and leads to a promenade on the south shore of the bay.

 Subway D, Q to Sheepshead Bay.

 Laribet Landing, Miramar YC, Sheepshead Bay YC, Varuna YC

 Il Fiornetto, Lundy's, Limans, Mario & Luigi's, Randazzo's

Holocaust Memorial Mall West End Ave. At the top of the bay, headstones pay tribute to those murdered in the Holocaust. Vista.

Dead Horse Bay

The calm waters of Dead Horse Bay attract wind and kite surfers. Spectators can enjoy the colorful action from the shore of Plumb Beach. Dead Horse Bay gets its name from the horse rendering industry that once occupied the shore. The city's largest marina, with about 600 slips, lies in the protected cove of Deep Creek. Floyd Bennett Field is a reclaimed natural area on the bay built on the landfill and salt marshes of Barren Island, which is an island in name only. Treasure of the notorious pirate Gibbs is buried somewhere on the island.

 Subway D, Q to Sheepshead Bay; 2, 5 to Flatbush Ave. to Q35 Green Bus Line.

Shore Pkwy. Gwy passes Plumb Beach and links with the Rockaway Gateway Gwy to Floyd Bennett Field and over Marine Pkwy. Bridge.

 Gateway Marina, Deep Creek YC

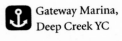 Sunset view from a tee at the driving range of Gateway Sports looks west out over the bay.

Plumb Beach (GNRA) Belt Pkwy. Just past exit #9. It is composed of a single dune, salt lagoon and large mudflat where horseshoe crab breed in late spring. The beach is the main place for kite-boarding and windsurfing within city limits. Beach, birding, habitat, parking, restrooms, sun bathing, surfing and vista.

Floyd Bennett Field (GNRA) Flatbush Ave. 1,448 acres. The city's first municipal airport was the site of many great feats in aviation history. Named for the navigator and pilot of Admiral Byrd's polar expeditions, the field was the eastern terminus for all coast-to-coast record flights. Wiley Post (1933) and Howard Hughes (1938) both circled the globe in record time from the airfield. It is today home to the NYPD Aviation Unit, blimp dockage and the Historic Aircraft Restoration Project. The eight "Hangar Row" buildings are to house a new community sports complex. The grounds have nature trails, community gardening and camping (reserved for youth groups). Beach, biking, birding, camping, fishing, habitat, hiking, historic site, car-top launch, nature center, parking, picnic areas, restrooms and vista. 718-338-3799 nps.gov/gate

Jamaica Bay

Jamaica Bay is a 20 square mile embayment separated from the Atlantic Ocean by Rockaway Peninsula. The shore is marshy and the bay has many shallow islands. Since the 1950s, much of the marshland skirting the bay has been landfilled. The bay supports a large and diverse wildlife population of birds, butterflies, shellfish and finfish. The remaining wetlands of Jamaica Bay provide vital habitat, filter and clean the water and serve as a natural defense against flooding in upland communities. Pollution is a problem in the bay. The salt marshes are disappearing at an alarming rate and no one knows why. An effort to protect and buffer the bay has sparked the acquisition and preservation of land surrounding the fragile waterbody. About 35 acres of wetlands are being restored and planted with native grasses. The city has designated Jamaica Bay a Special Natural Waterfront Area where preservation is a priority. The state has designated Jamaica Bay a Significant Fish and Wildlife Habitat. Marine Park, Floyd Bennett Field, Plumb Beach, Canarsie Pier and Bergen Beach on the bay are part of Gateway National Recreation Area, which encompasses 26,000 acres of protected parkland under the jurisdiction of the National Park Service. The park is named for the natural "gateway" to New York Harbor formed by two arms of land reaching across the water from Breezy Point and Sandy Hook, N.J. Park units cover three boroughs and two states. Brooklyn unit is headquartered at Floyd Bennett Field. It is home to Gateway Environmental Study Center and Ecology Village, which is one of the few places to campout in New York City.

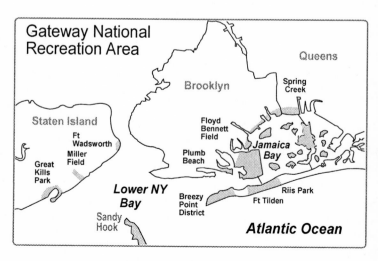

Shell Bank Creek

Shell Bank Creek borders the protected peninsula of Gerritsen Beach. The shore is lined with boats and boat clubs. Access to the water is limited to residents and club members. It is difficult to drive through the narrow one-way streets and most of the sightlines to the water are blocked. Many of the homes in Gerritsen have waterfront yards and private boat docks. The community also enjoys private Kiddie Beach.

 Subway D, Q to Kings Hwy. to B31 Bus to Gerritsen Ave.

 Anchor YC, Riviera, Shellbank YC, Tamaqua Marina, Venice Marine

 Dockside Café, Jordan's Lobster Dock, Clemente's Maryland Crabhouse, Lobster Harbor, TGI Friday's

Gerritsen Creek

Gerritsen Creek is an inlet of Jamaica Bay that flows through Marine Park. The brackish water and salt marshes of Gerritsen support a wide range of shorebirds. The western shore is made up of recreational and natural areas. A golf course takes up the eastern shore of Mill Creek. In the center of Mill and Gerritsen creeks is White Island, a protected habitat. Wooden pilings in Gerritsen Creek are all that remains of the first tide-powered gristmill in America. It was built in 1645 by Wolf-ert Gerritsen, the Dutch farmer for whom the creek is named.

 Gristmill is visible at low tide from the Salt Marsh Center.

Marine Park (GNRA) Flatbush Ave. at Gerritsen & Fillmore Ave. The former horse racing estate of the Whitney family was donated to the city in 1920 with the provision that it be a public park.Ball fields, basketball, birding, bocce, cricket, fishing, golf, habitat, hiking, nature center, playground, restrooms and tennis. Forever Wild Area.

Marine Park Golf Course
2880 Flatbush Ave. 718-338-7149

Salt Marsh Nature Center
3302 Ave. U. Contains a mile long trail through tall cordgrass, salt marsh and tidal flats. Leashed dogs are allowed on the trail. Educational programs, habitat, hiking, historic site and vista. 718-421-2021

Mill & East Mill Basin

East Mill Basin is 4,700 feet long and empties into Mill Basin, which reaches 13,500 feet and drains to Jamaica Bay. Mill Island, at the center of the basins, is an exclusive community where circular streets lead to large homes with backyard boat anchorages The area was an important industrial center prior to WWII. A wooden house built by Dutch immigrant J. M. Schenck in 1675 stood at East 63rd Street and is now on display at the Brooklyn Museum.

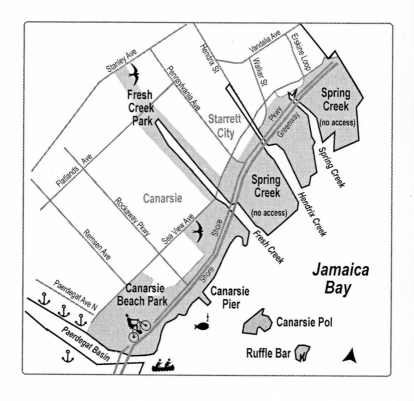

 Bus B41 Flatbush Ave. to Ave. U at Kings Plaza.

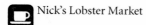 All Seasons Marina, Bay End Dock, Corvette, Dan Dimeglio, Mill Harbor YC, Pilgrim YC

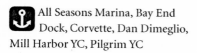 Nick's Lobster Market

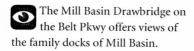 The Mill Basin Drawbridge on the Belt Pkwy offers views of the family docks of Mill Basin.

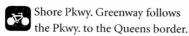 Shore Pkwy. Greenway follows the Pkwy. to the Queens border.

Four Sparrows Marsh Ave. U. 66.5 acres. The seaside, swamp, song and sharp-tailed sparrows nest in their protected namesake salt marsh. Birding and habitat. Forever Wild Area.

Bergen Beach (GNRA) Three miles of beachfront bridle paths and a small beach extend from the banks of Mill Basin west to the mouth of Paerdegat Basin. Birding, fishing, habitat, horseback riding and vista.

Jamaica Bay Riding Academy
7000 Shore Pkwy. 718-531-8949

Paerdegat Basin

Paerdegat means "horse gate" in Dutch. Initially a tidal creek, the mile-long dredged basin is 450 feet wide with water depths of 14 feet. A wastewater control plant anchors the head of the basin. The shores are city-owned and lined with marinas and yacht clubs that are granted the concession by City Parks. Sebago Canoe Club is one of the region's oldest clubs dedicated to human-powered boating. Paddlers, rowers and sailors use the club's launch access to Jamaica Bay.

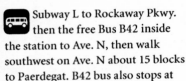

Subway L to Rockaway Pkwy. then the free Bus B42 inside the station to Ave. N, then walk southwest on Ave. N about 15 blocks to Paerdegat. B42 bus also stops at Canarsie Pier.

Shore Greenway bike path runs from Canarsie Pier to Pennsylvania Ave. along Jamaica Bay.

Diamond Point YC, Hudson River YC, Midget Squadron YC, Paerdegat YC, Sebago Canoe Club

Paerdegat Basin Park 160 acres. The park is comprised of the basin bound by Bergen, Ralph, Paerdegat N & Flatlands Ave. No public access. Habitat.

McGuire Park Bergen Ave. Sports fields on the western edge on the basin. Ball fields, cricket, habitat, hiking, playground, picnic area, restrooms, tennis and volleyball.

Canarsie Beach Park & Pier (GNRA). 132 acres. One of the best fishing piers in the city and a good vantage for viewing the marsh islands of Jamaica Bay. Ball fields, beach, birding, fishing, habitat, hiking, parking, picnic tables, pier, ranger station, refreshments, restrooms and vista. 718-763-2202

The Creeks

Fresh Creek and Hendrix Creek are straight channels dredged into wetlands. Spring Creek is actually three connected creeks—Old Mill, Ralph and Spring—that mark the border of Brooklyn and Queens. The Pennsylvania and Fountain Avenue landfills, both superfund hazardous waste sites, are being converted to natural habitat and open space. It entails a 10 year process before the land will be open to public use.

Fresh Creek Preserve Louisiana, Flatlands & Seaview Aves. A landing at Louisiana Ave. allows views the salt marsh. Birding and habitat. Buffer the Bay.

Spring Creek Park A largely inaccessible natural area extending from Fresh Creek to Queens. Birding and habitat. Forever Wild Area, Buffer the Bay Program.

Queens

Waterfront History

By Jim Driscoll

Since the county of Queens was made up of very independent towns and villages until 1898, and is still the least unified borough of New York City, it is impossible to speak of the Queens shoreline as a single entity.

Jamaica Bay and Rockaway. Members of the Canarsie Tribe were the first inhabitants of this area. The earliest European settlers of Rockaway included Richard Cornell. There is a landmarked Cornell Cemetery in Far Rockaway. Some of the islands in Jamaica Bay were occupied by fisherman in the 19th Century. The Rockaways were attracting visitors for their sea breezes as early as 1800. The improvement in transportation by the arrival of the Long Island Railroad furthered its development as a middle and working class resort by 1900. The 1920s saw the destruction of the shell fishing industry on Jamaica Bay. The New Deal era led to development of Jacob Riis Park. After WWII suburban housing projects and Idlewild Airport were built along the Bay.

The North Shore. The earliest inhabitants of the North Shore were the Matinecoc Indians who had settlements that extended from present-day Flushing along northern Long Island. The Dutch and the English began settling in the area around 1645. The earliest settlers of Bayside didn't actually settle on the bay, but settled in an area called the Alley. This was a waterway that traveled from Little Neck Bay as far inland as the Alley Pond. There were summer hotels on Little Neck Bay in the mid-19th century that attracted vacationers from Manhattan. The most popular was the Crocheron. The Matinecocs used Little Neck Bay for shell fishing and local residents would continue to fish in the Bay down to the modern era when pollution destroyed the shell fish business.

Across from Bayside is Douglaston. In the mid-19th century this was mostly an estate belonging to George Douglas. The arrival of the Long Island Railroad led to further development. Douglas Manor, an upscale real estate development on Little Neck Bay, was developed in the early twentieth century. This early suburbanization of the area prevented the commercialization of the coast. The Shore Road in Douglaston is one of the few scenic shore roads in the city.

By the middle of the 19th century, factories were built in College Point. The first, the Poppenhusen hard rubber factory was established along the waterfront in 1854. By the end of the 19th century shorefront picnic grounds, such as Witzels Point View, were popular destinations for outings by Manhattan political and social groups. A ferry service to Manhattan and the Bronx continued until the opening of the Bronx-Whitestone Bridge in the late 1930s. Whitestone developed more slowly than the other villages in this area. A number of wealthy businessmen, such as Samuel Leggett, built mansions along the beautiful shoreline in the early 1800s. The area became more developed after the arrival of the Long Island Railroad in 1868. Industries and resorts started appearing along the coast, but

Broad Channel Island   South Street Seaport Museum

much of the coastline remained residential. Beechurst, a suburban community at the eastern end of Whitestone, that advertised its coastal attractions, was established in the early 20th century. This community remains completely residential.

The Upper East River. The first inhabitants were American Indians who farmed on the upland and gathered fish and shellfish from the waters of the East River. The earliest European settlement was probably the village of Flushing, which was established by the English and Dutch in 1645. This was an important village from the start because of its location on Flushing Creek (a tidal estuary). The creek was an active waterway from colonial days. Steamboat traffic from Flushing to lower Manhattan began in the 1820s. Much of the creek was done away with when dams were built to create to artificial lakes on the World's Fair Grounds in the late 1930s. Although rowing meetings took place on Flushing Creek until the beginning of the 20th century, more and more it was being taken over for commercial use. By 1900 gravel yards and asphalt factories start dotting the shore.

To the west of the creek is Flushing Bay. The western shore of the bay used to be called North Beach and beginning in the 1880s was the site of a Coney Island-style amusement park. LaGuardia Airport was built in the 1930s. Further west is Bowery Bay. There were two islands off the shore of the Bay: Berrian's Island and Rikers Island. Berrian was eventually attached to the mainland by landfill is the now the site of a huge Con Edison Plant. Rikers Island, originally farmland, is now attached to Queens by bridge and is the home of a city prison. By the 1870s, the Steinway family moved their piano factory to northern Astoria along the water, now just east of the Con Ed plant, and built a company town to go with it.

At the extreme western end of this part of the waterfront is Old Astoria. The village of Astoria, which is located near the shores of Hallett's Cove, was incorporated in 1839. It was a residential area but there were some factories and other commercial activities along the shore. Separating the village and Ward's Island is the famous Hell Gate channel. Long famous as a graveyard for ships, the Army Corps of Engineers detonated a series of explosions in the 1870s and 1880s that destroyed submerged rocks and made it a relatively safe passage.

West Queens. Dutch and English farmers arrived in the middle of the 17th century. Three of the early communities were Ravenswood, Hunters Point and Dutch Kills. Ravenswood was the name of a community of beautiful estates on the East River that disappeared by the early 20th century as the area became more commercial. It is now known mostly as the site of huge Con Edison Plants. The commercial development of Hunters Point took off with the arrival of the Long Island Railroad and regular ferry service to Manhattan in the 1850s. By the 1870s the shore of Hunters Point was lined with oil refineries including one owned by

Standard Oil. The area around the Dutch Kills, a branch of the Newtown Creek, underwent a similar development with the arrival of railroad service and a growing need for industrial space.

The Queens and Brooklyn coasts of Newtown Creek have been industrial centers since the mid-19th century. The first settlement in Queens was in Maspeth near the creek in 1642. Destroyed by the Indians, a second settlement was on Smith Island just off the East River coast. In the early 1800s DeWitt Clinton had his summer residence in Maspeth near the creek. Spurred by the need for industrial production more and more factories were being built along Newtown Creek beginning in the 1860s. Smith Island (later called Furman Island) was attached to the mainland. The Furman estate was once known for its trout streams, now it was filled with warehouses and factories. The industries in this area were of the dirtiest type—oil refining, manufacturing fertilizers, tanning, acid production, etc. By 1900 the creek was an environmental nightmare.§

Jim Driscoll is Vice President of the Queens Historical Society.
Sources: New York City Comprehensive Waterfront Plan; the Queens Borough Chamber of Commerce; various books by Vincent Seyfried; Various old newspaper articles..

Go Coastal:
Queens

Queens has the greatest land area of the five borough and over 7,000 acres of city parkland, a few patches of state land and large tracts of national park area. The borough contains 30% of the city's waterfront on two coasts, encompassing 196 miles of shoreline on Jamaica Bay, Atlantic Ocean, Long Island Sound, Little Neck Bay, Flushing Bay, East River and Newtown Creek.

Jamaica Bay

Jamaica Bay is an embayment of tidal wetlands that covers 13,000 acres off the coasts of Queens and Brooklyn. The bay is about 8 miles long and 4 miles wide and opens to the Atlantic Ocean and Lower Bay through Rockaway Inlet. It was created by the formation of the Rockaway peninsula, which is the western-most part of a barrier beach system that extends for 60 miles along the southern shore of Long Island. The mean water depth is 13 feet with a tidal range of 5 feet. The fragile eco-system is over 1,000 years old. It is one of the most impacted and valuable coastal resources in New York City. The sheltered waters, marsh islands and inlets of Jamaica Bay are a major migratory bird stopover on the Atlantic flyway and provide important habitat for fish and shellfish. The wetlands buffer the effects of storms and ocean waves

on the shore and protect the residential areas from flooding. The bay has endured a century of dredging, landfilling, development and other encroachments. A watershed of about 85,000 acres drains to the bay and four wastewater treatment plants dump millions of gallons into the water each day. Efforts are underway to control erosion, restore wetlands and acquire riparian buffer zones between the bay and surrounding uplands. Scientists are conducting a pilot restoration project at two-acre Big Egg Marsh that could provide insight into saving the bay's tidal marshes. Many of the marsh islands in the bay only emerge at low tide. The size and shape of the islands have been fluid over time and are rapidly eroding. The low-lying marsh areas are protected and may be visited on a permit-only basis for the purpose of nature study. Robert Moses rescued the bay's shore from development to create a refuge and

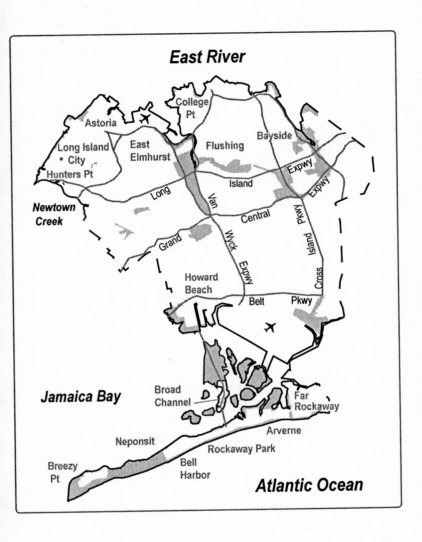

East River

College Pt

Astoria

Long Island City
Hunters Pt

East Elmhurst

Flushing

Bayside

Expwy

Expwy

Newtown Creek

Long

Island

Van

Central

Pkwy

Grand

Wyck

Island

Expwy

Cross

Howard Beach

Belt

Pkwy

Jamaica Bay

Broad Channel

Far Rockaway

Arverne

Neponsit

Rockaway Park

Breezy Pt

Bell Harbor

Atlantic Ocean

parks. It later became part of Gateway National Recreation Area, a 26,000 acre preserve created by an act of Congress in the 1970s and run by the National Park Service. It encompasses a wildlife refuge, historic forts and airfields, many cultural and natural resources and extensive beaches that offer a wide range of recreation opportunities. Gateway areas in Queens include Jamaica Bay Wildlife Refuge, Jacob Riis Park, Fort Tilden and Breezy Point.

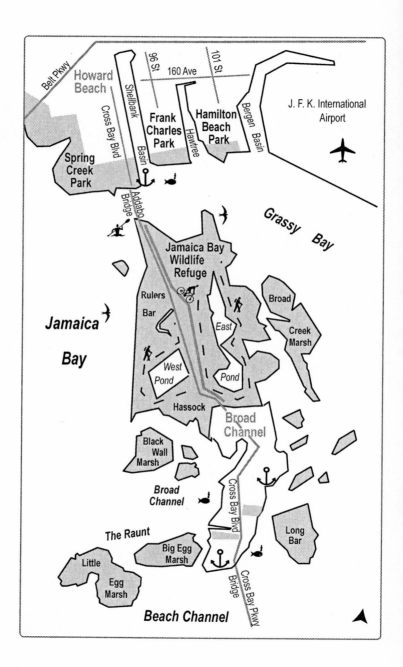

Belt Pkwy

Howard Beach

96 St

160 Ave

101 St

Shellbank Basin

Cross Bay Blvd

Frank Charles Park

Hamilton Beach Park

Hawtree

Bergen Basin

J. F. K. International Airport

Spring Creek Park

Addabo Bridge

Grassy Bay

Jamaica Bay Wildlife Refuge

Rulers Bar

Broad

Creek Marsh

Jamaica

Bay

East

West Pond

Pond

Hassock

Broad Channel

Black Wall Marsh

Broad Channel

Cross Bay Blvd

The Raunt

Long Bar

Little

Big Egg Marsh

Egg Marsh

Cross Bay Pkwy

Bridge

Beach Channel

Grassy Bay

Grassy Bay comprises a labyrinth of inlets and marshland within Jamaica Bay, east of Cross Bay Boulevard. Shellbank Basin is a mile-long man-made channel that runs behind the commercial strip in Howard Beach. The shores of Shellbank Basin are crowded with private club docks and pleasure craft. It was once homeport of Mafia boss, John Gotti's yacht *Not Guilty.* Spring Creek Park stretches from the Kings County line to the western mouth of Shellbank Basin and Charles Park flanks the east bank. The busy thoroughfare is lined with clam bars, nail salons, yacht clubs and the only Starbucks with a roof-top tanning deck in the New York area. Howard Beach is a residential community that began as a fishing colony of squatters' shacks on the eastern banks of Hawtree Creek. The area was transformed in the 1890s by developer Bill Howard who called it the "Venice of Long Island." Today, a few fishing shacks remain along the shore alleys and dead-end streets of tiny Hamilton Beach. JFK International Airport was built on the marshes of Jamaica Bay surrounding Bergen Basin in 1942. Hawtree and Bergen Basins are the site of sand dune and salt marsh restoration. Deep borrow pits originally dug in Grassy Bay to provide clean fill for airport expansion are now being restored to their natural depth in order to improve water quality.

 Subway A to Howard Beach.

 The Shore Pkwy Greenway to Cross Bay Blvd.

 Capt. Mike's Marina, Howard Beach Motor Club, L'il Cricket Marina, Lynn Boatyard, Old Mill YC, Riley's YC

 And Then Michael's, Lenny's Clam Bar, Starbucks, Vincent's Clam Bar

 The A subway train as it travels over Grassy Bay, the longest stretch between stations, offers views of the stilt houses in Broad Channel.

Frank Charles Park (GNRA) 98th St. from Shellbank Basin to the western outlet of Hawtree Creek. Once home court to Vitas Gerulaitis. Ball fields, basketball, beach, birding, bocce, fishing, hiking, playground, habitat, restrooms, tennis, track and vista.

West Hamilton Beach Park (GNRA) Hawtree Basin. End of 104th St. & 165th Ave. Accessible by a wooden bridge and narrow streets. Ball fields, basketball, beach, handball, hiking, fishing, picnic area, restrooms and vista.

Bergen Basin Observation Trail 10 acres. Vacant land near the mouth of Bergen Basin that contains a freshwater pond and is slated to provide new waterside access. Birding, habitat, hiking and vista. ✗

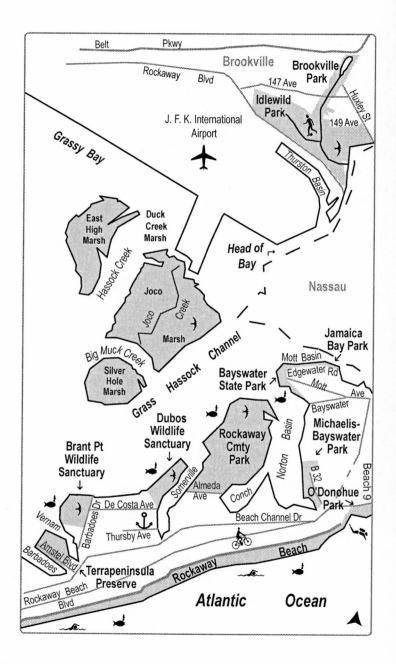

Belt Pkwy

Brookville

Rockaway Blvd

Brookville Park

147 Ave

Idlewild Park

Huxley St

149 Ave

J. F. K. International Airport

Thurston Basin

Grassy Bay

East High Marsh

Duck Creek Marsh

Hassock Creek

Head of Bay

Nassau

Joco

Joco Creek

Marsh

Jamaica Bay Park

Big Muck Creek

Silver Hole Marsh

Grass Hassock Channel

Mott Basin

Edgewater Rd

Bayswater State Park

Mott Ave

Bayswater

Dubos Wildlife Sanctuary

Rockaway Cmty Park

Norton Basin

Michaelis-Bayswater Park

Brant Pt Wildlife Sanctuary

B 32

Beach 9

O'Donohue Park

Somerville

Almeda Ave

Conch

Vernam

Barbadoes Dr

De Costa Ave

Beach Channel Dr

Thursby Ave

Amstel Blvd

Barbadoes

Terrapeninsula Preserve

Rockaway Beach

Atlantic Ocean

Rockaway Beach Blvd

Broad Channel

Broad Channel is the only inhabited island in Jamaica Bay. A population of 3,000 residents live in a 20 block long by four block wide neighborhood on the southern half of the island. Because of the marshy ground many of the homes were built on stilts and connected by wooden gangways. The island was used as a fishing village by the Canarsie and Jameco Indians and homesteaders, fishermen and squatters later took over the city-owned land. After years of trying to evict the island's residents, the city allowed Channelites to purchase their lots for as little as $500 and up to $2,500. The northern half of the island on Ruffle Bar and the surrounding islets form Jamaica Bay Wildlife Refuge, one of the most important urban wildlife sanctuaries in the country. There is a patchwork of oddly named marshes dotting the bay, including Black Wall Marsh, Broad Creek Marsh, Canarsie Pol, Duck Creek Marsh, Duck Point Marsh, East High Marsh, Elders Point Marsh, JoCo Marsh, Little Egg Marsh, Nestepol Marsh, Pumpkin Patch Marsh, The Raunt, Silver Hole Marsh, Stony Creek Marsh, Subway Island, Winhole Marsh and Yellow Bar Hassock. Smitty's Fishing Station, the largest boat rental in the Tri-State region, has half and full day rentals for fishing and exploring the bay.

 Subway A to Broad Channel. S Shuttle transfer.

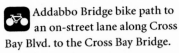 Addabbo Bridge bike path to an on-street lane along Cross Bay Blvd. to the Cross Bay Bridge.

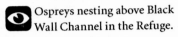 Anabus Boat Club, Channel Marine, Iroquois YC, North Channel YC, Smitty's Fishing Station

Ospreys nesting above Black Wall Channel in the Refuge.

Jamaica Bay Beach (GNRA) Cross Bay Blvd. Southern foot of the Addabbo Bridge. There is water access from either side of the road. Religious artifacts litter the small beach where Indo-Caribbean Hindus make offerings. Biking, birding, fishing, habitat, launch, parking and vista.

Jamaica Bay Wildlife Refuge (GNRA) Cross Bay Blvd. 9,155 acres. In migratory season waterfowl and shorebirds flock to these feeding grounds, where over 300 species have been spotted. The 1.5-mile West Pond trail winds through habitat and terrapin turtle breeding areas. The East Pond trail is more secluded. Birding, educational programs, habitat, hiking, parking, picnic area, restrooms and vista. 718-318-4340 nps.gov/gate

Broad Channel Community Park Cross Bay Blvd. at E 16th Rd. 15 acres. Basketball, handball, playground, tennis and vista.

Broad Channel Park Cross Bay Blvd. & 20th Rd. 17 acres. On Broad Channel waterway. Ball fields, basketball, blading, fishing, playground and vista.

Grass Hassock Channel

On the bayside of Rockaway peninsula a string of parks and preserves buffer the shore and provide public waterfront access. Wetlands flank the airport, which opened in 1948 as Idlewild Airport on the grounds of Idlewild Golf Course. It was renamed JFK International Airport in 1963. Cordgrass, creeks and wetlands envelop the airport property. Thurston Basin and Hook Creek drain to Head of the Bay within the terminal security zone. Runway 22 extends into the bay on JoCo Marsh, the nesting area of the only laughing gull colony in New York State. Silver Hole Marsh is a prime fishing spot.

 Subway A to Far Rockaway/Mott Ave or Beach 25th St.

 A proposed Far Rockaway North Shore Greenway would extend along the bayshore and an elevated boardwalk may be built on Somerville Basin. ✖

 Kennedy Airport Ferry from Pier 11/Wall St. ✖

 View of jets taking off and landing over the bay from Bayswater State Park.

Idlewild Park Preserve Head of the Bay Basin. Rockaway Blvd. & Springfield Ave. 100 acres. A largely undeveloped wetland with winding creeks that will get a new trail system. Birding, habitat, hiking, nature center, paddling and vista. Forever Wild Area ✖

Jamaica Bay Park Head of Bay Basin. Edgewater Rd. 148 acres. An undisturbed wetland accessible by a narrow path on the shorefront. Birding, fishing, habitat and vista.

Bayswater Point State Park Mott Basin. Mott Ave. 12 acres. Trail systems through wetlands, beaches and woodlands at the tip of Mott Point Peninsula. Birding, beach, cricket, educational programs, fishing, habitat, hiking, restrooms and vista. 212-694-3722

Michaelis-Bayswater Park Norton Basin. Beach Channel Dr. at Beach 32nd St. 27 acres. City park fronting Norton Basin. Ball fields, basketball, birding, handball, playground, restrooms, tennis and vista. 718-318-4000

Rockaway Community Park Almeda Ave. 253 acres. Also called the Almeda wetlands, located on a spit of land between Norton and Conch Basins, on the former Edgemere landfill. Ball fields, basketball, biking, birding, fishing, tennis and vista.

Dubos Point Sanctuary Sommerville Basin. 34 acres. A wildlife preserve named for Pulitzer Prize winning microbiologist and ecologist Rene Dubos. Best access along the shore. Birding, fishing and habitat. Buffer the Bay, Forever Wild Area.

Brant Point Wildlife Sanctuary Vernam Basin. 24 acres. The park supports wildlife considered vital to the ecology of the shore. Birding, fishing and habitat. Buffer the Bay.

Terrapeninsula Preserve (GNRA) Vernam & Barbadoes basins. Amstel Blvd. 22 acres. Coastal dune and tidal marsh. Birding, habitat and vista. Forever Wild Area

Beach Channel

Beach Channel is a narrow waterway separating Broad Channel from Rockaway. It is a main channel for boat traffic on Jamaica Bay. Jet skis are allowed to operate in the waters closest to Rockaway, where federal restrictions do not apply. Beach Channel Drive edges the bay, connecting the Cross Bay and Marine Pkwy bridges. There are parks, playgrounds and public access areas along much of the shore. Beach Channel High offers classes in oceanography and marine sciences. A paved boat ramp at the school has closed, which had provided the areas only public launch.

 Subway A change to S Shuttle to Beach 105 St.; Bus B116.

 Veterans Memorial Bridge or Marine Park Bridge path.

 Belle Harbor Yacht Club

 The Wharf, Pier 92

 View of distant Manhattan skyline from the Wharf.

Beach Channel Playground Beach Channel Dr. at Beach 80th St. Ball fields, basketball, handball and vista.

Tribute Park Beach 116th St. Tribute to Rockaway residents lost 9/11/01.

Beach Channel Park Beach Channel Dr. from Beach 116th to 126th St. 13 acres. Esplanade and lawn along the seawall. Biking, bocce, fishing, habitat and vista.

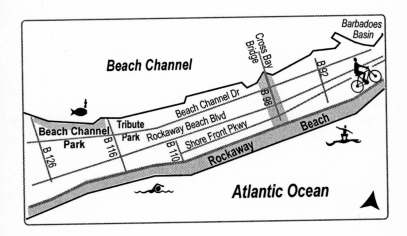

Rockaway Inlet

Rockaway Inlet is the passage that connects Jamaica Bay to the Atlantic Ocean. The Indian name for the 11-mile-long peninsula was "Reckanawa-haha," meaning "the place of laughing waters." Rockaway has steadily grown westward as ocean tides have moved and deposited sand from barrier beaches to the east. The beach from Fort Tilden to Rockaway Point is protected habitat for the Piping Plover. The private residential cooperative communities of Breezy Point and Roxbury are located amid miles of federally maintained seashore at the western tip of Rockaway peninsula. In 1919, the first transatlantic flight launched from the Rockaway Naval Air Station, later Jacob Riis Park. The coastal waters offer some of the best sailing conditions in the city. Party boats drift the Inlets tides setting hooks for bass and fluke. The shallow bars off the coast have been the cause of thousands of shipwrecks, such as the *Black Warrior* and *Cornelia Soule* off Rockaway Point, which attract marine life that in turn attracts scuba divers and fishermen.

Subway A to S shuttle at Broad Channel to Rockaway Park/116th St then Q35 Green Bus line.

Rockaway Greenway at Marine Park Bridge to Riis Park.

Seasonal service to Riis Park by NY Waterway.

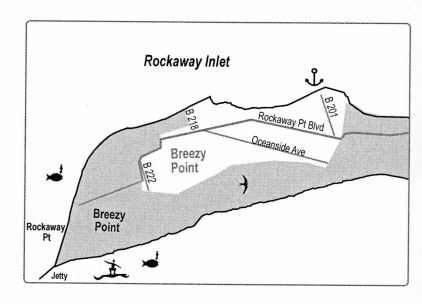

Belle Harbor Yacht Club, Rockaway Point Yacht Club

Kennedy's on the Bay, Sugar Bowl

An observation deck rising 60 feet above sea level atop Fort Tilden's Battery Harris East is popular for hawk and raptor watching.

Jacob Riis Park (GNRA) Beach Channel Dr. 225 acres. The first beach developed for motorists is a mile long sandy beach divided by jetties into 14 bays flanked by a concrete boardwalk and large recreation area. The newly renovated Moorish-style bathhouse and historic clock tower are city landmarks since the 1930s and on the National Register of Historic Places. Nude bathing is tolerated at the western end of the beach. Ball fields, barbecue grills, basketball, beach, biking, birding, golf, handball, outdoor pool, paddling, fee parking, picnic area, refreshment, restrooms, sunbathing, swimming, tennis, volleyball and vista.

Breezy Pt. Executive Golf Course Beach 116th St. 18-hole pitch and putt on the beach promenade.

Fort Tilden (GNRA) Beach 169th St. & Rockaway Pt. Blvd. 317 acres. The only functioning beach ecosystem in the city, the beach has 20-foot high dunes and white sand beaches. The former Nike missile base is now a popular natural area for surf casting and hawk watching. Ball fields, basketball, beach, biking, birding,

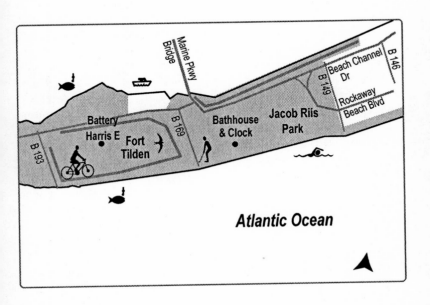

cricket, educational programs, fishing, habitat, hiking, historic site, permit parking, picnic area, ranger station, restrooms, sunbathing, tennis, volleyball and vista. 718-318-4300

Breezy Point Beach (GNRA) Rockaway Point Blvd. Inside the gated community, there are two miles of protected national seashore and a long rock jetty and 25-foot tall light tower at the very tip of the peninsula. The beach is closed to the public each spring to safeguard nests of endangered Piping Plovers. Gain access to fishing parking lots and off-road permits ($50) to drive the beach, available at the Fort Tilden Ranger Station. Beach, birding, fishing, habitat, hiking, permit parking and vista.

Atlantic Ocean

The Rockaway Peninsula is a barrier beach extending from Far Rockaway to the tip of Breezy Point. It is made of sand and sediment pushed west along the southern coast of Long Island from as far as Montauk. The beach is completely engineered. Jetties, and groins extend every block to help fight erosion. Rockaway Beach once rivalled Coney Island as America's most popular playground. It was known as the "Irish Saratoga" in the late 1800s because of the large number of Irish immigrants that settled there. In 1882, the world's largest hotel, the Rockaway Beach Hotel, was built on four blocks of beachfront with room for 8,000 guests.

Unfortunately the hotel never really opened, but was foreclosed on, torn down and sold for scrap. From 1901 to 1985, world-famous Rockaway Playland amused visitors to the seashore. Within five years of Playland's closing, the Ramones were hitching a ride to rock Rockaway Beach and the city began bulldozing 41 blocks of oceanfront summer cottages in the name of urban renewal. The site in Averne sat vacant for 30 years and is currently in development to contain residential properties. One of the few remaining rows of historic summer cottages built after WWI resides at Beach 101st Street and about 100 bungalows survive in Far Rockaway from Beach 17th to Beach 24th Street. Today, the beach is bound by public housing, nursing homes, Irish pubs and mansions. The main drag is at Rockaway Park Beach 116th Street. The coast is prone to severe rip tides, which cause dangerous swimming conditions along the entire beach. Rockaway is the only place suitable for surfing in New York City. The legal break is off the jetty at Beach 90th Street. Surf lessons and board rentals are available at nearby Tsunami Surf Shop. The artificial Rockaway Reef is prime fishing ground about two miles off the coast. Scuba divers venture east to shore dive out of Beach 8th and 9th Streets, near the Atlantic Beach Bridge. There is a deep lagoon and 10 feet of visibility, and the water is teaming with marine life, even tropical fish washed up in the Gulf Stream. In season, parking is extremely difficult near the beach.

Subway A to Broad Channel change to S shuttle to Rockaway Park: Beach 90, 98, 105 or Beach 116.

 Shore Front Pkwy. runs 1.6 miles from B 73 to B 109, the south side of the roadway may be closed seasonally, for summer recreation. Rockaway Boardwalk: bikes are permitted from 5 a.m. to 10 a.m. only during the summer season.

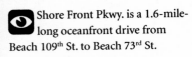 The Beach Club, Sand Bar

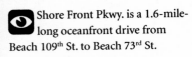 Shore Front Pkwy. is a 1.6-mile-long oceanfront drive from Beach 109th St. to Beach 73rd St.

Rockaway Beach Beach 126th St. to Beach 3rd St 97 acres. The wide city beach extends 7.5 miles along the Atlantic Ocean and attracts four million visitors per season. The 6-mile-long boardwalk from Beach 19th to Beach 129th Sts. is the world's second longest behind Atlantic City. Whale-amena Beach, a 13-foot-high, 19-foot-long stucco whale relocated from the Central Park Children's Zoo marks the entrance to Beach 95th St. Barbecue grills (Beach 17, 88 and 98), basketball, beach, biking, birding, blading, fishing, handball, playgrounds (Beach 9, 17, 44, 59, 97 and 106 Sts), refreshment, restrooms, showers, surfing, swimming, volleyball and vista. 311 or 718-318-4000

O'Donohue Park Seagirt Blvd. Beach 9th to Beach 20th St. 2.5 acres. Ball fields, basketball and playground.

Long Island Sound

Little Neck Bay

Little Neck Bay is a harbor inlet of the Long Island Sound between Queens and the Great Neck Peninsula. About 1,400 acres in size, the bay is a fish and waterfowl habitat and a popular recreational boating area. Captain Kidd is said to have anchored in Little Neck Bay where his band of pirates used secret passages built beneath Bayside homes to smuggle stolen goods. Prohibition rumrunners used the bay for their nefarious activities as well. The shore is studded with waterfront estates and historic homes. On the eastern coast of the bay, Douglaston peninsula is bound by two protected wetlands of tidal coves, salt marshes, woodlands and freshwater ponds at Alley Pond and Udall's Cove. Alley Creek is a tidal creek that forms a narrow ravine as it flows to Little Neck Bay. Natural springs within Alley mix with the saltwater of Little Neck Bay. The home owners in exclusive Douglas Manor on the peninsula share ownership of the waterfront. A waterfront promenade runs parallel to the Cross Island Parkway from Alley Pond to Fort Totten at Willet's Point.

 LIRR to Douglaston or Bayside.

 The 3-mile-long Little Neck Bay path from Alley Pond Park to Little Bay Park. The Brooklyn-Queens Greenway will cross existing parks to

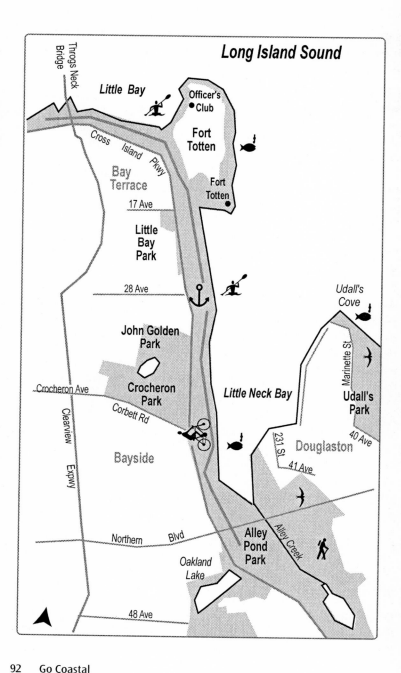

Long Island Sound

Throgs Neck Bridge

Little Bay

Officer's Club

Fort Totten

Cross Island Pkwy

Bay Terrace

Fort Totten

17 Ave

Little Bay Park

28 Ave

Udall's Cove

John Golden Park

Marinette St

Udall's Park

Crocheron Ave

Crocheron Park

Little Neck Bay

40 Ave

Clearview

Corbett Rd

Douglaston

231 St

41 Ave

Bayside

Expwy

Northern   Blvd

Alley Creek

Alley Pond Park

Oakland Lake

48 Ave

link Alley Pond and Coney Island. It is in place for 22 miles from Highland Park to Fort Totten. ✕

⚓ Bayside Marina, Douglaston YC

👁 Shore Road offers a scenic drive through Historic Douglas Manor rising above Little Neck Bay.

Udall's Park Preserve Marinette St. & Douglas Rd. 50 acres. 2.5 miles of nature trails through a unique wetland environment. Birding, fishing, habitat, hiking and vista.

Alley Pond Park Northern Blvd. 624 acres. The "Alley" is a narrow corridor surrounded by hills and divided by roadways. It is a protected wetland habitat with an extensive trail system. Native brook trout have been reintroduced to a cold water stream in the preserve. Ball fields, biking, birding, educational programs, fishing, habitat, hiking, nature center, paddling, parking, picnic area, restrooms, tennis, urban ranger activities and vista.

Alley Pond Environmental Center 718-229-4000 alleypond.com

Crocheron Park 36th Ave. 45.8 acres. One of the city's prettiest parks, the former home of the Crocheron Hotel where weekend clam bakes drew ferry traffic from Manhattan, it contains landscaped lawns and a freshwater lake. Ball fields, biking, birding, habitat, hiking, esplanade, ice skating, parking, picnic area, playground, restrooms, tennis and vista. 718-225-2620

John Golden Park 215 Pl. & 33rd Ave. Once the estate of Broadway producer John Golden "Mr. Bayside," who donated the land to the city. Ball fields, parking, picnic areas, tennis and vista.

Fort Totten Totten Ave. 120 acres. The seaside 19th century military complex closed in 1995 and 90% of the property is to be designated city park. Environmental studies found mercury pollution in the water and soil, which has delayed transfer of the land. The fort remains home to one of the nations largest active reserve commands, the 77th Army Reserve. On the National Register of Historic Places and the Battery and Officer's Club are NYC Landmarks. Paddlers launch kayaks from the small pebble beach at the entrance gate. Biking, birding, blading, fishing, habitat, hand launch, hiking, historic site, museum, parking, picnic areas, restrooms and vista.

Fort Totten Historical Center Tours by appointment. 718-352-0180

Officer's Club The 1870 castle-shaped building was the inspiration for the Army Corps of Engineers' insignia. Home to the Bayside Historical Society. 718-352-1548

Little Bay Park Cross Island & Utopia Pkwy. 50 acres. A narrow park and walkway on the shore of Little Bay stretching from Fort Totten to the base of the Throgs Neck Bridge. Ball fields, basketball, biking, birding, blading, esplanade, fishing, hand launch, marina, and vista.

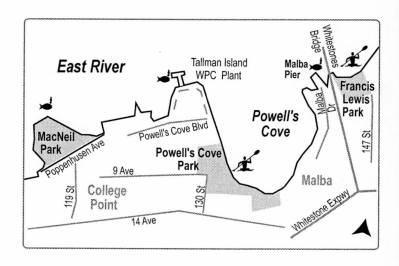

Upper East River

Powell's Cove

Powell's Cove is a petite bay bound by reclaimed wetlands on the western shore. It provides a rich habitat for birds and fish and welcomes exploration of its natural areas. Whitestone, on the eastern bank of the cove, is named for a large white boulder visible in the water where the East River meets the Long Island Sound. The Whitestone Bridge was built to carry traffic to the 1939 World's Fair. A park under the bridge is named for Whitestone's most famous resident, Francis Lewis, a signer of the Declaration of Independence. The discreet enclave of Malba is on the south shore where homes have waterfront lots and private

docks. Malba is an acronym created from the first letter of the surname of the five men who developed the town. Malba Field and Marine Club, founded in 1914, had a pier, dock and boathouse that were destroyed by arson in 1992. Though landlocked, the all-male club is still listed on the register of American Yacht Clubs. Fire also destroyed 100 years of memorabilia at the Ariel Tennis and Rowing Club on the cove.

 LIRR to Flushing Station

 Bus QBx1 has racks to shuttle bikes over the Whitestone Bridge, otherwise neither the Throgs Neck or the Whitestone have bike/ped. access.

 College Point Yacht Club, Beechurst Yacht Club

View of the Whitestone Bridge from Malba Pier

Francis Lewis Park Parsons Blvd. 17 acres. A shady retreat with waterside walking and viewing areas and a small strip of beach. Basketball, beach, biking, bocce, fishing, habitat, handball, hand launch, playground, restrooms, water spray and vista.

Malba Pier Foot of Malba Dr. there is a small pebble beach at low tide. Fishing and vista.

Powell's Cove Park 130th St. and 9th Ave. 52.5 acres. A restored tidal wetland with wooden cinder paths through wildflower meadows, salt marsh and open fields. Cordgrass separates on a narrow oath to where kayakers launch. Biking, birding, habitat, hand launch, hiking and vista.

Tallman Island WPC Plant 127-01 Powell's Cove Blvd. A landscaped waterfront path around the pollution treatment plant that leads to a well-used, but unkempt fishing pier. Fishing and vista.

Flushing Bay & Creek

Flushing Bay extends four miles inland to the village of Flushing. The shallow bay, from 4 to 8 feet deep, is an anchorage for small boats and the World's Fair Marina. The bay is one of the most polluted water bodies in the city. A dike, originally built to protect the harbor from waves, restricts the natural circulation of water in the bay. College Point is a hilly peninsula on the northeastern shore of the bay. The town was developed by Conrad Poppenhusen, who built a rubber factory and worker's housing, roads, railroads and the nation's first free kindergarten there. The landmark Poppenhusen Institute, built in 1868 as the town hall, today serves as a community center and museum of local history. Flushing Creek flows through Flushing Meadows-Corona Park and downtown Flushing to drain into Flushing Bay. The creek is narrow with average water depths ranging from 5 to 16 feet. The park is built on filled marshland. Flushing Creek feeds the twin man-made lakes, in the park's southern section. In the 1800s, the land along the creek bloomed with acres of fruit trees in America's first commercial nursery, which decades later became the famous "valley of ashes" described by F. Scott Fitzgerald in *The Great Gatsby*. The remains of stone silos from the ashpits can be found amid the wrecks at auto junkyards that now line the creek at Willets Boulevard. Flushing is the geographical center of the city and the fastest growing business district. The thriving Asian community centers on Main Street, and has 47 acres of neglected waterfront that have been slated for renewal.

 Subway 7 to Willets Point/Shea Stadium or Main St/Flushing; LIRR to Flushing Station.

 Flushing Bay Promenade runs along the water's edge from

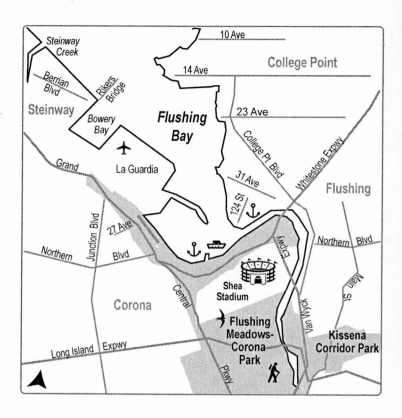

Harpers St. to LaGuardia. Flushing Meadow paths connect to Kissena Park and the B-Q Greenway.

 Seasonal Shea Stadium shuttle to World's Fair Marina.

 Anchorage Marina, Arrow YC, World's Fair Marina

 World's Fair Marina Restaurant

 MacNeil Park overlooks LaGuardia takeoffs and

Rikers Island down East River to the midtown Manhattan skyline.

Hermon A. MacNeil Park

Poppenhusen Ave. at 119th St.
29 acres. The hillside park has shade trees, waterside paths and spectacular views. Once the site of Mayor Fiorello LaGuardia's summer home, the park is named for the world-renowned sculptor of Indians and creator of the George Washington statue on the Washington Square Arch. Ball fields,

basketball, biking, blading, bocce, esplanade, fishing, handball, picnic area, playground, restrooms and vista.

Flushing Bay Promenade
27th Ave. overpass to Harper St. 28 acres. A 1.5-mile uniquely designed linear promenade that encircles Flushing Bay. Best access is World's Fair Marina, where several Dragon Boat teams practice and race. Biking, boat ramp, excursion boats, fishing, habitat, hand launch, marina, paddling, restaurant and vista.

Downtown Flushing Esplanade
35th Ave. to 40th Rd. 36 acres. Plans for the eastern shore of Flushing Creek to open new public space, access and sightlines, and connect downtown Flushing with the Bay Promenade. �֍

Flushing Meadows-Corona Park
Grand Central Pkwy. & Van Wyck Expwy. 1,225 acres. The site of the 1939 and 1964 World's Fairs and the first home of the UN in New York. It is the city's second largest park and home to the Unisphere, NY Mets, U.S. Open Tennis, Queens Botanical Gardens, Theater in the Park, NY Hall of Science and acres of open space. The world's largest scale model of New York City is exhibited in the Queens Museum. Meadow Lake features dragon boat racing, paddle and rowboat rentals, and one of the regions best sailing schools. Willow Lake is a largely inaccessible natural area. Ball fields, barbecue grills, biking, bike rentals, birding, boat rentals,

cricket, esplanade, golf, habitat, hiking, historic site, paddling, parking, picnic area, playground, restrooms and sailing. 718-760-6561

Bowery Bay

There is no public access to the industrial shore of Bowery Bay. The waterfront is dominated by LaGuardia Airport and Con Edison. The waters are too contaminated for fishing or recreational use. The airport was built in 1939 on the site of North Beach and Gala Park—an amusement park and beer garden shut down by Prohibition. The Marine Air Terminal was LaGuardia Airport's first terminal opened in 1942. It served Pan Am's waterborne B-314 sea-to-land aircraft. The landmark Art-Deco terminal has one of the largest WPA created murals entitled *Flight* by James Brooks. The road to Rikers Island crosses the western end of the bay. Though it is accessed through Queens, the prison island is actually part of the Bronx. Just west of Bowery Bay, Steinway Creek is reached by a dirt road off Berrian Boulevard. The eastern bank of the creek contains a petroleum storage facility. The creek flows to Steinway and Sons Piano Factory, established by German cabinet-maker Henry Steinweg in the 1880s. Timber is barged down the creek for the manufacture of pianos in a process that has changed little in the companies 150 years.

 Subway N to Ditmars Ave.; R to Steinway St. Astoria.

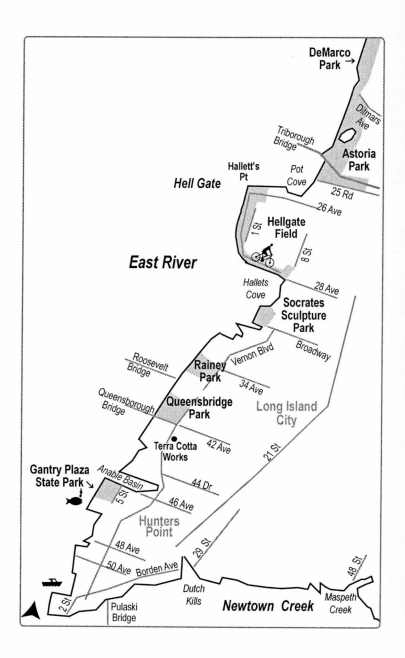

DeMarco
Park

Ditmars
Ave

Triborough
Bridge

Astoria
Park

Hallett's
Pt

Pot
Cove

25 Rd

Hell Gate

26 Ave

1 St

Hellgate
Field

8 St

East River

Hallets
Cove

28 Ave

Socrates
Sculpture
Park

Broadway

Roosevelt
Bridge

Rainey
Park

Vernon Blvd

34 Ave

Queensborough
Bridge

Queensbridge
Park

Long Island
City

Terra Cotta
Works

42 Ave

21 St

Gantry Plaza
State Park

Anable Basin

44 Dr

5 St

46 Ave

Hunters
Point

48 Ave

29 St

50 Ave

Borden Ave

48 St

2 St

Pulaski
Bridge

Dutch
Kills

Newtown Creek

Maspeth
Creek

Lower East River

The villages of Hunters Point, Astoria, Ravenswood, Steinway, and Dutch Kills were consolidated into Long Island City. In 1895, the Mayor of the new municipality was nicknamed "Battle Axe" Gleason after he chopped down a fence erected by the Long Island Railroad at the Borden St. ferry slip. The colorful, but corrupt politician was later jailed at Miller Hotel, now the Waterfront Ale House. One of the East River's most accessible shores, the waterfront contains a string of seven city parks that provide over 121 acres of public space. All of the East River parks in Queens are being refurbished. The land elbows south at Hell Gate, where the East River, Harlem River and Long Island Sound converge. Formed by a fault deep below the water's surface, it is one of the deepest and most treacherous areas in the harbor. Over 1,000 ships have sunk in Hell Gate. Three of the city's great bridges span the Hell Gate: Triborough, Hell Gate and Queensboro. Hallett's Point projects into the river at Hell Gate and is bound by the shallow waters of Pot Cove and Hallet's Cove. A small beach has formed on shore of Hallett's Cove.

 Subway 7, E, G, N, Q, R, V, N, W or F to Queensbridge.

 A 6 mile greenway is planned on the East River, stretching from Astoria Park south to the mouth of Newtown Creek. ✵

 View of the Hell Gate Bridge from Astoria Pool and the short Shore Rd. scenic drive offering river and skyline views.

Ralph DeMarco Park Shore Blvd. 20th Ave. to Ditmars Blvd. 6.2 acres. A narrow grass strip and waterfront path with sitting areas. Esplanade, fishing and vista.

Astoria Park Ditmars Blvd. & Hoyt St. 65 acres. Acquired by the city in 1913, the picturesque park extends from the Triborough Bridge to the Hellgate Railroad Bridge. The huge Art-Deco pool, built for the 1939 Olympic trials, is the city's largest public pool roomy enough for thousands of bathers. Ball fields, bandstand, basketball, biking, blading, dog run, esplanade, fishing, hiking, parking, picnic area, playground, pool, restrooms, tennis, track and vista.

Hellgate "Whitey Ford" Fields 26th Ave. and 1st St. 3.5 acres. Ball fields, parking, track and vista.

Hallett's Cove Park Vernon Blvd. Basketball, esplanade, playground and vista.

Socrates Sculpture Park Broadway at Vernon Blvd. 5 acres. Renowned outdoor sculpture park devoted to large-scale works. Educational programs, events and vista. 718-956-1819 socratessculpturepark.org

Rainey Park 34th Ave. & Vernon Blvd. 9 acres. A shady riverside park. Ball fields, esplanade and vista.

Queensbridge Park 40th Street.
20 acres. Located under the Queensboro Bridge, the park's crumbling
seawall has barred people from the
riverside. It is finally being repaired.
The Costco next door has a waterfront
walk that connects to the park. Ball
fields, basketball, handball, picnic area,
playground, putt-putt, restrooms,
volleyball and vista.

Terra Cotta Works 42-16 Vernon
Blvd. The landmark building once
housed a leading manufacturer
of ornamental terra cotta, which
supplied the bricks for Carnegie Hall.
Silvercup Studios now owns the property and future plans include a public
esplanade on the waterfront. ✘

Anable Cove

Queens West is a 74-acre residential and commercial complex that
commands the southern boundary
of Hunters Point. The preserved scaf-
folds of old barge gantries once used
to load railcar floats serve as reminders of the area's industrial past. The
red neon Pepsi-Cola sign has glowed
across the East River since 1937. It
was moved a few blocks to the south
until completion of the Arquitecton-
ica residential complex. The smoke-
stacks of the former Schwartz Chemical Factory are another prominent
feature of the Queens waterfront.
The stacks were painted by artist,
Georgia O'Keefe in the series "Across
the River." Waterfront tennis clubs,
Fila Sports and Tennisport, co-exist

with Queens West, but may fall victim
to development in the future.

 Subway G to 21st St. or Court
Sq.; 7 to Vernon Blvd.

 Hunters Point, at the foot of
Borden Ave. & 2nd St. ferry to
E 34th St. & Pier 11/Wall St. Also
Water's Edge offers guests free water
shuttle from E 34th St. to 44th Dr.

 Doubbles, Tennisport,
Waterfront Crab House,
Water's Edge Restaurant

 View of United Nations and
Queensboro Bridge from
Gantry State Park.

Anable Basin 44th Dr. 3.5 acre. A
mastodon bone was unearthed during
the construction of the canal in 1868.
A former city dock repair facility will
be allowed to return to its natural
ecology and open public access. Birding, habitat and vista. ✘

44th Drive Pier A public pier used by
Water's Edge Restaurant. Excursion boat
and vista.

Queens West Waterfront Park
47th Rd. to 50th Ave. 20 acres. The residential complex covers 1.25 miles of
waterfront that will include 20 acres
of public open space. Only a small
section has been realized to date.
212-803-3100 queenswest.org ✘

Peninsula Park 1 acre. A grass
promontory adjacent to Gantry Park.
Biking, esplanade, fishing, habitat
and vista.

Gantry Plaza State Park 48th & 49th
Ave. 2.5 acres. Two historic gantries
and four distinctive piers. The Overlook and Cafe piers offer viewing and
seating areas. The Sunning Pier has
lounge chairs and the Fishing Pier has
a fish cleaning station with running
water. Basketball, blading, fishing,
handball, historic site, picnic area,
playground, sunbathing and vista. No
bikes or pets permitted in state parks.

Newtown Creek

Newtown Creek is a 3.5 mile long
tidal creek between Queens and
Brooklyn. Legend holds that Captain
Kidd buried treasure on the creek's
shore. The creek has been home to
one of the heaviest concentrations
of industry in the country. From the
1880s up until the mid-20th century,
Newtown was one of the nation's
busiest and most polluted waterways.
It remains today an exclusively industrial corridor with hardly any public
access. Pleasure craft occasionally
wander into the channel and the relatively flatwater draws neighborhood
kayakers.

Dutch Kills is an arm of Newtown
Creek that stretches a half mile north
to Queens Plaza. One of the earliest
settlements in Queens was founded
along the "kill" the Dutch name for
stream. The first gristmill in Queens
operated on Dutch Kill. The original mills stones, the oldest artifacts
in the borough, are now imbedded
at Queens Plaza North. Sunnyside

Rail Yards were built in the marshes
surrounding Dutch Kills effectively
destroying any trace of the colonial settlement. The creek's headwaters are in West Maspeth named for
the Mespeatches Indians, one of the
13 tribes that inhabited Long Island.
Mespeatches means "at the bad water
place" so named because of the stag-
nant swamps in the area. Maspeth
Creek is a shallow half mile, 400 foot
wide channel. It is one of the most
polluted sections of Newtown Creek.

 Subway 7 to Hunters Point Ave.
or G to 21st St; LIRR to Long
Island City Station

 There is a bike/ped. path
on the Pulaski Bridge over
Newtown Creek to Brooklyn.

The Pulaski Bridge marks the
midway point for runners of
the New York City Marathon and
provides a unique view of the creek
and midtown Manhattan skyline.

Phelps-Dodge (Laurel Hill) 42-02
56th Rd. 35 acres. The site of a copper
smelting plant that abuts Maspeth
and Newtown creeks. It is a brownfield and Superfund site, where
hazardous chemical wastes were
dumped and it is being decontami-
nated for reuse as an industrial park.

Street-end Parks Small parks will
be built at street-ends at 2nd St., 49th
St., 58th Rd. and Vernon Blvd. directly
across from the Manhattan Ave.

Staten Island

Waterfront History

By Carlotta DeFillo

S taten Island has 35 miles of waterfront. It is bordered by Newark Bay and the Kill van Kull on the north, Upper New York Bay, the Narrows, Lower New York Bay and the Atlantic Ocean on the east, Raritan Bay on the south and the Arthur Kill or Staten Island Sound on the west. Several smaller islands sit offshore. Shooters Island near Mariners Harbor was home to Standard Shipbuilding Corp. and Prall's Island is a bird sanctuary. Off South Beach lie the man-made Hoffman and Swinburne Islands. These two islands were built for use as the quarantine station in 1872, and abandoned in 1933. During World War II they were used for military training, only to be abandoned again at war's end.

The earliest inhabitants of Staten Island were Algonkian-speaking Native Americans who set up camps along the shores in the areas of Tottenville, Prince's Bay, Great Kills, Arrochar, Stapleton, West New Brighton, Mariners Harbor and Fresh Kills. They harvested berries, fish, oysters and clams, and even ran the Island's earliest ferries. The first Europeans set foot on Staten Island in Tompkinsville at the Watering Place, a spring of fresh water near the shore, before 1623.

The earliest public ferry was in operation in Stapleton by 1708, and by the 1770s ten ferry lines connected Staten Island to New Jersey, Manhattan and Brooklyn. The best-known Island ferryman was Cornelius Vanderbilt, who started an empire from his single sailboat ferry, starting in 1810. Staten Island became part of New York City in 1898 and a new fleet of ferryboats arrived in 1905. The fare had been a nickel since 1897, and that fare remained in effect until 1975, when it was raised to 25 cents. Currently the world-famous ferry ride is free!

As early as the 1670's the excellent fishing, clamming and oystering possible in the waters around Staten Island encouraged new settlers. Oystering was second only to farming as the Island's largest occupation until the 1920s. Some of the areas historically known for the oystering trade, as well as for magnificent homes of local sea captains, were Mariners Harbor, Rossville, Prince's Bay, Tottenville and Howland Hook.

Shipbuilding and ship repairs were important industries on the Island's shores since Colonial times. In the early 1900s existing shipyards expanded and new yards like Brewer Drydock, Downey's Shipyard, and Staten Island Shipbuilding, all in Mariners Harbor, came into existence. Caddell Drydock in West New Brighton dates to the early 1900s and is still active today. On the South Shore many smaller boatyards built and repaired boats for oystermen around Tottenville during the 1800s and into the early 20th century: Ellis', Brown's, Butler's and Latourette's, to name a few. Piers lined the east

Snug Harbor
© Noble Maritime Collection

shore starting at St. George by 1872. Pouch Terminal in Clifton was founded in 1916 and in Tompkinsville and Stapleton the City of New York built deepwater piers in 1921. In 1937 the New York Foreign Trade Zone was established in Stapleton.

In addition to industry, the waterfront has provided ample opportunities for recreation. Staten Island Athletic Club, the first on the Island, was founded in 1877 in a boat club building in New Brighton. Several cricket and tennis clubs also developed on the North Shore waterfront. Over the years Rosebank, Stapleton and New Brighton have all housed many seaside sports and athletic clubs. In the late 1800s huge resort hotels flourished in St. George, New Brighton and Huguenot, on the south shore. Summer resort areas arose in South Beach and Midland Beach in the late 1800s and early 1900s. Many small camps were founded, each including such amenities as bungalows or tent camps, hotels, bathing pavilions, fishing piers, bandshells, casinos, rollercoasters and carousels. Although most of the amusements are gone and the bungalows have been converted to year-round homes, the boardwalk and beaches are now parkland and have been recently renovated.

South shore recreation areas thriving today include Lemon Creek, Wolfe's Pond Park and Gateway National Recreation Area, which includes Miller Field in New Dorp, Great Kills Park and Fort Wadsworth, now both a national park and the nation's oldest continuously manned military installation. The Island takes pride in its shoreline parks that preserve many open spaces for public use, from Tottenville's Conference House, to the Alice Austen House overlooking the shores of New York Harbor and the Narrows.§

Carlotta DeFillo is Librarian and Historic Interpreter of the Staten Island Historical Society/Historic Richmond Town.

Sources: Staten Island: a Resource Manual for School and Community New York City Board of Education, 1964. Leng, C. W. and Davis, W.T.D., Staten Island and its People vols I-II, History Publication Co., New York, N.Y., 1929. Sachs, Charles, Made on Staten Island The Staten Island Historical Society, Staten Island, N.Y., 1988. "Staten Island Sites and Scenes," The Staten Island Tourism Council, Pamphlet, n.d. Unprocessed Archival Collection on Oystering Industry

Go Coastal:
Staten Island

Staten Island has been a part of New York City since 1687 when the Duke of York offered the island as a prize in a sailing contest, which the team from Manhattan won. The island has twice the land mass of Manhattan and is the least populated of the five boroughs. It is the southern-most spot in New York State at Wards Point, and the highest point on the eastern seaboard south of Maine, at Todt Hill. The island has 35 miles of waterfront and the channels around it carry more commercial traffic than the Panama Canal.

Upper New York Bay

Upper New York Bay extends from the coast of St. George in the north to the Verrazano-Narrows in the south. Staten Island offers the city's most stunning views of the inner harbor and Manhattan skyline from its shore and from its hilltop summits. The first stop for most visitors to Staten Island is the ferry terminal at Saint George. The facility is being modernized with new amenities, restaurants and a harbor viewing deck. Within a short walk of the ferry, the landmarked St. George Historic District is notable for its terraced landscape and its rich variety of early suburban architecture. Located around Westervelt Avenue, Carroll Place and St. Mark's Place, the houses reflect Queen Ann, Italianate, Colonial and Victorian styles. The North Shore Esplanade extends down the shore from the ferry to connect with recreational, cultural and historic sites. Maritime services are still active along much of the Upper Bay shore, including Millers Launch, Sandy Hook Pilots and Reynolds Shipyard. The seeds of Cornelius Vanderbilt's fortune were sown on the coast at Stapleton, where the young entrepreneur started his ferry service between Staten Island and Manhattan. The former Navy Homeport dominates a mile of waterfront. FDNY Marine Unit 9 and the landmark *Fire Fighter* operate from the Homeport docks. The 100-year-old Ocean Yacht Club is housed in an antiquated structure across from the fenced enclosure of the former naval base. The clubhouse once stood at the water's edge, but lost its water rights when Homeport was built. It now exists as a yacht club in name only.

 SIRT Staten Island Rapid Transit 14-mile, 21 stop commuter

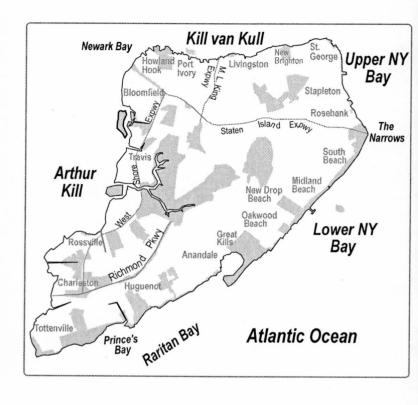

rail operated by MTA. $2 fare is paid at St. George only. 718-966-SIRT

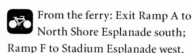
From the ferry: Exit Ramp A to North Shore Esplanade south; Ramp F to Stadium Esplanade west.

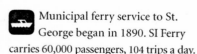
Municipal ferry service to St. George began in 1890. SI Ferry carries 60,000 passengers, 104 trips a day.

Patricio's Restaurant

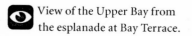
View of the Upper Bay from the esplanade at Bay Terrace.

Stadium Esplanade Jersey St.
52 acres. A mile-long waterfront park with footpaths winding through gardens and native plants, seating areas, viewing platforms and a bikeway that stretches west from the ferry terminal. Biking, fishing, habitat, hiking, parking and vista.

Richmond County Bank Ballpark
Field of dreams to the SI Yankees, a single A affiliate team of the NY Yankees, 6,500 seat stadium built atop the CSX tracks. 718-698-9265 siyanks.com

North Shore Esplanade

Attractive walkway and artwork along the waterfront from the ferry to the Lighthouse Museum extending to Pier 6. Pier 1 has been restored for fishing and a memorial to the Staten Island victims of September 11, 2001 stands vigil against the view of the Manhattan cityscape. Biking, blading, esplanade, fishing, historic site and vista.

National Lighthouse Museum

One Lighthouse Plaza. 6.3 acres. The museum occupies the weathered structures of the former U.S. Lighthouse Depot, which was established to test and inspect fuels, lamps and lenses for lighthouses. Four of the six buildings are on the National Register of Historic Places. Pier 1 harbors the *Nantucket* —the largest lightship ever built. Historic site, historic ship, museum, pier and vista. 718-556-1681 lighthousemuseum.org ✶

Cromwell Recreation Center

Pier 6. Murray Hulbert Ave. City Parks recreation center housed on a large enclosed pier. 718-816-6172

Stapleton Homeport Front St.

36 acres. A mile of waterfront developed by the Navy in the 1980s at a cost of $200 million and decommissioned in 1994. It was the nation's first Free Trade Zone. A federal anchorage offshore is used by containerships awaiting berthing or favorable tides. No public access, except during Fleet Week. Plans for reuse are in review. ✶

The Narrows

The Narrows is the tight reach that connects the Upper and Lower Bays. Bluffs rise high above the mile wide strait and offer good public access and unobstructed water views. From these shores Alice Austen honed her photography skills and the New York Yacht Club successfully defended the America's Cup for the first time. There is a kayak launch at Buono Beach and excellent shorecasting for striped bass, bluefish, flounder, porgy and blackfish. The winding paths of Von Briesen Park offer the best vantage for seeing the great number of vessels that pass through the Narrows and the Peregrin falcons that nest there. Fort Wadsworth, the country's oldest military installation, has guarded the entrance to the inner harbor for over 200 years. The Coast Guard is still active at the garrison where they operate Harbor Traffic Control monitoring harbor activity. The Staten Island Unit of Gateway National Recreation Area extends along the south shore and includes: Fort Wadsworth, Miller Field, Great Kills Park, and Hoffman and Swinburne islands.

 SIRT to Fort Wadsworth; Bus S51

 Fort Wadsworth ✶

 The Carriage House

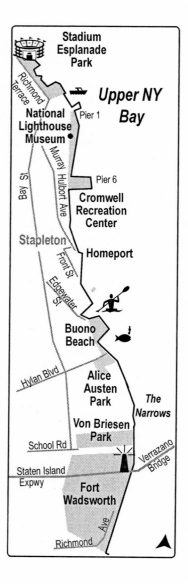

View from the front porch of Harbor House Bed & Breakfast, across from Buono Beach.

Buono Beach Foot of Hylan Blvd. A pebble beach and small boat launch named for Mark Buono, a S.I. resident killed in Vietnam. Fishing, habitat, hand launch and vista.

Alice Austen Park 2 Hylan Blvd. 4 acres. Two houses in the park are part of City Parks Historic House Trust. Beach, educational programs, esplanade, gardens, fishing, historic site, museum and vista.

Clear Comfort Cottage The 18th century cottage of self-taught photographer Alice Austen is today a museum and gallery. 718-816-4506

McFarlane-Bredt House Former quarters of the NY Yacht Club, in need of repair and not open to the public.

Von Briesen Park Foot of Bay St. 10 acres. "First House on the Left, America," is the address owner Arthur von Briesen (1843–1920), founder of the Legal Aid Society, coined for his mansion sited on the bluffs overlooking the Narrows. Birding, esplanade, hiking and vista.

Fort Wadsworth (GNRA) Bay St. 18th century seacoast defense batteries, Battery Weed and Fort Tompkins, stand on the cliffs above the Narrows. Admission is free. Ball fields, beach, biking, educational programs, events, fishing, hiking, historic site, lighthouse, picnic area, refreshments, restrooms, tours and vista. 718-354-4500 nps.gov/gate

Lower New York Bay

Lower New York Bay is a vast body of water that flows from the Narrows to the open sea. Long stretches of barrier beach, nature preserves and public park face the bay. South and Midland are the big public beaches, which once drew tens of thousands of summer visitors to Happyland Amusement Park and other seaside resorts. The beach extends past the summer cottages at Cedar Grove Beach and the restored dunes at Oakwood Beach. It is possible to walk the six mile long continuous beach from South Beach to Great Kills.

Hoffman and Swinburne islands are visible from the beaches, residing about one-mile offshore. The United States Maritime Service had a training school for merchant marines on Hoffman Island from 1938 to 1947. Both islands were once quarantines and are today bird sanctuaries within Gateway National Recreation Area and closed to the public. There are serious shoals between the islands that makes navigation difficult, but offers great fishing.

 Bus S51, S76 from St. George

Biking is permitted on FDR Boardwalk and there is a bike lane on the fire road that runs parallel to the beach. The Beach Greenway, a 6 mile path from Fort Wadsworth to Great Kills Park, still has many on-road gaps. ✖

 View of the Old Orchard Shoals Lighthouse and Verrazano Bridge from the new Ocean Breeze Fishing Pier at Midland Beach.

South Beach & Midland Beach
Father Capadanno Blvd. Two contiguous huge swimming beaches on the south shore. FDR Boardwalk, built by WPA workers in 1938, stretches 2.5 miles from Fort Wadsworth ending at a deep-water fishing pier at Midland Beach. Ball fields, beach, biking, blading, bocce, fishing (Oct. to May), habitat, handball, parking, picnic area, pier, playground, refreshments, restrooms, shuffleboard, swimming and vista.

Miller Field Park (GNRA) New
Dorp Ln. 187 acres. The former Vanderbilt estate, it was used as an airfield and a seaplane base during WWII. Miller Field is named for the first aviator killed in combat in France, James Ely Miller. Ball fields, beach, biking, birding, educational programs, fishing, habitat, hand launch, hiking, historic site, lighthouse, parking, picnic area, playground, restrooms and vista. 718-351-6970

The Bluebelt 12,000 acres.
A protected watershed drainage basin used to control and filter storm water runoff along the island's south shore. The project of the NYCDEP encompasses streams, ponds, lakes and wetlands. It has created a green corridor while preserving valuable wetlands and preventing flooding.

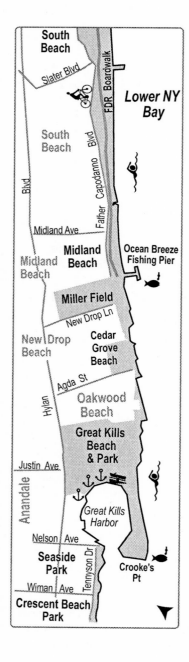

Great Kills Harbor

Great Kills is a well protected natural harbor. The narrow entrance channel opens to a circular basin about one mile around. It is a deepwater federal anchorage, with moorings managed by City Parks. Marinas and yacht clubs crowd the shore and community groups have worked to open waterfront space for public use. The harbor is the place on Staten Island to board a party boat, fishing charter or dive boat. Dunes separate the yacht harbor from the Lower Bay at Crooke's Point, which is a mile long sand spit at the southern tip of Great Kills Park. It was called Plum Island for the beach plums that grow there before landfilling married it to Great Kills forming the harbor. The park is part of Gateway National Recreation Area's Staten Island unit. It is an important bird and butterfly migration landing spot. The White Trail in Great Kills Park is a moderate 7.5 mile hike that connects with trails in the Staten Island Greenbelt at its northern end.

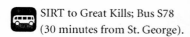 SIRT to Great Kills; Bus S78 (30 minutes from St. George).

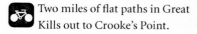 Two miles of flat paths in Great Kills out to Crooke's Point.

Atlantis Marina & YC, Mansion Marina, Nichols Great Kills Park Marina, Richmond County YC, Staten Island YC

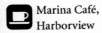 Marina Café,
Harborview

Lands end at the rock jetty at
the tip of Crooke's Point offers
great views of Great Kills Harbor and
the Lower Bay.

Great Kills Park & Beach (GNRA)
From Miller Field to Ebbetts Ave.
253 acres. The park encompasses a
1.5-mile stretch of white sand beach,
miles of nature trails and a wide
esplanade along the edge of Great
Kills Harbor. The Ranger Station
is open year-round and there is
no fee to enter the park. A permit
($50) is required for parking in the
boat ramp lot, off-hour fishing and
access to Crooke's Point. Ball fields,
barbecue grills, beach, beachcombing, biking, birding, bridle paths,
educational programs, esplanade,
fishing, habitat, hand launch, hiking,
marina, model airplane field, nature
center, parking, picnic area, refreshments, restrooms, swimming, trailer
launch and vista. 718-987-6790
nps.gov/gate

Seaside Nature Park Tennyson Dr.,
Nelson to Cleveland Ave. 14 acres. A
former vacant lot transformed to a
landscaped park with winding paths
through woodlands and wildflowers.
Fishing, habitat and vista.

Crescent Beach Park Tennyson
Dr. 68 acres. A tiny waterfront park
named for the crescent-shaped sandbar that separates it from the harbor.
Biking, fishing, and vista.

Raritan Bay

The southwest coast of Staten Island
was shaped by the southern limit of the
Wisconsin glacier during the last ice
age, which is represented by the terminal moraine that crosses the island.
The Raritan Bay waterfront contains
beaches, dunes, wetlands, freshwater
ponds and sub-tidal mudflats protected
from the open sea by the Sandy Hook
bar. Raritan Bay is an arm of Lower
New York Bay that is about 12 nautical
miles in length and eight nautical miles
wide. It extends from the Raritan River
in New Jersey to the Ocean. The bay is
shallower than the waters of the Lower
Bay. It is rich in marine life and draws
fishing boats throughout the long
season. Horseshoe crabs spawn on the
beaches in late spring and threatened
sea turtles feed in the bay during the
summer. Raritan Reach is the middle
of the main shipping channel, which
marks the accepted boundary between
New York and New Jersey. Fishing
regulations of both states apply in the
bay. About 100 commercial clammers
ply the waters of Raritan harvesting
over half of the clams produced in
New York State, about 80,000 bushels
a year. Hard clams seeded in the bay
are relocated to cleaner waters about
21 days prior to harvest and sale.

 SIRT to Annadale
Bus S78

 Wolfe's Pond Park has 8 miles
of multi-use mountain biking
trails through hilly terrain.

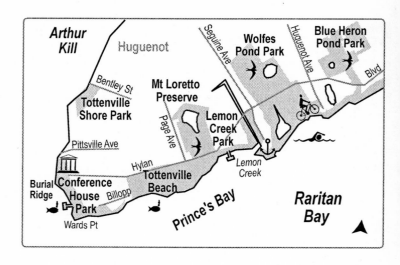

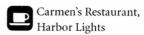 Carmen's Restaurant, Harbor Lights

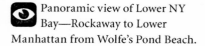 Panoramic view of Lower NY Bay—Rockaway to Lower Manhattan from Wolfe's Pond Beach.

Blue Heron Park 48 Poillon Ave. 222 acres. A quiet haven for waterfowl and wading birds. Nature trails wind through woodlands, meadows and swamps to freshwater ponds that drain to Raritan Bay. Birding, educational programs, habitat, hiking, nature center, picnic areas, restrooms and vista. Forever Wild Area. 718-967-3542

Spanish Camp Hylan Blvd. Poillon & Lipsett Ave. 17 acres. A few historic bungalows remain at the former summer retreat of the Spanish Naturopath Society, a group of nature-loving Communists, and home to candidate for sainthood of Dorothy Day, who was founder of the Catholic Worker movement. Day is buried at nearby Resurrection Cemetery. Historic site and vista.

Wolfe's Pond Park & Beach
Hylan Blvd. & Cornelia Ave. 317 acres. Natural terrain with freshwater ponds, bogs, woodlands and the island's largest old growth forest just yards from the beach and oceanfront promenade. The freshwater pond was originally a tidal inlet that silt and sand dammed cutting off the salt water. Ball fields, barbecue grills, beach, biking, birding, blading, fishing (Oct.-May), freshwater fishing, habitat, model yacht pond, parking, picnic area, playground, refreshment, restrooms, row boat rentals, swimming, tennis and vista. Forever Wild Area. 718-984-8266

Prince's Bay

Prince's Bay (also known as Princess Bay) was the hub of the island's oyster trade in the 1800s, employing over 15,000 watermen who raked the bottom of the bay for the mollosk. A typhoid outbreak closed the beds in 1916. Today, it is against the law to take oysters from the bay. Lemon Creek is a tidal-freshwater creek that empties in Prince's Bay. Since the 1950s, the creek has been summer home to the city's only colony of Purple Martin, the largest members of the swallow family in North America. The birds nest in multi-family birdhouses built atop poles 20 feet high. Some of the elaborate perches are constructed by Rikers Island inmates of mahogany donated by piano-maker Steinway & Sons. Jet skis and motor boats are not allowed within 100 feet of shore.

SIRT Princes Bay, Pleasant Plains; Bus S74 & S78

Lemon Creek Marina, Princess Bay Boatmen's Association, Sandy's Marina

 View of the bay from the 85' high red clay bluffs at Mt. Loretto and the view of the cliffs from the end of Sharrott Ave.

Sandy Ground 1538 Woodrow Rd The oldest free black community in the country settled near the headwaters of Lemon Creek in the 1830s by oystermen of Prince's Bay. 718-317-5796

Lemon Creek Park 440 Seguine Ave. 106 acres. A large natural area and salt marsh with boating and fishing access. Beach, birding, boat ramp (Bayview Ave.), fishing pier (Sharrott Ave.), habitat, hiking, historic site, marina, parking, horse-back riding and vista. Forever Wild Area.

Equestrian Center 718-317-1121

Seguine Mansion The Greek Revival mansion overlooking the bay was built in 1838 by a successful bay oysterman. A Historic House Trust property. Tours by appt. 718-667-6042

Mount Loretto Preserve (NYSDEC) 6581 Hylan Blvd. 194 acres. The highest ocean-facing cliffs in New York State, the red clay sea cliffs rise 85 feet above a narrow mile-long beach at the former Catholic orphanage. The grounds comprise 200 year old beech trees and five distinct ecosystems. Beach, birding, fishing, habitat, hiking, historic site, educational programs, lighthouse, nature center, parking, restrooms and vista. 718-482-4953 dec.state.ny.us/website/reg2/loretto

Tottenville Beach Hylan & Page Ave. Two-mile-long beach extending from Mt. Loretto to Conference House Park. Beach, beachcombing, birding, fishing, habitat, parking, picnic area, restrooms and vista.

Conference House Park 7455 Hylan Blvd. 265 acres. The southernmost point of NYC and NYS, the park was the site of an 8,000 year old Lenape

Indian settlement and burial ground at Wards Point. Beaches, birding, events, fishing, habitat, historic site, parking, picnic area, restrooms and vista. 718-984-6046

Billopp House The historic 1680 fieldstone manor house of British Loyalist Capt. Billopp famous for the failed peace conference between John Adams, Benjamin Franklin, Edward Rutledge and Admiral Lord Howe on Sept. 11, 1776. National and City Landmark, and part of the Historic House Trust. 718-984-2086 conferencehouse.org

Arthur Kill

The Arthur Kill is a major shipping channel 14 miles long, reaching from Raritan Bay to Newark Bay and separating Staten Island from New Jersey. An average of 50 vessels transit the channel daily. The watercourse is 500 feet wide and dredged to a depth of 41 feet. It is vulnerable to pollution because of weak water currents. One of the largest oil refineries in the world is located on its banks. An oil spill in 1990 leaked more than a million gallons of fuel oil into the water. Restoration is ongoing to repair the damage to the shore's natural areas. Most of the waterfront contains abandoned industrial sites, which have returned to a natural state. Tidal creeks penetrate vast wetlands and protected breeding grounds for wading birds. Streets in Charleston and Rossville often end at dirt paths that lead through cord grass to the water, but there are few places to access the Arthur Kill coast. The shore at Kreischer Cove contains Port Mobil, a large oil tank farm that separates Clay Pits Pond from the Arthur Kill. In 1854, Balthazar Kreischer built the city's largest brick factory and a company town near the shore's rich clay deposits. The Kreischer mansion and a row of landmarked worker's houses on Kreischer Street survive today. To the north, the corroded hulls of scrapped ships are scattered along the coast in a ghost fleet known as the "Graveyard of Ships." Maritime artist John Noble assembled a barge from the ruins of derelict ships, which he used as a floating studio from which to record the activity of the port. The wreck field is from Witte Marine Salvage, which mined scrap metal from derelict vessels on the banks of the Arthur Kill since the 1930s. Local outfitters offer kayak tours to the half sunken ferries and tugs.

 SIRT Tottenville (last stop); Bus S74 & S78 to end of Hylan Blvd.

 Port Atlantic Marina, Tottenville Marina

 View of the Graveyard of Ships from Blazing Star Cemetery.

Tottenville Shore Park Arthur Kill Rd. & Bentley St. 9 acres. Scenic park that reaches to the salt marshes surrounding the ramps and base of the Outerbridge Crossing. Habitat.

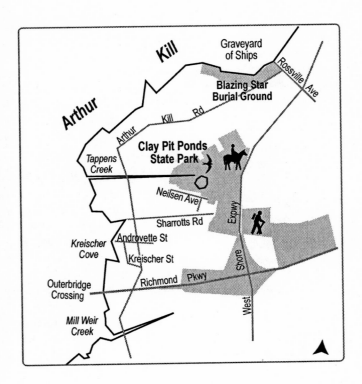

Clay Pit Ponds State Park Preserve
83 Nielsen Ave. 260 acres. Nature
trails and 5-miles of bridle paths run
through freshwater wetlands, sandy
pine barrens, woodlands and spring-
fed creeks that drain to Arthur Kill.
Birding, educational programs, habitat, hiking, historic site, horseback
riding, nature center, picnic area,
restrooms and vista. 718-967-1976

Blazing Star Burial Ground Arthur
Kill & Rossvile Rd. 12 acres. One
of the island's oldest cemeteries,
containing 41 graves that date from
1750. The site is a New York City
Landmark. Birding, habitat, historic
site and vista.

Harbor Herons Complex 2,195
acres. A complex of tidal and
freshwater marshes, ponds, creeks
and islands that support the largest breeding population of colonial
water birds in the northeastern
United States. The variety of nesting
and migrating wading birds include:
great, snowy and cattle egrets; glossy
ibis; blue, green, black-crowned and
yellow-crowned night herons. The

protected rookery encompasses the Isle of Meadows, Prall's Island, Gulfport Marsh, Goethal's Bridge Pond State Preserve, Saw Mill Creek, Old Place Creek, Mariner's Marsh, Shooter's Island, Granitville Swamp and Teleport Woods.

Fresh Kills Creek

Fresh Kills Creek is a brackish tidal estuary that flows north and south of the Isle of Meadows to empty in the Arthur Kill. The creek flows through the 2,200-acre Fresh Kills Landfill, the biggest landfill in the world and one of the largest man-made constructs on the planet. Opened in 1948, the compressed garbage has been piled into four mounds that are now taller than the Statue of Liberty and visible from outer space. The landfill closed in March 2001 and it will take 30 years before the refuse decomposes completely. Repair of the ecosystem and reclamation of Fresh Kills for public use as a nature preserve and park are in the early planning stages. Fresh Kills Creek flows three miles inland and branches north into Main Creek and south into Richmond Creek. Main Creek is navigable at high tide and offers miles of canoe routes. The creek flows through the southern reach of the Staten Island Greenbelt and the southern end of the serpentine ridge. Serpentine is a greenish rock formed by the collision of the continental plates of Africa and North America over 300 million years ago.

Fresh Kills Park 2252 Richmond Ave. 813 acres. The Native Plant Center and demonstration gardens in the park preserve over 275 species of native plants, trees and shrubs, as well as rescue seeds and plants from construction sites throughout the city. Birding, gardens, picnic areas and habitat. 718-667-5169

William T. Davis Wildlife Refuge Travis & Richmond Ave. 260 acres. The city's first wilderness sanctuary, named for one of Staten Island's most noted naturalists. Main Creek canoe access is at Signs Road in near the parking area. Birding, educational programs, habitat, hand launch, hiking, nature center, paddling, parking, restrooms, trails and tours. Greenbelt. 718-667-2165

Richmond Creek

Richmond Creek is a tidal estuary that curves through Latourette Park to Mill Pond in historic Richmond Town. This is the southern part of the Staten Island Greenbelt. The creek is canoeable its entire length at high tide. Early settlers arrived by water to establish Richmond Town as the seat of government for the Staten Island colony. Goods once moved to Arthur Kill by way of the creek. A 19th century stone-arch bridge carries Richmond Hill Road over Richmond Creek.

 Bus S74 to Richmond Hill Rd.

Joseph J. Holka Overlook on the Greenbelt blue trail at Todt Hill is the vista made famous by Staten Island native and Hudson River School painter Jasper Cropsey in *Looking Oceanward* in 1895.

Staten Island Greenbelt 2,800 acres. A preserve encompassing 12 parks interlaced with 35 miles of foot trails through mixed terrain that includes woodlands, wetlands and meadows, as well as historic and recreational sites in natural areas and city parks, including Latourette, W. T. Davis Refuge, Willowbrook Park, Clove Lakes Park and headquarters at High Rock Park. 718-667-2165 sigreenbelt.org

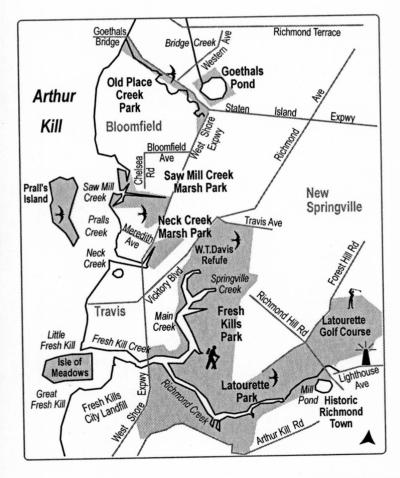

Latourette Park

1001 Richmond Hill Rd. 540 acres. The park has five sections, including Richmond Town, woodlands, marshlands, hills and the gold course. The Latourette family lived on the land since the 1600s. The federal-style mansion of David Latourette, built in 1836, is now clubhouse of the 18-hole golf course. Biking, birding, habitat, hiking, historic site, golf, parking, picnic area, refreshment, restrooms and vista. Greenbelt. 718-351-1889

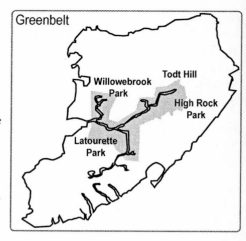

Historic Richmond Town

441 Clark Ave. 100 acres. NYC's only historic village is a living museum containing 27 restored buildings, many open to the public, and costumed interpreters depicting Colonial life. Educational programs, historic site and tours. Greenbelt 718-351-1611

Lighthouse Hill Points of Interest:

Upland from the headwaters of Richmond Creek, the hilltop places provide dramatic views from the summits of the serpentine ridge.

Staten Island Lighthouse The active 1912 lighthouse sits 200 feet above sea level.

Crimson Beech House 48 Manor Court. The only house designed by Frank Lloyd Wright in the city. It is a prefab building in the hilltop neighborhood.

Jacques Marchais Center
338 Light House Ave. The largest collection of Tibetan art outside of Tibet. 718-987-3500.

Todt Hill Ocean Ter. At 410 feet, the second highest peak on the East Coast.

Neck Creek Marsh Park Meredith Ave. 17 acres. Tidal salt marsh drained by Neck Creek, also called the creek between Chelsea and Travis. Birding and habitat.

Saw Mill Creek Marsh Park Chelsea Rd. 111 acres. Restored salt marsh. Birding, habitat, urban ranger canoe programs and vista. Forever Wild Area. Harbor Heron Complex.

Old Place Creek Wetlands 70 acres. The creek is a tributary of the Arthur Kill that winds through wetlands and a rare grove of Persimmon trees. Birding and habitat. Harbor Heron Complex.

Kill van Kull

The Kill van Kull is a 4-mile-long tidal strait and major shipping lane that links the Arthur Kill and Newark Bay to Upper New York Bay. The half-mile wide channel separates Staten Island from the Bayonne Peninsula in New Jersey. It is spanned by the Bayonne Bridge, the second longest steel-arch bridge in the world. An endless flotilla of barges, tugs and containerships navigate the federal channel, which is being dredged to 50 feet by blasting through bedrock.Kill van Kull is the main route for ships unloading at Howland Hook and New Jersey's Port Newark and Port Elizabeth. Howland Hook Containerport was reactivated in 1996 and is now the fastest growing marine terminal in the Port. The 187 acre facility is expanding to the adjacent Port Ivory property. The success of the Howland Hook facility has sparked construction of a rail link between the Staten Island Rail and the Chemical Coast Line (CSX) to link with the national freight network. Industrial areas flank wetlands at Arlington Marsh and Mariner's Marsh. Shooter's Island, now an avian sanctuary, is located in the middle of the channel as it opens into Newark Bay. Authority over the island is split between New York and New Jersey. There is a long tradition of ship building in the coastal communities of Mariner's Harbor, Port Richmond and West Brighton. Marine support services; tug and barge companies, drydocks and other traditional maritime businesses line the shore today. The tugyards of the East Coasts top towing companies: Moran, McAllister, K-Sea, and Reinuer, work the East Coast from the shores of the Kill van Kull. Caddell Dry Dock and Repair, at the foot of Broadway, has been an important shipyard for 100 years. It is where South Street Seaport's Wavetree and the celebrated Fireboat John J. Harvey were restored, and it is the repair yard of Staten Island ferries. Richmond Terrace runs parallel to the waterfront. It was once lined with ship captain's houses. A short row still stands on the Terrace from Van Name to Van Pelt Avenue. Water access is restricted by railroad tracks and industrial structures. An abandoned gypsum plant, now a brownfield site in need of cleanup, takes up 29 acres of waterfront. There are few place to view the water, with the exception of street-ends at Harbor Road and Nicolas, Broadway, Port Richmond and Bard Avenues.

 Bus S40 (Ramp D at St. George) runs on Richmond Terrace

 North Shore Greenway path extends from Snug Harbor to St. George Terminal.

 Snug Harbor landing is used by scheduled excursion boats and cultural center events.

 R. H. Tugs

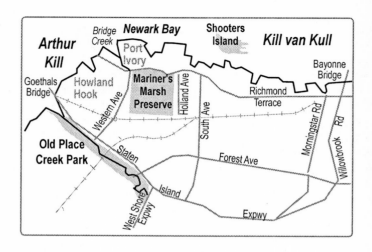

Best close-up views of working ships being pushed, pulled and towed by tugs is from poolside at Faber Park or at the bar of R. H. Tugs.

Mariner's Marsh Park Richmond Terrace at Holland Ave. 107 acres. Upland freshwater wetland encompasses ten ponds, sweet gum trees and Bittersweet vine accessible by trail. Birding, educational programs, fishing, habitat, parking and restrooms. 718-447-6374

Faber Park 2175 Richmond Terrace. 4.25 acres. Landscaped lawns and waterfront esplanade along the seawall offer views of the Bayonne Bridge. Biking, esplanade, fishing, pool, parking, picnic area, playground, restrooms, showers, swimming and vista. 718-442-9613

North Shore Waterfront Park Tompkins Ct. 9.5 acres. The former Blissenbach Marina site purchased by the Port Authority to transform into a new waterfront park. ✗

Snug Harbor Cultural Center 1000 Richmond Ter. 83 acres. Opened in 1833, Sailor's Snug Harbor was the country's first home for retired and disabled merchant mariners. As many as 1,000 retired seamen lived in the self-sufficient community. Herman Melville's brother, Thomas administered the institution from 1867 to 1864. Since 1976, the campus has served as an arts and cultural center. It contains a National Register Historic District of 26 landmark buildings. The five Greek Revival structures facing Richmond Terrace were the dormitories that housed the "Snugs." August Saint Gaudens sculpted the bronze statue of the institution's benefactor, Capt. Robert Randall in 1884. An

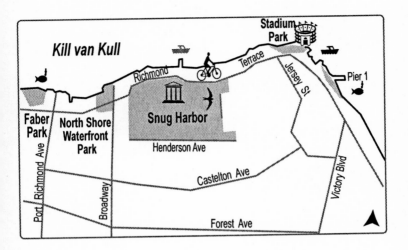

iron fence encircles the campus and there is a boat dock for excursions on the Kill van Kull. Admission is free. Amphitheater, biking, birding, dock, educational programs, events, gardens, historic site, historic ship, museum, refreshments, restrooms, parking, picnic area, refreshment, restrooms and vista. 718-448-2500 snug-harbor.org

Snug Harbor Points of Interest:

Governor's House & Cottages
The large house and five identical Victorian cottages on the western side of the campus once housed the help. Most have been restored and today provide extended stays for visiting artists.

Neptune Fountain Designed by J.W. Fiske, the 1893 zinc statue is on view at the Visitor's Center. A bronze recast adorns the grounds.

Newhouse Center The oldest building, constructed in 1833 retains the original skylight dome and ceiling murals, It is now a contemporary art gallery.

Noble Maritime Collection
Museum featuring the works and studio barge of noted maritime artist John. A. Noble. It contains a recreated dorm room. 718-447-6490 johnanoble.com

Staten Island Children's Museum
The Block Harbor exhibit in the museum helps kids explore the waterfront. 718-273-2060

Staten Island Botanical Garden
The Chinese Scholars Garden was constructed in China by master gardeners, shipped and assembled at Snug Harbor. 718-273-8200 bibg.org

Get
Wet

Annual Aquatic Events

January
Frostbite Sailing Series
National Boat Show
New Year's Day Polar Bear Swim

February
NYRA Indoor Rowing Championships
St. Valentine's Day Erg Regatta

March
Beneath the Sea Scuba Show

April
Bronx River Flotilla
Earth Day
Gowanus Canal Clean-up
Manhattan College Crew Regatta
NY Surf Fishing Contest
RYC Annual Flounder Tournament
Staten Island Fishing Flea Market
Sunset Swing

May
Balance Bar Adventure Sprint
Bike Week
CCA Striped Bass Tournament
Great Kills Blessing of the Fleet
Floating the Apple Coxwain Training
International Migratory Bird Day
Macallan-Striped Bass Derby
Maritime Day
National Safe Boating Week
NYC Extreme Adventure Race

River to River Festival
Sailors Ball
Sheepshead Bay Blessing of the Fleet
Shorewalker's Great Saunter

June
Aquarium Month
CircusSundays @ Waterfront Museum
City Island Fleet Weekend
Conference House Art Show
Environmental Bike Tour
General Slocum Memorial Ceremony
Hudson River Park Day
Liberty World Challenge Outrigger Race
Manhattan Island Marathon Swim
Mermaid Parade
National Fishing & Boating Week
National Seafood Month
NYC Powerboat Rally & Poker Run
NYRA Championship Rowing Regatta
NYS Free Fishing Days
Wild Onion Adventure Race
World Ocean Day

July
Bike Messenger Ride
Coney Island Fireworks Fridays
Cove to Cove Swim
Go Fish Festival
Hook to Horn Row
Intrepid Ultimate Summertime Party

July 4th Fireworks at City Beaches
Macy's 4th of July Fireworks
Music at Castle Clinton
NYC Water Festival at Battery Park
Old Mill YC Ladies Fluke Contest
Rockaway Sandcastle Contest
Seaport Summer Concert Series
Seaside Park Concert Series
Shad Creek Assn. Fluke Tourn
Siren Music Festival
South Beach Sandcastle Contest
Tamaqua Shark Tournament

August

Brighton Beach Jubilee
Coast Guard Day
Great Hudson Swim
Harrison St. Paddle Regatta
Hong Kong Dragon Boat Fest

Liberty Dragon Boat Race
National Marina Day
NY Stunt Kite Championships
NYC Triathlon
Power Squadron Rendezvous
Rockaway Volleyball Championships
Tamaqua Bass & Bluefish Tourney
Tugboat Challenge at the Intrepid
Tugboat Film & Video Series

September

Bronx River Golden Ball
Butterfly Migration
International Coastal Cleanup Day
Lady Liberty Sail Regatta
Little Red Lighthouse Festival
Little Red Lighthouse Swim
Marine Aquarium Hobbyist Day
Mayor's Cup Schooner Race

Etienne Frossard

Million Dollar Duck Race
National Estuaries Day
NY/NJ Sail Expo
NY Superboat Grand Prix
Old Mill YC Fluke Derby
Stonewall Sails
Underwater Cleanup Day

October

Tsunami's Duke K. Surfing Contest
Mariner's Marsh Fall Festival
NYC Oyster Festival
Port Industry Day
Red Bull Flutag
Sea Sunday at Seamen's House
Staten Island Waterfront Festival
Tour de Bronx

November

Erie Invitational Row
Metro Championship Crew Regatta
NYC Surf Film Festival

December

American Star Race of Whitehall Gigs
Audubon Christmas Bird Count
Seamen's Church Christmas-at-Sea

Waterside Attractions

Art in the Anchorage Cadman Plaza West. Live performances are held in the cathedral-like vaults of the Brooklyn Bridge anchorage. creativetime.org

AquaNights New York Aquarium. Summer music series amid the fish tanks, featuring jazz, blues, rap and more, staged Fri. evenings. 718-265-3459 nyaquarium.com

Astroland Amusement Park
1000 Surf Ave. Coney Island. Open daily from June to Labor Day, and weekends April, May and Sept. An amusement park built on the site of Feltman's Restaurant (inventor of the hot dog). Host of the Siren Music Fest and of the Cyclone Roller Coaster. The Astrotower offers views from 275 feet above the beach. 718-372-0275 astroland.com

Bargemusic Fulton Ferry Landing. Year-round chamber music concerts aboard a converted railroad barge that offers spectacular views of lower Manhattan and Brooklyn Bridge. 718-624-2083 bargemusic.org

Blues & Barbecue Hudson River Park, Pier 54. Blues artists perform while BBQ restaurants serve specialties. hudsonriverpark.org

Brooklyn Bridge Park Summer Film Series Empire/Fulton Ferry State Park. Free Thursday night movies, July-Aug. 8:30 p.m. Valet bike parking. bbpc.net

Hudson River Rocks Hudson River Park, Pier 54. Free open air concert series. hudsonriverpark.org

Inwood Shakespeare in the Park Inwood Hill Park 218th St. & Indian Rd. Free outdoor performance of the Bard's plays. 917-918-0394

Moon Dance Hudson River Park Pier 25. Tango, mambo, and swing dance lessons July-August on Sundays, from sunset to 10 p.m. hudsonriverpark.org

Cyclone, Coastal Roller Coaster. Designed by Vernon Keenan and built by Harry C. Baker in 1927 at a cost of $100,000, the coastal amusement is the most famous and most copied roller coaster ever built. Three cars carry 24 passengers over 2,640 feet of wooden track for 1:50 minutes of ride-time that reaches speeds of 60 miles an hour, heights of 85 feet and has 12 steep drops. It was built on the site of the world's first roller coaster, the Switchback Railway. Cyclone was operated by Jack and Irving Rosenthal until 1971, briefly run by the City Parks Dept., and in 1975 the classic ride was restored by Dewey and Jerome Albert, owners of Astroland Amusement Park. An official New York City Landmark since 1988, it is listed in the New York State Register of Historic Places and is a National Historic Landmark.

Music at Castle Clinton Battery Park. Concerts on Thurs, July-Aug, free tickets are distributed at 5 p.m. day of performance. 212-835-2789

Outdoor International Film Festival Socrates Sculpture Park. July–Aug Wed. evenings at 7 p.m. free film, music, dance and local food at the park. socratessculpturepark.org

Riverflicks Summer film series at Hudson River Park, Fridays on Pier 25 and Wednesdays on Pier 54, food is available onsite or pack a picnic. 212-533-PARK hudsonriverpark.org

Riverside Park Films 104th St. Free Wednesday night movies in the park. 212-870-3070 riversidepark.org

River to River Festival Free events along the downtown waterfront, May to September. rivertorivernyc.org

Sandcastle Contests Sand sculpting competitions held at Orchard, Rockaway and South beaches. sandtools.com

Seaport Concerts Rock, pop, jazz and soul music on historic piers. 212-732-8257 southstreetseaport.com

Seaside Summer Concerts Seaside Park. Free summers concerts Thurs 7:30 p.m. brooklynconcerts.com

Sideshows by the Seashore Surf Ave. & W 12th St. Open weekends. 99-seat Coney Island theater featuring classic circus sideshow acts. 718-372-5159

Submerge Festival Series of traveling films, videos and photography celebrating underwater environments. geocities.com/submergefestival

Sundays at Snug Harbor Free outdoor concerts on Sun 6 p.m. July to Aug. 718-448-2500 snug-harbor.org

Sunset Jams Robert Wagner Park. Music on Fridays at 6:30 p.m. July & August. bpcparks.org

Tugboat Film & Video Series Screenings of experimental film and video at coastal sites around the city. 212-408-0219 workingwaterfront.org

Aquatic Life

New York has a diverse and interesting population of sea life in an area that mixes the East Coast's longest river, with a deep-water canyon that falls off the continental shelf very close to shore.

This area is ever changing with tidal combat against the river's flow and temperature fluctuations that can range from near freezing in winter to sub-tropical in summer. Within this area of change animal life comes and goes, visiting briefly to spawn and retreat, like the Atlantic shad, or others, taking residence permanently, to move about from shallow or deep adjusting to season and temperature.

A sample of New York sea life gives a snapshot at best, completely different at another time of year. But many animals can be listed as residents of New York since they so influence our impression of New York sea life; others are exotic visitors, up from the south, carried into the bay on a wayward swirl of the Gulf Stream.

Harbor Seal *Phoca vitulina.* Harbor seals are making a comeback in New York. Sightings around the city are becoming more common, even some distance up the Hudson. This seems

strange to many New Yorkers, but they're not called harbor seals for nothing! At one time they were so commonplace and such a competition to fishermen, that a bounty was placed on their noses. Hunters would get a cash reward for every nose presented. This practice and hunting for their skins eliminated them almost completely from areas around humans. Their population shrank to strongholds further north and offshore islands. The Marine Mammal protection Act now protects them from any human interference or hunting. They are now in New York waters every year. They can often be seen "hauled–out" and sunning themselves on Hoffman and Swinburne Islands, a few hundred yards off Midland Beach, Staten Island.

Whales are infrequent visitors, but sometimes do pass through the maze of shipping traffic that crisscrosses the harbor. Recently, the Aquarium staff spotted a humpback in Caesar's Bay, just south of the Verrazano Bridge and in easy view of the Belt Parkway. This whale was swimming strongly and with purpose. What purpose could it have so close to Gotham? We can only guess, but it was an exception to other incidents of sick or injured whales washing in or straying into New York City disoriented or dying. These offshore animals happen in only by chance or ill luck. With the busy traffic, it is probably just as well.

Seahorse *Hippocampus erectus.* Many would not believe it, but the lined seahorse is native to New York. Most people think of seahorses in tropical waters, but we have a species that survives our cold winters and can be found in estuaries and along the piers in the Hudson River. In fact, scientists used to call this species, *Hippocampus hudsonius.* The scientific name being derived from the Greek: hippo = horse, campus = wriggling monster, and hudsonius for the river where it is found.

Like the flounder, sea horses are "normal" fishes just oriented in a different way. Stretch out a seahorse, and it looks just like a pipefish, and pipefish are not too far from "normal"- Gills on both sides. Pectoral

Don Riepe

fins on each side (the ears of a seahorse). Dorsal fin on the back and vent underneath. Both pipefish and sea-horses have an exoskeleton that look like armor plate. Seahorses have a prehensile tail that they wrap around plants or hold onto pilings. Seahorses eat small shrimp, which they snap up as they swim by

Horseshoe crab *Limulus polyphemus.* Like a relic from prehistoric seas, the horseshoe crab lives much the same as its ancestors must have over 250 million years ago. It is not actually a "crab" It is an arthropod, that has the characteristic jointed legs like the crabs, but have feeding appendages called chelicerae that group it to the spiders and scorpions.

Horseshoe crabs are common along the Atlantic coast and can be found along the NYC shore all summer. So common in many places that they used to be harvested by the ton for fertilizer. Today they are recognized as an essential element in the ecology of the shore, especially because their eggs are such an important food source for shore birds. Horseshoe crabs are collected for medical research where their blood is used in tests for detecting bacterial contamination. Their blood happens to be "blue" because oxygen is carried by a copper-based, hemocyanin, rather than the iron based, hemoglobin, that colors human blood red.

The dangerous looking tail of the horseshoe crab is actually a harmless tool that it uses to right itself when it is flipped over. In the surf where it is often found, this is a common occurrence.

Moon jelly *Aurelia aurita.* Educators no longer refer to these animals as jellyfish so that they are not confused as being "fish". The confusion is unlikely, particularly as they are most commonly seen- as a gelatinous blob washed onto the beach. Sometimes they proliferate the waters and swimmers bump into them in the surf. This usually sends them screaming back to shore. While some species are, in fact, very dangerous, the common moon jelly is harmless and if it could be observed; is quite beautiful. Aquariums are now displaying these animals so that the public can appreciate their delicate beauty. The moon jelly is a clear and transparent disk, something like a glass Frisbee. It has small tentacles that while they do have stinging cells, they are completely harmless to humans.

Sea turtles eat moon jellies. Sometimes the nearsighted turtles will consume plastic bags that resemble a transparent jelly- One more reason to prevent such trash from entering our waters.

Paul L. Sieswerda, Curator
New York Aquarium

Charles William Beebe, Naturalist & Ocean Explorer (1877-1962) The first person to observe deep sea life, when Beebe made his world record descent 3,028 feet beneath the ocean in the Bathysphere with Otis Barton on August 15, 1934. Born in Brooklyn, Beebe began exploring underwater with a homemade diving helmet made of wood in the 1920s. He attended three years at Columbia University in 1899, became Assistant Bird Keeper at the new Zoological Park (Bronx Zoo), and was later named director of the Department of Tropical Research. Beebe and friend, Teddy Roosevelt worked out the idea for a deep-sea submersible over lunch one afternoon. The design for the Bathysphere was realized by engineer and dive partner, Otis Barton.

Aquariums

Aquarium at Staten Island Zoo
614 Broadway Staten Island
718-442-3100. From shrimp to sharks, in a wrap-around aquatic experience featuring marine life from all over the world. 🚌 Bus S48, S53

NY Aquarium Wildlife Conservation Society. Surf Ave. & W 8th St. Brooklyn 718-265-FISH nyaquarium.com. The oldest continuously operating aquarium in the country, it was originally located in Castle Clinton on the southern tip of Manhattan. The 14-acre Coney Island site opened in 1957 and is now home to over 8,000 animals, including giant Pacific walruses, Beluga whales, sharks, sea jellies and native sea life. 🚇 Subway F, W to Stillwell Ave. Check schedule for changes due to station renovation.

- **Aquatic Animal Health Center** Veterinary services, perform large-scale procedures and recuperate animals. Opening 2005. ✘

- **Osborn Laboratory of Marine Sciences** Marine research arm of the Wildlife Conservation Society, that researches such topics as dolphin cognition, satellite tagging of sharks, and coral reefs.

The River Project Estuarium
Pier 26, Hudson River Park
212-233-3030 riverproject.org. Open daily 11 a.m. to 5 p.m. A marine biology field station that explores the inter-pier and under-pier habitats of Manhattan's Hudson River waterfront with a 3,000 gallon aquarium system that houses a living laboratory, which includes river species exhibits, fish monitoring, oyster restoration and avian habitat. 🚇 Subway 1, 9 to Franklin St.

Beaches

❝ The seashore is an incredible place for edible wild plants, whether you're exploring empty lots in East Rockaway, or hiking through Pelham Bay Park, Jamaica Bay Wildlife Sanctuary, Marine Park, Fort Tilden Park, Floyd Bennett Field or Plum Beach. I've been leading Wild Food and Ecology Tours throughout the Greater NY area since 1982, and the seashore habitat is one of my favorites for finding common renewable wild edibles in abundance.

Sunshine and sandy soil makes this an ideal place for root vegetables, and some of the superabundant delicacies you'll find near the seashore include wild carrots, common evening primrose root, and wild parsnips. Fruits and berries thrive in these ecosystems too. They include wild blackberries and dewberries, autumn olive berries, beach plums, and rose hips of the wrinkled rose. There are even wild apricot trees in Marine Park.

There are plenty of shoots and greens you can also gather throughout these habitats. Purslane, lamb's-quarters, curly dock, sheep sorrel, field garlic, poor man's pepper, field peppergrass, Japanese knotweed, wild asparagus, pokeweed, black locust blossoms, milkweed, and garlic mustard are just a few that come to mind. There are even edible seaweeds you can gather at low tide or after a storm. And at the bottom of the food chain, they're a lot safer than the fish! They include rockweed, kelp, sea lettuce, and Irish moss. ❞

"Wildman" Steve Brill,
author of *The Wild Vegetarian Cookbook* and *Identifying and Harvesting Edible and Medicinal Plants in the Wild* (wildmanstevebrill.com)

Beach Season:	Memorial Day to Labor Day
Lifeguards on Duty:	10 a.m. to 6 p.m.
Summer Average Air Temps:	75F 24C
Summer Average Water Temp:	67F 19C
Topfree:	Riis Park
Bikes:	Allowed 5 a.m. to 10 a.m. only
Dogs:	Off-season only, except Ft. Tilden

Don Riepe

Beaches are constantly in motion, endlessly eroding and replenishing. Barrier beaches, such as Rockaway and Coney Island, are reshaped by long-shore sand transport, where wave action moves sand down the shore. The sand migrates east to west, from Montauk along the length of Long Island to Coney Island. Two decades of sand accumulation has added a mile of westward growth to the tip of Breezy Point. Sand comes from rocks and varies in size, shape and color. Most of the sand on city beaches is a blend of quartz, magenite, garnet and other materials. Except Staten Island, where sand comes from brown stone sediment that has washed down the Newark Basin.

The beach is made up of the dry sand above the high water mark called the backshore and the intertidal area, which is just below the low tide line. The berm is where the two areas meet on the crest of the beach. Dunes form beyond the backshore. The city's last natural dune eco-system is at Fort Tilden. Storms and winter nor'easters strip beach sand to offshore sandbars. Only beach nourishment programs, sand fences and dune building reduce erosion and help the beach to regenerate. Jetties, seawalls and groins disrupt the natural sand flow and cause erosion down current. In 1922, Coney Island was the nation's first beach replenishment project that used sand from offshore deposits.

Beachcombing

- The strand or wrackline is where shells, seaweed and debris are deposited by the high tide.

- Breezy Point is the best city beach for shelling. Shells found on city beaches include: quahogs, surf clams, Atlantic slippers, common jingles, bay scallops, blue mussels, Atlantic ribbed mussels, cockle shells, razor clams, oyster and moon snails.

The Strand

- The Official New York State shell is the bay scallop (*Argopecten irradians*).
- The American Museum of Natural History has the third largest collection of mollusks in North America. The New York Shell Club meets at the museum on the 2nd Sunday of each month at 2 p.m.
- In the 17th and 18th century, Native Americans established wampum making stations along the seashore, where wampum beads were made from cutting, drilling and polishing the purple interior of the quahog shell.

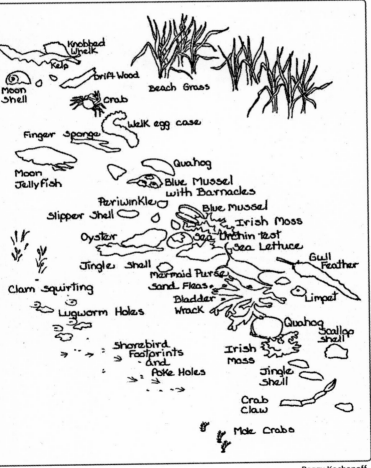

Peggy Kochanoff

Beaches

The barrier beaches of New York City provide miles of public seashore. City Parks and Recreation maintains 14 miles of swimming beaches. The National Park Service administers the beaches in Gateway National Recreation Area. Swimming is only permitted at guarded beaches during the summer season.

Cigarette butts, food wrappers and beverage caps are the most prevalent debris found on city beaches. Much of it comes from street litter that goes down storm drains and catch basins, ending up in the rivers, and finally washing up on area beaches.

Bronx

Orchard Beach *Long Island Sound*
Pelham Bay Park 718-885-2275. A mile-long beach with a promenade and band shell near the Pelham Bay salt marshes and hiking trails. Basketball, beachcombing, beach volleyball, biking, hand boat launch, handball, handicap access, fee parking, lifeguards, nature center, paddling, picnic area, playground, refreshments, restrooms, rowing and vista.
Subway 6 to Pelham Bay Park then BX12 Bus (summer only); NY Express Bus/Pelham Bay.

Brooklyn

Brighton Beach *Atlantic Ocean*
East Seabreeze Walk to Corbin Place 718-946-1350. A wide stretch of white sand beach and rock jetties bound by the boardwalk, Russian cafés, senior housing and luxury condos. Beach volleyball, biking, lifeguards, picnic area, playground, refreshments, restrooms, showers, sunbathing, swimming and vista. Subway Q to the Brighton Beach; Bus B1, B68.

Coney Island Beach *Atlantic Ocean*
Surf Ave. from W 37th St. to Brighton 718-946-1350. America's first and most famous public beach was originally a private beach accessed only by paying a fee for a changing room. The beach stretches two miles and is framed by the Riegelmann Boardwalk, iconic amusement rides, clam shacks, handball courts and Steeplechase Pier. Beach volleyball, biking, fee parking, fishing, handball, lifeguards, playground, pier, refreshments, restrooms, scuba diving, showers, sunbathing, swimming and vista.
Subway F, Q & W to Stillwell Ave.

Wet Weather Advisory

Refrain from swimming at area beaches at least 12 hours following heavy rains when pollution levels are much higher because stormwater runoff mixes with wastewater from sewage plants. A wait of up to 48 hours is advised at beaches on Eastchester Bay in the Bronx. The Department of Health tests the water quality at area beaches throughout the summer and advises of beach closures due to pollution.

Coney Island Creek Park *Coney Island Creek & Gravesend Bay* Bayview Dr. Coney Island. A narrow beach of fine white sand and restored dunes where anglers wade into the water to cast and couples seine for bait fish. The beach features stunning views of the Verrazano Bridge beyond a Stonehenge of old pier pilings. It is the best access to the private sands of Seagate Beach along the beach at low tide. No facilities. Fishing and vista. 🚌 Subway W to Bay 50th St. Bus B74.

Manhattan Beach *Atlantic Ocean* Oriental Blvd. 718-946-1373. A compact family beach and promenade. Ball fields, barbecuing, beach volleyball, fee parking, fishing, lifeguards, picnic area, playground, restrooms, swimming, tennis courts and vista. 🚌 Subway D, Q to Brighton Beach; Bus B1 Eastbound.

Plumb Beach (GNRA) *Dead Horse Bay.* Belt Pkwy. A wild beachscape consisting of cobbled shore, sand dunes, mud flats and calm waters that are favored by wind and kite boarders. Beachcombing, biking, fishing, free parking, habitat, kite surfing, restrooms, sunbathing, windsurfing and vista. 🚌 Subway D, Q to Sheepshead Bay. Entrance is just past eastbound Exit #9 on Belt Pkwy.

Seagate Beach *Atlantic Ocean* Resident-only beach in the gated community of Sea Gate located on the western end of Coney Island. Beachcombing, fishing, lighthouse, private beach club, sun bathing,

swimming and vista. 🚌 Subway W to Bay 50th St. Bus B74.
   Seagate Beach Club 3716 Atlantic Ave. 718-372-4477. Cabana/beach club.

Queens

Breezy Point (GNRA) *Atlantic Ocean & Rockaway Inlet* Beach 222nd St. 718-318-4300. Private co-op community and over 1,000 acres of protected beachhead for endangered shorebirds. Off-road permit parking ($50) obtained at Ft. Tilden. Beachcombing, fishing, habitat, private beach clubs, surfing, swimming and vista. 🚌 Subway A to Beach 116th St. to Q35 Green bus.

   Breezy Point Surf Club Rockaway Pt. Blvd. Beach 718-634-7200 Cabana/beach club.
   Silver Gull Club 1 Beach 193rd St. 718-634-2900. Cabana/beach club

Fort Tilden Beach (GNRA) *Atlantic Ocean* 718-318-4300. A wide expanse of unguarded beach protected by high dunes that attracts shore casters and intrepid sunbathers. Fishing line recycling bin located at the Ranger Station. Ball fields, beachcombing, biking, carry in/carry trash policy, cricket, dogs allowed, ferry, fishing, habitat, nature trails, parking by permit, picnic area, restrooms, sunbathing and vista. 🚌 Subway 2 to Flatbush (last stop) to Q35; A to Rockaway Park to Q22 Bus.

Jacob Riis Park *Atlantic Ocean* Beach 169th St. 718-318-4300. A mile of sand beach and boardwalk. The bathhouse and clock have been NYC Landmarks since the 1930s. Nude bathing is tolerated on the eastern end. Ball fields, barbecuing, beach volleyball, biking, carry in/carry out trash policy, permit parking ($50/yr), handicap access, lifeguards, paddling, picnic area, restrooms, showers, sun bathing, swimming and vista. 🚌 Subway 2 to Flatbush Ave. transfer to Q35 Bus.

Rockaway Beach *Atlantic Ocean* Beach 9th St to Beach 149th St. 718-318-4000. Barrier seashore stretching 7 miles with 5 miles of boardwalk. Action centers at Beach 116th St. Surfable break at Beach 90th St. and scuba diving at Beach 9th St. Barbecue grills, beachcombing, beach volleyball, biking, lifeguards, handicap access, playgrounds, refreshments, restrooms, showers, scuba diving, sun bathing, surfing, swimming and vista. 🚌 Subway A to Beach 116 St; Bus Q21, Q22. Limited street parking.

Staten Island

Great Kills Beach (GNRA) *Atlantic Ocean & Great Kills Harbor* Hylan Blvd. A long stretch of sand beach, dunes and nature trails in a 1,200-acre National Park. Beachcombing, biking, boat launch & trailer ramp, fishing, habitat, lifeguards, marina, nature trails, parking, picnic area, refreshments, restrooms, sunbathing, swimming and vista. 🚌 SIRT to Great Kills; Bus S78.

South & Midland Beaches *Lower Bay* Father Capodano Blvd. 718-987-0709. A spacious beach that frames the entire south shore of Staten Island, well beyond the designated public beach areas. WPA built, FDR Boardwalk runs 2.5 miles ending at the Midland Beach fishing pier. Beachcombing, bocce, fishing, picnic area, pier, refreshments, restrooms, sunbathing, swimming, volleyball and vista. 🚌 SIRT to South Beach; Bus S78.

Tottenville Beach *Atlantic Ocean* Page Ave. An apron of beach just north of Conference House park. Beachcombing, lifeguards, parking, picnic area, restrooms, sunbathing, swimming and vista. 🚌 SIRT to Tottenville; Bus S78.

Wolfe's Pond Beach *Prince's Bay* Hylan Blvd. 718-984-8266. A rocky shore with low-lying dunes. Beachcombing, habitat, picnic area, restrooms, sun bathing, swimming and vista. 🚌 SIRT to Prince Bay; Bus S78.

Beach Events

Annual International Beach Clean-up	718-471-2166
Amercan Littoral Society NY Chapter (alsnyc.org)	September
Sand Sculpting Contests	sandtools.com
City beaches	July -August

Birding

   ❝ Birding in New York City is an exhilarating experience in any season. Songbirds migrating through drop down in our parklands to fuel up for the next leg of the journey while migrating hawks swirl above. Shorebirds and waterbirds winter in our bays and along our shores. Long-legged waders establish rookeries on uninhabited islands in the harbor. Five hundred and seventy-eight miles of waterfront and several hundred large and small parks provide habitat for over 300 species, one third the number of species that can be seen in North America. New York City is a stopover for migratory birds on the route known as the Atlantic Flyway. **❞**

          Marcia T. Fowle, co-author of *New York City Audubon Society Guide to Finding Birds in the Metropolitan Area*

New York City is an avian crossroads. In the 1920s, a group of birding enthusiasts, including ornithologist Joseph Hickey, naturalist Allan Cruickshank and Roger Tory Peterson formed the Bronx County Bird Club to pursue their interest. Thanks to their efforts, birding is today the second most popular outdoor activity in the country. Membership in city birding clubs exceeds 9,000. Each spring, millions of migrating birds pass through the city enroute to breeding grounds. The scene reverses in the fall when the birds head south to winter nest sites. Traveling largely at night, they follow a 10,000 mile route along the Eastern Seaboard, called the Atlantic Flyway, which is one of four major avian routes in North America. The peak migrating seasons are late April and early September. The birds rest and feed in natural areas along the city's coast. No one is completely sure how they navigate, whether by sun, star, magnetic field or other means. During migration season, the Empire State Building turns off its lights on cloudy nights when birds are drawn to the lights and in danger of flying into the building. The main threats to local and migrant bird populations are loss of habitat, human disturbances and predators. At JoCo Marsh, where JFK Airport Runway 22 bisects the marshy home of the only laughing gull colony in NY State, the gulls pose a threat to aircraft from bird strikes, when a bird can get sucked into the engine and bring down a jet. The Port Authority has engaged falcons, gull predators, which fly over the field in an attempt to coax the colony to relocate.

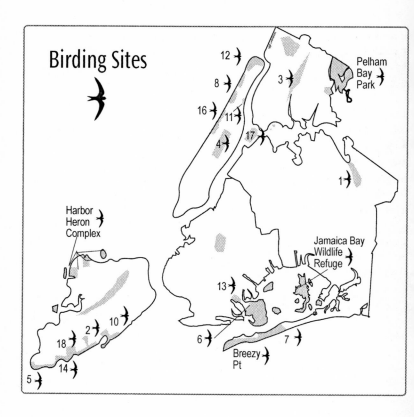

Birding Sites

12 | 8 | 16 | 11 | 4 | 17 | 3 | Pelham Bay Park | 1

Harbor Heron Complex

Jamaica Bay Wildlife Refuge

13 | 2 | 10 | 18 | 6 | 7 | Breezy Pt | 5 | 14

Top Birding Sites

The state has designated the most significant habitats for the survival of birds and conservation of bird species as Important Bird Areas:

Breezy Point Vital habitat for endangered Piping Plover and Common Terns among the dunes from March to August. The nesting areas are closed to the public in the spring when about a dozen monogamous pairs of plovers lay eggs and rear their young on the shore. Birding passes are sold at the Fort Tilden Ranger Station.

Jamaica Bay Wildlife Refuge
Over 300 species have been recorded, including shorebirds, gulls, terns, and water fowl. Monarch butterflies pass through each September.

Harbor Herons Complex A network of protected nesting islands and foraging areas for colonial wading birds, especially herons, egrets and ibis. The complex encompasses Goethals Bridge Pond, adjoining wetlands such as Old Place Creek, Graniteville Swamp, Sawmill Creek Marsh, and nearby nesting islands, including Isle of Meadows, Prall's Island and Shooters Island on Staten Island. Also included are North and South Brother, Hoffman and Swinburne islands.

Pelham Bay Park A wide range of habitat supports populations of wading birds, wren, rail and owls. It is a well-known winter owl and fall hawk watch site. The park is the largest natural area in the region and over 200 species have been recorded along the many nature trails.

Other City Birding Sites

1 Alley Pond Park, Queens
2 Blue Heron Park, Staten Island
3 Bronx Park, Bronx
4 Central Park, Manhattan
5 Conference House Park, Staten Isl
6 Floyd Bennett Field, Brooklyn
7 Fort Tilden, Queens
8 Fort Washington, Manhattan
9 Four Sparrows Park, Brooklyn
10 Great Kills Park, Staten Island
11 Highbridge Park, Manhattan
12 Inwood Hill Park, Manhattan
13 Marine Park, Brooklyn
14 Mount Loretto, Staten Island
15 Prospect Park, Brooklyn
16 Riverside Park, Manhattan
17 Ward's Island
18 Wolfe's Pond Park, Staten Island

Don Riepe

Roger Tory Peterson, Painter & Naturalist (1908-1996). Peterson moved to New York to pursue a career as a commercial artist. He attended the Art Students' League and the National Academy of Design. He was a founding member of the Bronx County Bird Club in the 1920s. In 1934, Peterson combined his painting skills and love of birds to create *A Field Guide to the Birds*. The book, initially rejected by four publishers, presented a simple system for identifying birds that revolutionized bird-watching. The Peterson Identification System was so successful that it has been applied to all manner of flora and fauna, and was employed in WWII to identify enemy aircraft.

Birding Clubs & Programs

Audubon Society NYC Formed in 1979, it is one of the country's largest chapters with 8,000 members. 212-691-7483 nycas.org

Brooklyn Bird Club Founded 1909, highlights birding spots. Bird walks, field trips, school and youth programs. 718-875-1151 brooklynbirdclub.org

Linnaean Society of NY Founded 1878, named for the scientist who invented the system for classifying plants and animals. Meets monthly at American Museum of Natural History. 212-252-2668 linnaeansociety.org

MetroBirds Personalized birding trips in NYC. metrobirds.com

Prospect Park Audubon Center at the Boathouse The first urban Audubon center in the country. Programs for adults and children. prospectparkaudubon.org

Queens County Bird Club Meets at Alley Pond the 3rd Wednesday of the month. 718-939-6224 qcbc.all.alt

Rare Bird Hotline Alert birders of sightings. 212-979-3070

Urban Park Rangers Bird walks and educational programs in city parks for adults and children. Call 311

Birding Events

Audubon Society Christmas Bird Count		audubon.org/bird/cbc/
An all-day census of early winter bird populations. An 103 years old tradition by birding clubs throughout United States		December 25
Great Backyard Bird Count		birdsource.org/gbbc/
National bird count and identification event		February
International Migratory Bird Day		birds.fws.gov/imbd/
Celebration of annual bird migration		May/October

Boat Building & Modeling

❝Boat building in New York City has not been active for some time. However, there is still much heritage in City Island, and along the waterfront. Yacht design continues on 5th Avenue.

In 1929, a very seasoned yacht broker by the name of Drake Sparkman approached a fledgling yacht designer named Olin Stephens regarding a joint venture in yacht design and brokerage. Although Olin was only twenty-one at the time, he eagerly accepted this proposal, which began three quarters of a century of business, which continues in New York City.

Through the contacts of Drake Sparkman, new designs were commissioned in 1929, which included the Manhasset Bay One Design, developed for the Manhasset Bay Yacht Club, still an active racing class today. Other commissions followed and many for local yachtsmen or local yacht clubs such as The New York Yacht Club, Larchmont Yacht Club and Knickerbocker Yacht Club. Today over 2700 designs have sprung from the drawing boards of Sparkman & Stephens and countless broker deals.

Olin Stephens's father, a member of the Larchmont Yacht Club, commissioned one of the most famous designs, a yacht called *Dorade*. *Dorade* went on to win the Transatlantic Race of 1931, which was a momentous accomplishment for a yacht of only 52' of length. At the height of the Depression, New York was looking for any uplifting news, and the Mayors office rewarded these young yachtsmen with a reception at City Hall, and a ticker tape parade up Broadway.

At the time of the company's inception, boat building was in full swing in the New York Metropolitan Area. This included builders such as the Henry B. Nevins and Minneford Yards of City Island as well as the Consolidated Shipyard located on the Harlem River.

In the early 30s, six meter racing yachts were very active in the waters of Long Island Sound. These were generally designed by local designers such as Sherman Hoyt, Henry Gielow and Clinton Crane. It was fortuitous that four clients came to Olin Stephens in the Fall of the Great Stock Market Crash of 1929 for new six meter designs. In all, 37 six-meters were designed by Sparkman & Stephens. It is interesting to note that the first 18 six meters designed by S & S were built at the Nevins Yard in City Island, between 1929 and 1938. Later, 2 winning 12 meter America's Cup contenders, *Constellation* and *Intrepid*, were built at The Minneford Yard of City Island.

Many have asked, "Why would a yacht design and brokerage firm locate in New York?" when many chose more yacht friendly locations such as Newport, Rhode Island or Fort Lauderdale, Florida. The primary reason for staying in New York is we are accessible year round and not just for seasonal periods. **"**

Courtesy of Sparkman & Stephens, Inc. New York, NY © 2003
(sparkmanstephens.com)

Boat Building Workshops

Floating the Apple built its first Whitehall Gig in 1992 in a midtown warehouse and wheeled it across 42nd Street to launch in the Hudson River. Thanks to the efforts of dedicated volunteers, dozens of Whitehalls now ply city waterways. Boat building workshops are conducted with local schools and youth groups to impart environmental education, maritime skills, science, math, and woodworking.

East River Apprenticeshop
GMDC 1155 Manhattan Ave. Boat building with City-as-School alternative high school constructing Whitehalls and Dories. 718-383-4388 erashop.com

East River C.R.E.W. School and youth boat building. 212-369-0058 x170 maxpages.com/eastrivercrew

East River Kayak Club GMDC 1155 Manhattan Ave. 16-week-long kayak building workshop, where members build mahogany sea kayaks. Also youth kayak building programs. 718-389-5277 e-riverkayak.org

Floating the Apple Worldwide Plaza, W 49th St. Volunteers build Whitehalls in programs open to all age groups. 212-564-5412 floatingtheapple.org

New York Restoration Project
31 W 56th St. School and youth boat building. 212-333-2552 nyrp.org

Rocking the Boat 60 E 174th St. School and youth boat building. 718-466-5799 rockingtheboat.org

Seaport Boat Shop South St. Seaport Volunteer shipwrights participate in the restoration and maintenance of historic ships berthed at Pier 16 and learn traditional maritime trades. 212-748-8690 southstseaport.org/ volunteer

Traditional Small Craft Association
Preserves the traditional skill of small craft building. Chapters: Floating the Apple and South Street Seaport. tsca.net

Olin J. Stephens, Yacht Designer (1908-). Born in the Bronx, Olin Stephens is known as "Mr. America's Cup" and often considered the greatest yacht designer of the 20th century. Olin's record 6 victories in the America's Cup is unlikely to ever be met. Largely self-taught, Stephens began work with his brother Rod and later collaborated with yacht broker Drake Sparkman to form Sparkman and Stephens in 1929. America's Cup winners, *Ranger* (1937), *Columbia* (1958), *Constellation* (1964), *Intrepid* (1967), *Courageous* (1974), and *Freedom* (1980) were conceived in Stephen's office at Nevins Yard in City Island.

Boat Modeling

There were no line drawings in yacht design. Vessel features were worked out on scale models. These design tools became presentation pieces for owners. In the late 1800s, there was enormous demand for quality scale models. H. E. Boucher Manufacturing Co. of New York started as a naval architecture firm and developed into one of the premier model building companies in the world, and the primary modelers for the New York Yacht Club. The Navy also found scale models useful in teaching ship identification and war gaming. By the 1880s the sport of building specialized competition models was in full swing. Conservatory Water in Central Park was one of the earliest dedicated ponds for model yachting. Radio-controlled regattas are held on the pond and model boat rentals are available. The demand for early models by collectors is high. A 1916 scale model created by Boucher sells today for about $70,000.

Model Collections

Forbes Magazine Gallery 52 5th Ave. Free admission. Over 500 antique toy boats and models, representing all the great makers from 1870s through the 1950s. 212-206-5548

India House Collection One Hanover Square. Merchant ship collection. Tours by appointment only. 212-269-2323 indiahouseclub.org

Noble Maritime Collection Snug Harbor, Staten Island. Over 600 small (4"-6") ocean liner models.

Maritime Industry Museum SUNY Maritime 6 Pennyfield Ave. Models of merchant vessels. 718-409-7218 maritimeindustrymuseum.org

Museum of the City of New York Marine Gallery 1220 5th Ave. Model ships from the 18th to the 20th century. 212-534-1672 mnyc.org

New York Yacht Club 37 W 44th St. 150 full rigged models and about 1200 builders and half models that represent a history of yachting in America. 212-382-1000

William H. Webb, Shipbuilder (1815-1899) Webb took control of his father Isaac's shipbuilding firm in 1840 and became one of New York City's foremost shipbuilders. He designed wooden boats and ships as varied in shape, size and purpose as fishing schooners, clipper ships, ferry boats and sea-going steamships. As iron became increasingly important to marine construction, Webb adapted and created ironclad naval warships. In 1894 he established Webb Academy and the Home for Shipbuilders on the Manhattan banks of the Harlem River. Thanks to Webb's generosity, Webb Institute, now located on the Long Island Sound, is a tuition free college offering degrees in marine engineering and naval architecture.

South Street Seaport The miniature fleet of model ships rivals the collection of historic ships docked at Pier 16 and includes hundreds of sailboats, miniature ocean liners and an assortment of ships-in-bottles. southstseaport.org

Model Boat Clubs & Shops

Brooklyn Battery Naval Brigade Combat club builds and contests model warships that date from 1906 to 1946. pittelli.com/warship/bbnb

Brooklyn Plastic Modelers Society Hobbyists build naval warships. hometown.aol.com/BPMSClub

Central Park Model Yacht Club Conservatory Water, Central Park East 72nd St. Founded in 1916, members sail radio-controlled model yachts on the famed Conservatory Waters pond in Central Park and store their models at Krebs Model Boathouse. In warm weather, a boat rental cart sets-up on the banks of the pond. 212-360-8133

Classic Ship Collection 230 E 15th St. Local agent for scale builder of classic ocean liners, freighters and more. 212-228-7353 classic-ship.de

Empire State Model Mariners Established 1988, club members build and sail R/C yachts. Meets first Friday of each month at Queens Botanical Gardens. 718-352-4209 home.nyc.rr.com/esmm

Maritime Craft Center Seaport Museum. Model ship building, restoration, repair and ship-in-bottle making demonstrations by volunteer craftsmen. southstseaport.org

Nautical Research Guild International group of ship modelers, maritime artists, nautical archeologists and historians. naut-res-guild.org

Ship Lore & Model Club South Street Seaport Museum. Meets 2nd Monday of the month at Seaport. 212-748-8648

Bridges

> ❝My favorite walk (for the moment) is along the Hudson from West 100th Street, up the west side of Manhattan, through Riverside Park and Fort Washington Park to the Little Red Lighthouse. Then we climb from Jeffery's Hook, some 200 feet up to the George Washington Bridge. The views are magnificent and uniquely breathtaking. No New Yorker should die without having walked over the George Washington Bridge. ❞
>
> Cy Adler, founder of Shorewalkers(shorewalkers.org) and author of *Walking Manhattan's Rim, The Great Saunter*

New York City bridges set the standard for bridges built all over the world. They are marvels of engineering that unite the boroughs and tie the city to the land. The elegant and grand designs and the geniuses who built them are an integral part of the city's culture. There are 75 bridges spanning the waterways of the city. King's Bridge was the first, constructed in 1693 across the Spuyten Duyvil Creek between Manhattan and the Bronx. It was demolished in 1917. Highbridge is the oldest standing bridge and the Brooklyn Bridge is the oldest open to vehicles. The Verrazano is the newest, longest and highest of the big bridges. The George Washington is the busiest, with over 300,000 crossings a day. The world record for longest single span was set and broken by the Brooklyn, Manhattan, George Washington and Verrazano bridges in turn. The Brooklyn

Bridge attracts the most jumpers. Robert Odlum was the first to jump to his death in 1885. A year later, barkeep Steve Brodie achieved fame when he claimed to have survived the leap. All of the East River spans have walkways and about 4,000 cyclists pedal across the four bridges to work each day. The Harlem River has the most bridges. Eleven of the 14 Harlem River bridges must open for tall ships. There are 25 moveable bridges in the city. Some are drawbridges, also called bascule bridges, and others use swing spans or vertical lifts. The Carroll St. Bridge is a landmark retractile wooden bridge over Brooklyn's Gowanus Canal. Opened in 1889, it slides back horizontally on wheels set on steel rails to open. A sail under or a walk over any of the city's major bridges affords a unique perspective to admire the graceful structure while enjoying the water views.

New York City Crossings

Bridges and tunnels connecting New York and New Jersey are operated under the jurisdiction of the Port Authority of NY/NJ. Interborough bridges and tunnels are controlled by the MTA. The NYC Dept. of Transportation administers the free East River crossings and most small moveable bridges. Marine traffic is handled 24 hours a day. Opening a bridge requires two to four hours notice requested by two-way marine radio directly to the bridge or by calling 212-361-7836 or on weekends 718-875-2234. The city's tunnels, submerged over 90 feet below water, also set engineering standards. The Holland, built in 1927, was the world's first mechanically ventilated long underwater vehicular tunnel. The Lincoln is the world's only three-tubed underwater tunnel and the Brooklyn Battery is the longest underwater auto tunnel in North America.

Bridges

1. Bayonnne Bridge
2. Brooklyn Bridge
3. Carroll St Bridge
4. Hell Gate Bridge
5. High Bridge
6. George Washington Bridge
7. Manhattan Bridge
8. Marine Pkwy Bridge
9. Queensboro Bridge
10. Triborough Bridge
11. Verrazano Narrows Bridge
12. Whitestone Bridge
13. Williamsburg Bridge

Fort Lee, NJ

Hudson River

East River

Bayonnne, NJ

Kill van Kull

Gowanus Canal

George Washington Bridge

© 1994 Dave "The Bridgeman" Frieder

Bayonne Bridge

(toll into NYC only)

Opened:	November 15, 1931
Engineer:	Othmar Ammann
Total Length:	8,275 feet
Water Clearance:	150 feet
Water Crossing:	Kill Van Kull

The second-longest steel-arch span in the world is slightly askew, not built on a right angle to the water but at a 58° angle connecting Port Richmond in Staten Island and Bayonne, NJ. Bike/ped. path open 24 hours, stairs. Staten Island: Morningstar Rd. at Hooker Place.

Othmar Ammann, Bridge Engineer (1879-1965) Ammann is responsible for six of the major and most significant bridges spanning New York City's waterways. He arrived in New York City in 1904 after earning an engineering degree in Switzerland, worked for Gustav Lindenthal, and served as bridge engineer to the Port Authority from 1925 to 1939. Ammann designed the graceful suspension bridges that mark the portals to New York Harbor, including the George Washington Throgs Neck, Bayonne, Whitestone, and Triborough bridges, and the Wards Island footbridge. The Verrazano was Ammann's last great bridge, completed when he was 86 years old.

Brooklyn Bridge

Opened:	May 24, 1883
Engineer:	W. Roebling
Total Length:	6,016 feet
Water Clearance:	135 feet
Water Crossing:	East River

The first suspension bridge ever built, the celebrated architecture lures more poets, artists, walkers and cyclists than any other city bridge. 🐜 Wide path elevated above traffic, with divided bike/ped. lanes. Manhattan: Park Row & Centre St. Brooklyn: Tillary & Adams Sts. or stairs at Cadman Plaza East & Prospect St.

Hell Gate Bridge

Opened:	September 30, 1916
Engineer:	Gustav Lindenthal
Water Clearance:	135 feet
Water Crossing:	East River

A 3.2-mile-long graceful steel-arch railroad bridge that is the strongest long span bridge in the world, its construction took more steel than the Manhattan and Queensboro bridges The bridge viaduct tracks across Randalls Island. The unique paint color "hellgate red" was created especially for the bridge.

High Bridge

Opened:	July 4, 1848
Engineer:	John Jervis
Total Length:	1,450 feet
Water Clearance:	114 feet
Water Crossing:	Harlem River

The landmark pedestrian bridge carried water from upstate reservoirs to the city until 1917, when WWI security concerns shut down the Old Croton Aqueduct system. It connects Highbridge Park near E 174th St. in Manhattan and High Bridge Park at E 170th St. in the Bronx. 🐜 Closed since the 1970s, when a stone thrown from the bridge killed a passenger aboard the Circle Line. Community efforts are working to reopen the span.

George Washington Bridge

(toll into NYC only)

Opened:	October 25, 1931
Engineer:	Othmar Ammann
Total Length:	7,140 feet
Tower Height:	604 feet
Water Clearance:	213 feet
Water Crossing:	Hudson River

LeCorbusier called it "the most beautiful bridge in the world." It is the world's heaviest bridge containing 113,000 tons of steel and 28,000 tons of Roebling cable wire. The open structural steel towers were intended to be faced with stone, but depression cost cutbacks prevented the extra expense. The bridge connects Manhattan at 179th St. and with the Palisades in Fort Lee, NJ. 🚲 Bike/ped. path on south-side, the north-side walkway is for pedestrians only.

Manhattan Bridge

Opened:	December 31, 1909
Engineer:	Gustav Lindenthal
Total Length:	6,855 feet
Water Clearance:	135 feet
Water Crossing:	East River

Art-deco suspension bridge with a street running through each anchorage. It is entered at Canal St. through an arch modeled after the Porte St. Denis in Paris, and links to Flatbush Ave in Brooklyn. 🚲 Bike/ped. path will eventually include a dedicated 10-foot-wide bike path on the north side.

Marine Parkway Gil Hodges Bridge

(Seasonal toll)

Opened:	July 3, 1937
Engineer:	David Steinman
Total Length:	4,022 feet
Water Clearance:	55 ft.; 150 ft. lifted
Water Crossing:	Rockaway Inlet

A steel lift truss span, named for the former first baseman of the Brooklyn Dodgers, carrying traffic from Flatbush Ave. to Jacob Riis Park linking Shore Greenway to Rockaway Greenway. 🚲 5-foot wide path.

Queensboro Bridge

Opened:	March 30, 1909.
Engineer:	Gustav Lindenthal
Total Length:	7,449 feet
Tower Ht:	350 feet
Water Clearance:	130 feet
Water Crossing:	East River

The National Landmark twin cantilever-truss bridge is a work of art, and the East River's busiest crossing. At one time trolleys stopped at stations located on the bridge that had stairways descending to Roosevelt Island. The caverns under the bridge, built in 1889 by Gustavino y Moreno, were a busy farmers market known as Bridgemarket until 1930. The bridge crosses over Roosevelt Island and is accessed at E 60th St. in Manhattan and Plaza/Crescent St. in Long Island City. 🚲 The north outer roadway is a car-free path.

Triborough Bridge (toll)

Opened:	1936
Engineer:	Othmar Ammann
Total Length:	13,820 feet
Water Clearance:	55 ft. - 143 ft.
Water Crossing:	East/Harlem Rivers

Actually three bridges in one— suspension span between Randalls Island and Astoria, truss bridge over the Bronx Kill and lift bridge over the Harlem River— joining Manhattan to Long Island and the Bronx. First years toll receipts brought in enough revenue to repay $37 million in federal loans. 🚲 Bike/ped. path is very narrow and long. Manhattan access: 124-126th Sts. Queens: Hoyt Ave. steep stairs. Bronx: 134th St. & Cypress Ave.

J **ohn A. Roebling, Engineer** (1806-1869), inventor of steel wire suspension cables, designed the Brooklyn Bridge and began construction in 1869. He died of tetanus poisoning from an injury incurred during construction that same year. John's son, **Washington Roebling, Engineer** (1837-1926) completed his father's bridge. He spent considerable time in the bridge caissons 80 feet below the surface of the East River and developed decompression sickness, or "the bends." Although the disease left Washington partially paralyzed and unable to speak by 1872, he continued to direct construction from his Brooklyn townhouse until completion of the bridge in May 24, 1883, relying on his wife. **Emily Roebling, Engineer** (1843-1903) learned higher mathematics and other points of bridge engineering while supervising the construction site daily. She kept all her husband's records, and represented him in business. Workers often came to her for construction advice.

Verrazano Narrows Bridge

(toll into Brooklyn only)

Opened:	November 21, 1964
Engineer:	Othmar Ammann
Total Length:	13,700 feet
Tower Ht:	693 feet
Water Clearance:	228 feet
Water Crossing:	The Narrows

The graceful span marks the gateway to the Upper Bay at The Narrows. The towers are farther apart at the top than at the base to compensate for the curvature of the earth, and the roadway is 12 feet lower in summer than in winter due to seasonal contraction and expansion. No access, but a footpath has been proposed.

Whitestone Bridge (toll)

Opened:	1939
Engineer:	Othmar Ammann
Total Length:	7,140 feet
Water Clearance:	150 feet
Water Crossing:	East River

The sleek bridge was built for the 1939 World's Fair with waterfront parks

created at each anchor in the Bronx and Queens. Bridge improvements through 2008, include returning the structure to its original appearance by removing stiffening trusses that were added to the bridge to prevent oscillation. No access. QBx1 bike-on-bus operates to carry bikes over bridge in summer months.

Williamsburg Bridge

Opened:	December 19, 1903
Engineer:	Leffert L. Buck
Total Length:	7.308 feet
Tower Ht:	310 feet
Water Clearance:	135 feet
Water Crossing:	East River

Inspired by architect Alexander Eiffel and called an "engineer's bridge," it is the largest of the East River suspension bridges. It carries 8 traffic lanes, 2 subway tracks, and a footpath at Delancy St. in Manhattan to Broadway & Roebling St. in Brooklyn. The asphalt bike/ped. path has steep ascent and stairs.

Burial at Sea

Jerry Garcia, L. Ron Hubbard, Rock Hudson and Ingrid Bergman are all buried at sea. Close to 300 bodies are committed to the deep in the waters around New York Harbor each year. There is no count of the cremated remains scattered over nearby waters. Marine funerals can take the form of scattering ashes on the waters at a favored fishing spot or placing a funeral urn at a preferred dive location. Ashes can become part of a fireworks celebration or an artificial reef. Ashes must be scattered at least three nautical miles from shore. Dispersal of cremate is not permitted from beaches or jetties. Nor is it allowed within the New York Bight or inland waters. Burial at sea of an intact body has to be in water at least 600 feet deep over 3 nautical miles from land. The casket must be weighted to ensure that the remains sink to the bottom permanently. A permit is not necessary, however the transport vessel has to notify the Environmental Protection Agency within 30 days. Wreaths and flowers left behind on the water must be decomposable. Viking-style funerals—sending the corpse to sea in a boat—must follow strict EPA and US Coast Guard guidelines for the disposal of ships at sea.

Marine Funeral Services

Celebrate Life! Places ashes in firework shells for dispersion at sea. 888-883-7060 celebratelife.net

Environmental Protection Agency Regulations governing disposal of vessels at sea and guidelines for a viking-style funeral. 212-264-9897 epa.gov/region02/water/oceans/burials.htm

Eternal Reef Green-Wood Cemetery, Brooklyn. Cremated remains are combined in memorial reefs that provide new undersea habitat. eternalreefs.com

Neptune Society Cremation services. 212-517-8262 neptunesociety.com

Sea Services Cremated remains placed in an organic memorial urn are delivered by divers to the ocean floor. seaservices.com

USCG Activities NY Free burial at sea services for veterans. 718-354-4030 uscg.mil or uscg.mil/mlcpac/ischon/da/burial%5Fat%5Fsea.doc

US Navy Mortuary Affairs Burial at sea for Navy vets and their families. 888-647-6676 chinfo.navy.mil/navpalib/questions/burial.html

Cruise Liners

“Arriving by sea into the Port of New York represented the start of a new life for millions of immigrants and for today's leisure passengers ranks as one of the greatest thrills one can have aboard any ship. Few places have such majesty, interest and energy as New York and the rich experience comes spectacularly to life while passing under the Verrazano-Narrows Bridge and into the Upper Bay.

Directly ahead, the Lower Manhattan skyline forms the elegant centerpiece, bracketed by downtown Brooklyn's smaller and older pile to the right, and to the left, the burgeoning new office construction on the New Jersey side.

While New York is still linked to the Old World by sea with regular sailings by the *Queen Elizabeth* 2, and beginning in April 2004 by the giant new 150,000 ton liner *Queen Mary 2*, it's pleasure cruises that form the principal traffic to and from the West Side Passenger Ship Terminal. Most sailings take place between late April and the end of October, and many of the regular weekly arrivals and departures occur on weekends. Manhattan and New Jersey have numerous places to watch and photograph the parade of ships in bound early in the morning and outbound between 4 and 5 p.m. **”**

Theodore W. Scull, World Ship Society, Port of New York

New York is the fifth busiest cruise port in the country. One million passengers sail in and out of the port each year. The cruise industry provided 11,289 jobs and contributed $902 million to the New York economy in 2002. The Passenger Ship Terminal handles about 250 vessel calls per year. It consists of piers 88, 90 and 92, capable of docking five cruise ships at 1000-foot-long berths on the Hudson River. Customs and other federal agencies have offices on site. The most popular destinations from the port of New York are Bermuda and New England, during peak season from May through October. The first ship to make New York its permanent homeport in several decades is the *Norwegian Dawn*, which offers weekly cruises to the Bahamas and Florida year-round. The world's largest cruise operator, Carnival offers 50 New York departures and wants to add more. The Manhattan ship terminal is operating at capacity and will be expanded, along with new berthing space at the Brooklyn Piers. Royal Caribbean has moved to docks in Bayonne, NJ.

Shipping News

Cruise passenger ship arrivals and departures were once prominently announced in major city newspapers. Today, few papers devote space to coverage of ship transits. The websites of the Passenger Ship Terminal and World Ship Society provide ship schedules.

Hundreds of New Yorkers observe and photograph the comings and goings of cruise ships in New York Harbor. Fort Wadsworth offers one of the best spots for capturing ships passing through The Narrows. On days when there are several departures, NY Waterway ferry to Weehawken, NJ offers a classic view of the liners sailing down the Hudson against the backdrop of the midtown skyline.

Passenger Ship Terminal (PST) 711 w 12th Ave. (46th to 54th St). Three finger piers, exhibit space, parking and rental cars. 212-246-5450 nypst.com

P & O Ports of NA Exclusive stevedore and terminal operator for the Passenger Ship Terminal under a 20 year contract with the Port Authority. poportsna.com

World Ship Society Port of NY Chapter (PONY) Founded in 1965, over 300 members pursue their enthusiasm for cruise ships. worldshipny.com

Cruise Lines with New York City Port o' Calls

Carnival Cruise Lines	800-498-6744	carnival.com
Celebrity Cruises	800-437-3111	celebritycruises.com
Costa Cruise Lines	305-358-7325	costacruises.com
Crystal Cruises	800-820-6663	crystalcruises.com
Cunard Line	800-528-6273	cunard.com
Festival Cruises	888-983-8767	festivalcruises.com
Holland America	800-426-0327	hollandamerica.com
Norwegian Cruise Line	800-327-7030	ncl.com
P&O Cruises	415-382-8900	pocruises.com
Princess Cruises	800-421-0522	princesscruises.com
Regal Cruises	800-270-7245	regalcruises.com
Royal Caribbean	800-327-6700	royalcaribbean.com
Seabourn Cruises	800-929-9595	seabourn.com
Silversea Cruises	800-722-6655	silversea.com

Dorothy Marckwald, Maritime Interior Designer. A native New Yorker and a graduate of Packer Collegiate Institute of Brooklyn, Dorothy's ground breaking designs set the standard for 20th century seagoing luxury. She joined the Madison Avenue design firm of Elsie Cobb Wilson in the early 1920s and was soon after celebrated for her art deco styling and uniquely American fashion for the express steamer *America*. Dorothy designed interiors for many vessels of naval architect Gibbs and Cox, Grace Lines' South American *Santa* liners, Farrell Lines, and American Export Line's *Constitution* and *Independence*. Marckwald ultimately fashioned the austere interior for the greatest ocean liner of the day, the 14,000 passenger *United States*, which was launched by United States Lines in 1951.

Clean Cruising

Cruise ships are like floating cities. A typical ship can produce up to 30,000 gallons of sewage a day and generate tons of solid waste, oily bilge water, wastewater from showers and galleys, and hazardous waste from onboard photo processing and dry cleaning. Just 12 miles from the coast, cruise ships can throw garbage overboard, and as near as 3 miles they can dump sewage into the sea. The air pollution from ship diesel engines is at a level equal to thousands of automobiles.

Passengers can check if the cruise company follows "green" practices. Passengers on ships who observe any dumping of plastic at sea, which is banned, should report it to the USCG National Response Center by calling 800-424-8802.

Ship-Spotting

Web cams are stationed at points around the harbor and provide a glimpse of ship activity.

Ambrose Light Buoy National Data Buoy Center. ndbc.noaa.gov

Circle Line Cam Camera mounted on Circle Line sightseeing boat. earthcam.com/usa/newyork/circleline

Empire State Building Views of *Intrepid* and Passenger Ship Terminal from webcams mounted on the Empire State Building. esbnyc.com

NY Skyline A porthole view of the Harbor. nj.com/nycskyline

Passenger Ship Terminal Live images of PST announcing arrivals and departures. home.att.net/~PIED-PIPER-TRAVEL/Webcam.html

USS Intrepid Live images from the mast of the great battleship. earthcam.com/usa/newyork/intrepid

Dining with a View

Waterfront Restaurants

Breathtaking views of the cityscape and New York Harbor set the stage for amazing on-the-water dining experiences in the world's largest restaurant market.

 Dock & dine available

Manhattan

American Park at the Battery
17 State Street Former utility building in Battery Park serves seafood and harbor views. 212-809-5508 americanpark.com

Bayard's & Blue Bar 1 Hanover Sq. Seaworthy upland fine dining restaurant surrounded by the maritime art collection of India House. 212-514-9454

Bridge Café 279 Water St. In operation since 1794, the city's oldest continuously run restaurant flanks the Brooklyn Bridge in the oldest wood-frame building in Manhattan. It is the former spot of the notorious Hole in the Wall bar described in "Gangs of New York." 212-227-3344

Boat Basin Café W 79th St. Riverside Park. Light fare and cocktails on the open air patio overlooking the houseboats and yachts at the marina

on the Hudson River. 212-496-5542 boatbasincafe.com

Carmine's Italian Seafood
140 Beekman St. 100-year-old fish house with a partial view of Fulton's Fish Market. 212-962-8606

Central Park Boathouse
Dining beside the park's freshwater pond. 212-517-2233

Chelsea Brewery Co. Chelsea Piers, Pier 59. A microbrew pub facing the powerboats docked at the marina on the Hudson River. 212-336-6440 chelseabrewingco.com

Club Gustavino 409 E 59th St. View of the tiled vaults under the Queensboro Bridge. 212-421-6644

F. illi Ponte 39 Desbrosses St. Italian food served in a room of exposed brick that looks out over the Hudson from Tribeca. 212-226-4621

14 Wall Street 14 Wall St, 31st Floor. Upscale French cuisine served in the former penthouse of J. P. Morgan featuring panoramic views of New York Harbor. 212-233-2780

Gigino at Wagner Park 20 Battery Pl. Moderately priced Italian fare and gelato on the green lawn of Wagner Park, offering spectacular views of

Nathan Handwerker, Restaurateur (1892-1974) A Polish immigrant who came to New York at the age of 20 in 1912. He did not invent the hot dog that credit goes to Charles Feltman in 1874. Handwerker is credited with opening America's first hot dog stand in Coney Island in 1916. Eddie Cantor and Jimmy Durante put up a $300 loan for Handwerker to open the original Nathan's, where he charged 5 cents for his garlic-spiced sausage on a roll. He made the ultimate "beach food" popular by installing signs that declared his hot dogs "world famous" long before they were. By 1955, Nathan's had expanded beyond Coney Island and today can be found all over the country.

New York Harbor and Statue of Liberty. 212-528-2228

Grill Room 225 Liberty St. World Financial Center. Wall-length windows deliver breathtaking harbor views. 212-945-9400

Harbour Lights 89 South St. Pier 17. A touristy, upscale seafood restaurant overlooking the East River and Brooklyn Bridge. 212-227-2800

Heartland Brewery 93 South St. Former site of Sloppy Louie's of *Up in the Old Hotel* fame, faces the river and historic ship slips. 646-572-BEER

Hudson River Club 4 World Financial Center. Formal setting, regional American cuisine and expansive harbor views. 212-786-1500

O'Neal's Riverside Park South Café 70th St. Plaza. Grilled burgers and sandwiches at Trump's new park at Riverside South on the Hudson.

Paris Café 119 South St. Seafarer's bar and seafood house built in 1873 that looks out on Fulton's Fish Market on the East River. 212-240-9797

Pen-Top Bar & Terrace Peninsula Hotel, 23rd Flr. 700 5th Ave. A well-heeled watering hole atop the hotel affords dramatic views of skyline and water. 212-903-3097

Pier 25 Snack Shack Hudson River Park. Outdoor grill at pier.

Pier 63 Maritime Bar W 23rd St. Outdoor bar on an old Lackawanna Rail Barge that serves as an anchorage for historic ships on the Hudson.

Rainbow Grill 30 Rockefeller Plaza 65th Flr. 5th Ave. Hudson River and skyline views in one of the city's most romantic rooms. 212-632-5100

Rise Bar Ritz-Carlton, 14th Flr. 2 West St. Battery Park. Al fresco lounge atop the Ritz Carlton takes full advantage of location and harbor panorama. 212-344-0800

Rooftop Restaurant Bentley Hotel 500 E 62nd St. Spectacular view of the Queensboro Bridge and East River.

Seaport Café Seaport. Euro-style outdoor café with seaport view. 212-964-1120

Sequoia South St. Seaport, Pier 17. Caribbean seafood on the East River. 212-732-9090

Skipper's Pierside Café South St. Seaport. Pier 16. Beer and burgers amid historic ship pier. 212-349-1188

SouthWestNY 225 Liberty St. World Financial Center. Indoor and outdoor seating looking out on North Cove marina. 212-945-0528

Steamers Landing Liberty & Albany St. Garden terrace with views of the Battery Park City esplanade and lower Hudson River. 212-432-1451 steamerslanding.com

Terrace in the Sky 400 W 119 St. A 1920s-style penthouse on top of Columbia's Butler Hall serves light French cuisine and views of the George Washington Bridge and upper Manhattan cityscape. 212-666-9490 terraceinthesky.com

The View at Marriott 1535 Broadway. The revolving restaurant on top of the Time's Square Marriott takes in the city and Hudson River. 212-704-8900

Top of the Tower 3 Mitchell Pl. Rooftop club crowning the Art Deco landmark Beekman Hotel features East River views and an outdoor terrace. 212-355-7300

Tubby Hook Cafe 348 Dyckman St. Dockside bar and grill with views of the George Washington Bridge down the Hudson and across to the Palisades. 212-567-8086 ⚓

Uguale 396 West St. Romantic restaurant serves Italian cuisine and Hudson River views. 212-229-0606

The Water Club 500 E 30th St at FDR Dr. Permanently moored barge decked out like a high-end yacht offering classic American kitchen and a rooftop Crow's Nest bar on the East River. 212-683-3333 thewaterclub.com

West 425 West St. at 11th Ave. Great place for sunset cocktails looking out on the Hudson River. 212-242-4375

UN Delegates Dining Room 1st Ave at 46th St. International cuisine served in the floor-to-ceiling windowed room on the East River. Open Monday through Friday only. ID required. 212-963-7626

Bronx

The Boat Livery 663 City Island Ave. Bud and boat rentals at bar/bait & tackle combo on Eastchester Bay. 718-885-1843 ⚓

City Island Lobster House 691 Bridge St. Arrive by boat or car to dine on the outdoor terrace overlooking the marina on the Long Island Sound. 718-885-1459 ⚓

Johnny's Famous Reef 2 City Island Ave. Popular fish shack with an outdoor patio looking out on the Long Island Sound. 718-885-2090

Harbor Restaurant 565 City Island Ave. Seafood, dock & dine and bay views just over the City Island Bridge. 718-885-1373 ⚓

Harbour Inn 50 Pennyfield Ave. Throgs Neck neighborhood restaurant and pub on the Long Island Sound. 718-892-9148

The Lobster Box 34 City Island Ave. Surf and turf menu with Italian flavors looking out on the Long Island Sound. 718-885-1952 lobsterbox.com

Marina del Ray One Marina Dr. Catering hall overlooking the Throgs Neck Bridge. 718-931-6500

Seashore Restaurant 591 City Island Ave. Serving fresh seafood since the 1920s, and welcomes dock and dine visitors. 212-885-0300 🛟

Sea View 636 City Island Ave. Seafood at a lunch counter at the City Island Bridge. 718-885-9263

Snuff Mill In the NY Botanical Gardens on the Bronx River. nybg.org

SUNY Maritime Hall 6 Pennyfield Ave. View of the Long Island Sound and Throgs Neck Bridge from the college dining hall. Open to the public for lunch on Thursdays only. 718-931-0080 sunymaritime.com

Tony's on the Pier 1 City Island Ave. Fish fry shack across on Long Island Sound. 718-885-1424

Wave Hill Cafe 675 W 252nd St. Light lunch and sweets served in the world-renowned gardens overlooking the Hudson River and NJ Palisades. 718-796-8538

Brooklyn

Alma 187 Columbia St. Mexican bar and restaurant with a roof deck serving family-style portions and a view of lower Manhattan across Brooklyn's working waterfront. 718-643-5400 almarestaurant.com

Brooklyn Ice Cream Factory Fulton Ferry Landing. Old-fashioned ice cream parlor in 1920s fireboat house under the Brooklyn Bridge. 718-246-3963

Bubby's 1 Main St. Comfort food and spectacular views of Lower Manhattan and the Brooklyn Bridge from DUMBO. 718-222-0666

Clemente's Maryland Crabhouse 3939 Emmons Ave. All-you-can-eat Maryland sweet crab and cold beer at a patio table at Venice Marina, located on Shell Bank Creek. 718-646-7373 🛟

Dockside Café 96 Ebony Ct. Homey local's bar and grill on Shell Bank Creek in Gerritsen Beach. 718-616-0091

Seafood Lover's Guide

The Seafood Lover's Guide evaluates the most popular seafood available in the New York region and ranks it on a scale from green to red (problematic species). Contact: Audubon's Living Oceans 888-397-6649 seafood.audubon.org; Wildlife Conservation Society 718-220-5155 wcs.org/gofish; Seafood Choices seafoodchoices.com

Freak Bar W 12th St. Coney Island. Open weekends at Sideshows by the Seashore in the 1917 terra cotta building that once housed the singing waiters of Child's Restaurants.

Giando On the Water 400 Kent Ave. Big, ornate Italian restaurant with on the Williamsburg banks of the East River. 718-387-7000 giandoonthewater.com

Grimaldi's 19 Old Fulton St. Enjoy curbside East River views while waiting for a table in Brooklyn's best and busiest pizza joint. 718-858-4300

Il Fornetto 2902 Emmons Ave. Terrace seating right on Sheepshead Bay. 718-332-8494

Istanbul 1715 Emmons Ave. Shish kabob on the Sheepshead Bay waterfront. 718-368-3587

Jordan's Lobster in the Ruff 2771 Knapp St. Lobster pound and restaurant on the banks of Shell Bank Creek. 718-934-6300

Lai Yuen 1033 4th Ave. Chinese food and a view of the Verrazano Bridge. 718-567-2300

Limans 2710 Emmons Ave. Turkish seafood specialties on Sheepshead Bay. 718-769-3322

Lundy Brothers 1901 Emmons Ave. A Sheepshead Bay tradition since it began on a wooden pier in 1916. Irving Lundy served the freshest seafood at the city's largest restaurant until the 1950s, when the establishment closed. The pink Moorish-style building was fully restored when the eatery reopened in 1995. 718-743-0022

Mario & Luigi's Seafood & Pasta 2007 Emmons Ave. Italian seafood on Sheepshead Bay, across from the fishing fleet. 718-891-4300

Montero's Bar 73 Atlantic Ave. Curb-side view of the harbor at this longshoremen's dive with old photos of the Brooklyn docks on the walls. 718-624-9799

Monte's Venetian Room 451 Carroll St. A wrap-around mural of Venice and red sauce Italian since 1906 at the Landmark Carroll St. Bridge on the Gowanus Canal. 718-624-8984

Moscow Café' Brighton 6th St. Ukrainian food on the Brighton Beach boardwalk. 718-934-3200

Nathan's 1310 Stillwell at Surf Ave. World-famous hot dogs served from its original location and from a boardwalk stand. 718-946-2202

Nick's Lobster Market 2777 Flatbush Ave. Lobster shack and pound on Mill Basin. 718-253-7117

Pete's Downtown 2 Water St. 1894 landmark restaurant below the Brooklyn Bridge. 718-858-3510 petesdowntown

Randazzo's Clam Bar 2017 Emmons. The 50 year old Italian clam shack is a Sheepshead Bay classic. 718-615-0010

River Café 1 Water St. Gourmet restaurant and outdoor terrace offering amazing views from a barge moored under the Brooklyn Bridge. 718-522-5200 rivercafe.com

Ruby's Old Thyme Bar W 12th St. Coney Island boardwalk beer joint.

Seaport Buffet 2027 Emmons Ave. All-you-can-eat on the Sheepshead Bay waterfront. 718-368-3388

Sunny's Bar The vintage dive has been a waterfront institution in Red Hook for three generations.

Tamaqua Bar & Marina 84 Ebony Ct. Clubby boaters bar on the docks of Shell Bank Creek. 718-646-9212 🐾

Tatiana Cafe 3152 Brighton 6th St. Seaside café on the Brighton Beach boardwalk. 718-891-5151

TGI Fridays 3181 Harkness Ave. Prime seating overlooking Shell Bank Creek. 718-934-5700

Volna 3145 Brighton 4th St. Blinis and vodka on the Brighton Beach boardwalk. 718-332-0341

Winter Garden 3152 Brighton 6th St. Russian supper club with an ocean view. 718-934-1781

Queens

And Then Michael's 163-35 Cross Bay Blvd. Year-round Italian seafood house opens seasonal tented outdoor clam bar on Shellbank Basin. 718-848-2800

Doubbles @ Fila Sports Center 44-02 Vernon Blvd. East River views from dining room of the private tennis club. 718-937-3001

Kennedy's On the Bay Beach 210th St. Breezy Point. Italian seafood and views of Jamaica Bay and Manhattan skyline. 718-945-0202

Lenny's Clam Bar 161-03 Cross Bay Blvd. Year-round clam shack opens seasonal outdoor tent on Shellbank Basin. 718-845-5100

Sand Bar 116th Beach St. Beach bar and grill on the Rockaway boardwalk.

Sugar Bowl Bedford & Oceanside Ave. Breezy Point beach bar.

Sunset Diner 116–11 Beach Channel Dr. Jamaica Bay views. 718-634-8500

Starbucks 157-41 Cross Bay Blvd. Roof deck on Shellbank Basin. 718-641-9332

Tennisport 51-24 2nd St. Private tennis club on the East River serving lunch and dinner Tues, Wed & Thur only. 718-392-1880

The Beach Club 129 Beach 116th St. Situated on the Rockaway boardwalk. 718-634-6500 thebeachclub.com

Pier 92 377 Beach 92nd St. Dockside dining overlooking Jamaica Bay. 718-945-2200 🐾

The Wharf 416 Beach 116th St. Deep fried fare looking out on Jamaica Bay. 718-474-8807 🐾

Water's Edge 44th Dr. Midtown. Manhattan views on an elegant barge moored on the East River banks of Long Island City. Free ferry from E 34th St. Pier, Manhattan. 718-482-0033

Waterfront Crab House 2-03 Borden Ave. Long Island City. Seafood and narrow East River views from outdoor tables. 718-729-4862

World's Fair Marina Restaurant World's Fair Marina. Indian-Asian menu served at the World's Fair Marina on Flushing Bay. 718-898-1200

Staten Island

The Carriage House Fort Wadsworth. Live music, food and drinks on an open deck under the Verrazano Bridge. 718-876-6489

Carmen's 750 Barclay Ave. Platters of paella served oceanside. 718-356-2725

Harbor Lights Wolfe's Pond Park. ✗

Harborview Restaurant 27 Mansion Ave. Steakhouse on Great Kills Harbor. 718-227-9771

Marina Cafe' 154 Mansion Ave. Seafood and panoramic views of Great Kills Harbor. 718-967-3077

Patricio's 691-695 Bay St. at Broad St. Platters of pasta and views of the Verrazano Bridge. 718-720-1861

R. H. Tugs 115 Richmond Terrace. Pub looking out on tugboats and supertankers plying the waters of the Kill Van Kull. 718-447-6369.

Waterside Barbecue Grills

- Alley Pond Park
- East River Park
- Inwood Hill Park
- Kaiser Park
- Flushing Meadows - Corona Park
- Manhattan Beach Park
- Orchard Beach - Pelham Bay Park
- Rockaway Beaches 17, 88 & 98
- Wards Island

Catch of the Day

City Seafood Market Locator nyseafood.org

Fulton Fish Market 200 Water St. One million pounds of fish are sold nightly at the oldest and largest wholesale fish market in the U.S., and the second biggest in the world after Tokyo. The market is slated to move to new quarters in Hunts Point, Bronx. Open 3 a.m. to 9 a.m. Scheduled tours conducted by Seaport Museum 212-748-8600

Grand Central Oyster Bar Built in 1913, the famed seafood house serves over 5,000 raw oysters per day. 212-490-6650 oysterbarny.com

Sheepshead Bay Fishing Boats Emmons Ave. Sheepshead Bay. The days catch sold dockside at bargain prices, right off the fishing boats each day around 4 p.m. when the fleet returns to the piers.

Excursion Boats

"Excursion boats are a little like cruise ships. One doesn't board an excursion boat to go somewhere. One boards an excursion boat because the voyage itself is a pleasant and relaxing way to spend an afternoon or an evening.

New York excursion boats come in a variety of shapes and sizes. There are high-speed craft that specialize in fast, breezy trips down the bay, there are sightseeing yachts that offer relaxing three-hour cruises around Manhattan Island, and there are voyages that offer everything from on-board concerts -- blues, rock, jazz or classical-- to lectures on specialized topics by experts in various fields.

A rather new style of excursion boat in New York are various dinner cruisers, as they are generally called, vessels that cast off just before lunchtime or dinner hour, and allow passengers to enjoy a fine meal as the captain navigates the vessel around the harbor. (Reservations are usually necessary and always recommended.)

Sometimes, though, an excursion boat can be something that is largely in the eye of the beholder! And so waterborne services that are designed and marketed as ferry services- vessels that carry people over and back across a river or bay can quickly become excursion boats if passengers choose to regard them as simply relaxing ways to take cruise around the harbor. **"**

Brian J. Cudahy has written many books on transportation history, his latest book is *How We Got to Coney Island*

Excursion Boats

Adirondack Depart Pier 62, Chelsea Piers. Regularly scheduled public sailings and sunset cruises aboard 80' schooner. 800-701-SAIL sail-nyc.com

Bateaux Depart Pier 61, Chelsea Piers. Glass enclosed French river boat, the *Celestial,* offers lunch and dinner cruises. 212-352-1366 bateauxnewyork.com

The Beast Depart Pier 16 - South Street Seaport & Pier 83 - Circle Line. A 30-minute power cruise of New York Harbor at speeds of 45 mph. 212-563-3200 circleline42.com

Chelsea Screamer Depart Pier 62, Chelsea Piers. Prepare to get wet aboard the 50-foot speedboat cruising New York Harbor, the Intrepid and Statue of Liberty. 212-924-6262 chelseascreamer.com

Circle Line Depart Pier 83, 42nd St. Famed 3-hour circumnavigation of Manhattan Island has been the most popular way to explore the city's waterways since 1954. The cruise travels a 35-mile route following the Hudson, Harlem and East rivers and sails into New York Harbor around the Statue of Liberty. Other excursions include: Semi-Circle Cruises and the Harbor Lights Cruises. 212-563-3200 circleline42.com

Eco-Cruise Sundays Departs 2nd St. Brooklyn. Urban Divers' monthly tour of the Gowanus Canal and Newtown Creek. geocities.com/ecocruisesunday

Executive Yacht Club & Spa Floating spa offers members 27 treatment rooms, steam rooms, saunas, swimming pools and meeting space aboard *Serenity II*. 212-571-CLUB eycspa.com ✄

Lettie G. Howard Depart Pier 16, South Street Seaport. Scheduled sailings aboard 1893 Fredonia-style schooner. 212-748-8590 southstseaport.org

NY Water Taxi Liberty Cruise Depart Fulton Ferry Landing, Brooklyn. Cruises of New York Harbor and the Statue of Liberty. 212-742-1969 nywatertaxi.com

NY Waterway Depart Pier 78, W 38th St. & Pier 17 South Street Seaport. Full and half circle Manhattan cruises, New York Harbor and special events cruises. 800-533-3779 nywaterway.com

Pioneer Depart Pier 16, South Street Seaport. Public sunset and evening sails aboard 1885 schooner. 212-748-8590 southstseaport.org

Riis Landing Cruise Depart Fort Tilden. Eco & Harbor Fortification Tours aboard the *Elsie K. Princess*. Also, Coney Island Fireworks, Monmouth Racetrack, West Point and Hudson River Foliage excursions. 718-318-7447 riislanding.com

Seaport Liberty Cruises Depart Pier 16, South Street Seaport. Sightseeing tours and one hour harbor cruise. 212-630-8888 circleline42.com

Shearwater Depart North Cove Marina, Battery Park City. Scheduled public sailings aboard 82-ft. 1929 Maine sailing schooner. 800-544-1224 sail-shearwater.com

Spirit Cruises Depart Pier 61, Chelsea Piers. Lunch, dinner and moonlight cruises. 212-777-2789 spiritcruises.com

Ventura Depart North Cove at Battery Park City. Public sunset sails each Friday at 6 p.m. 212-786-1204 sailnewyork.com

W.O. Decker **Tug Boat** Depart Pier 16, South Street Seaport. Tour the working waterfront aboard a six-passenger wooden tug. 212-748-8590 southstseaport.org

World Yacht Depart World Yacht, Pier 81 W 41st St. Dinner cruises. 212-630-8800 worldyacht.com

“ 4601 names of those lost in the desperate "Battle of the Atlantic" are visible from our Circle Line Ferry boat boarding at Pier #3. Names such as Tortorici, Weinburg, Vanderheiden, Thompson, Zabrowski, ordinary Americans, they put paid to FDR's promise to make America "the arsenal of Democracy". They were the children of Ellis Island. Minutes after departure, we close on the twenty-seven acre landfill their immigrant mothers remembered as the Island of Tears, and go face to face with Liberty Enlightening the World. Returning from the Statue, a stunning panorama, unmatched in human experience, confronts us, on misty days appearing of a sudden, the richest, most powerful, freest city of all. The likes of which no pharaoh, no Caesar, in his wildest reveries, ever commanded. Ah, sure it is, the Towers are no more, but this ever-changing scene, first espied by Henry Hudson on the 11th day of September, in the year 1609, remains breathtaking, lump in your throat, outdoor theater. A great Harbor becomes Cyclorama and I provide the voice-over. It may be the best job in the world. **”**

Tim Hollon, Narrator
Circle Line Ferry Boats' Harbor Cruise

Day Liners

Day liner steamboats carried passengers and tourists on the Hudson River for more than 150 years, sailing to ports between New York and Albany. Day Line referred to the time of departure, there was also a "Night Line" and "Evening Line."

The Floating Hospital

180-foot-long "Ship of Health," established in 1866 to care for New York Times newsboys, operates a dockside clinic and offers Summer Sails to underprivileged children The ship's future is uncertain.
212-514-7440 x110
thefloatinghospital.org

Circle Line Departs Pier 83. Seasonal Hudson River cruises to Bear Mt. 212-563-3200 circleline42.com

Hudson River Dayline Departs World Yacht Pier 81, W 41st St. Weekend cruises to Bear Mountain and West Point. 877-733-4735 hudsonriverdayline.com

New York Waterway Departs Pier 78. Seasonal destinations include: Kykuit and Lyndhurst Castle, Sleepy Hollow, Fall Foliage, West Point Football and to the beaches of Rockaway (Fort Tilden) and Sandy Hook. 800-533-3779 nywaterway.com

Seastreak Fall Foliage Cruise Departs Pier 81. Bear Mountain and West Point trips. 800-BOATRIDE seastreakusa.com

Party Cruises

Affairs Afloat, Inc	212-987-2628	affairsafloat.com
Blues Cruise	212-630-8888	bluecruiseny.com
City Lights Cruise	212-822-8573	citylightscruises.com
Coors Light Cruises	212-213-2002	Q104.3.com
Executive Bike Tours	732-741-2799	executivebiketours.com
Good2Go Booze Cruise	718-380-8863	good2godjsent.com
New York Harbor Cruise	212-288-1975	nyharborcruises.com
NYC Singles Cruises	212-288-0607	nycsinglescruises.com
Smooth Cruise	212-727-7768	spiritcitycruises.com

Charter Boats & Yachts

Atlantic Sail & Charter	212-786-1204	sailnewyork.com
Bacon Yacht Charters	212-873-7558	abaconnyachtcharter.com
Chelsea Piers Yacht Charters	212-645-6626	boatsnyc.com
Cloud Nine Charters	212-248-3800	cloud9charters.com
Dove Yacht Charters	212-445-5942	doveyacht.com
Eastern Star Yacht Charters	800-465-8556	easternstarcruises.com
Entrepreneur Yacht Charters	212-517-5998	entrepreneur2.com
Leilani Charters	718-332-2717	classicyachtleilani.com
Lots of Yachts	212-505-2214	lotsofyachts.com
Manhattan Yacht Charters	212-995-5470	metropolitanyacht.com
New York Boat Charters	212-496-8625	nyboatcharter.com
New York Boat Charter	212-595-2112	newyorkboatcharter.com
NYC Boat Cruise Charters	212-734-0605	nycboatcruise.com
Paddlewheel Queen	212-288-1975	paddlewheelqueen.com
Prada Yachts	212-489-9216	pradausa.com
Skyline Cruises	718-446-1100	skylinecruises.com
Southern Star Charters	212-787-8030	connexions.net
VIP Yacht Cruises	201-866-6264	vipyachtcruises.com
Yacht Owners of NY	212-736-1010	yachtsny.com
Ysi-Yacht Service	718-885-3294	yachtserviceintl.com

Ferries & Water Taxis

❝The City of New York consists of many islands, and while most of these are connected with each other by bridges, tunnels and causeways, there are also a number of ferry services that provide travelers with some wonderful waterborne options as they travel around the metropolitan area. Arguably the most famous ferry service in the known universe is one that connects the lower end of Manhattan Island with the borough of Staten Island, five miles down the bay. For many years the Staten Island Ferry was one of the best bargains in the city, as the one-way fare for a delightful half-hour ride was a mere five cents. Today it's an even better bargain, though, and the service charges no fare at all!

Recent years have also seen the emergence of many new ferry routes, and smart little boats now scoot back and forth across the Hudson and East rivers from many different landings. Many of the city's older ferry services were abandoned as bridges and tunnels were built in the early years of the twentieth century and ferry transport was regarded as old fashioned. Now, though, with bridges and tunnels operating at near capacity during peak rush hours, new ferry services have been established that allow passengers to bypass all the congestion, and enjoy a pleasant cruise while doing so. **❞**

Brian J. Cudahy, author of
Over and Back: The History of Ferryboats in New York Harbor

New York has the largest number of ferry riders in the country. More than 130,000 people commute by water each weekday. Ferries and water taxis offer a unique way to travel and sightsee in the Big Apple. The fabled Staten Island ferry transports 19 million passengers annually and is the city's fourth most popular tourist attraction. NY Waterway relaunched cross-Hudson service in 1986 and is today the largest private ferry operator in the country. Water taxis, resembling checker-board cabs, criss-cross the harbor adding new stops along the Hudson and East rivers. Fast ferries transport people to Broadway shows, baseball games, Thoroughbred races and the beaches of Rockaway. Service is expanding and new landings are in development. The terminals at St. George and Whitehall have been completely overhauled. Slips at World Financial Center and Battery Maritime are being modernized and a new terminal will wrap around the Lincoln Tunnel vents.

Commuter Routes

Ferries operate every 15-minutes during commuter rush hour Monday through Friday, from 6:30 a.m. to 9:30 a.m. and 4:00 p.m. to 7:00 p.m. Off-peak and weekend schedules vary. All boats are handicap accessible. Bikes may be taken for free on all ferries, except NY Waterway (cost is $1) and Seastreak ($3). Dogs are allowed on the Staten Island Ferry, but must be leashed, Seastreak and NY Waterway require that pets be in a carrier, while NY Water Taxi only permits therapy dogs to board.

Landings	Fee	Routes
Liberty Park Ferry Line		
World Financial Ctr	$5	Liberty Landing Marina (seasonal)
NYC DOT		
South Ferry/Whitehall	Free	St.George Terminal, Staten Island
New York Waterway		
Pier 11/ Wall St	$15	NJ: Belford, Harborside, Newport
WFC	$3	NJ: Colgate, Hoboken S & N, Port Imperial
Pier 11/ Wall St	$3-7	NJ: Colgate, Hoboken S, Port Imperial, Port Liberte
Pier 78/ W 38 St	$7-15	NJ: Belford, Colgate, Harborside, Hoboken N, Libery Harbor, Lincoln Harbor, Newport, Port Imperial
New York Water Taxi		
Pier 11/ Wall St	$5	Brooklyn: BAT 58th St, Fulton Landing, Red Hook
Hudson River Shuttle	$5	North Cove, Christopher St ✖, Chelsea Piers, Intrepid @ Pier 84, Riverside South @ W 69th ✖
E 34 St	$4	Hunters Point, Queens
East River Shuttle	$4	E 90 St, E 34 St, E 23 St, South St. Seaport, Pier 11
Seastreak		
Pier 11 & E 34 St	$18	NJ: Atlantic Highlands, Highlands, S. Amboy
Statue Of Liberty Ferry		
Castle Clinton/Battery	$10	Ellis & Liberty Islands (every 20 minutes)

NOTE: All rates and routes are subject to change. ✖ Future ferry/taxi landings are planned for Snug Harbor on Staten Island, Randall's Island, Battery Park Slip 6, and Williamsburg and Greenpoint in Brooklyn. In addition, shuttles may soon operate to both JFK International and LaGuardia Airports.

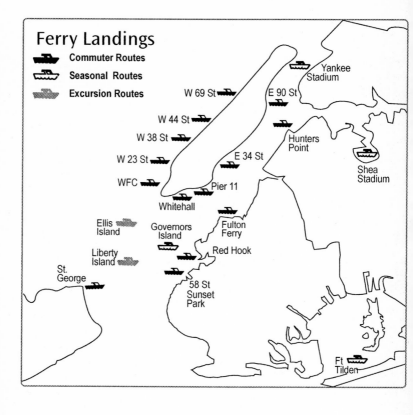

Ferry Landings

- Commuter Routes
- Seasonal Routes
- Excursion Routes

Yankee Stadium
W 69 St
E 90 St
Hunters Point
W 44 St
W 38 St
E 34 St
Shea Stadium
W 23 St
WFC
Pier 11
Whitehall
Ellis Island
Governors Island
Fulton Ferry
Liberty Island
Red Hook
St. George
58 St Sunset Park
Ft Tilden

Special Destination Ferries

A growing number of special event and seasonal ferries provide a unique transportation alternative to venues throughout the harbor. All ferry operators also offer boats for charter and schedule 4th of July and New Years Eve cruises.

Broadway Bound	800-53-FERRY	nywaterway.com
Cirque Du Soleil, Randall's Isl		risf.org
Monmouth Horse Races	800-262-8743	seastreakusa.com
Noble Harbor Launch	718-447-8223	johnnoble.com
Riis Park, Rockaway	800-53-FERRY	nywaterway.com
Sandy Hook Beach	800-262-8743	seastreakusa.com
Shea/Yankee Games	800-53-FERRY	nywaterway.com
West Point Football	800-262-8743	seastreakusa.com

Cornelius Vanderbilt, Entrepreneur (1794-1877). Born on Staten Island, Vanderbilt entered into business at the age of 16 with $100 that he borrowed from his mother and was the richest man in America at the time of his death. He began his career by ferrying passengers between Manhattan and Staten Island at a bargain rate. From 1818-1829, Vanderbilt was a steamboat captain in partnership with Thomas Gibbons–the man responsible for having the Fulton-Livingston New York ferry monopoly declared unconstitutional in 1824. As his wealth increased, "Commodore" Vanderbilt invested in railroads and financed steamship routes to Nicaragua and across the Atlantic, and continued to offer competitive rates.

Ferry & Water Taxi Operators

Liberty State Park Water Taxi
Service between Liberty State Park and North Cove in Battery Park City. 201-985-8000 llmarina.com

NY Water Taxi A fleet of low emission, low wake vessels. $15 day pass allows passengers to get and off the boat at stops throughout the day. New stops planned for the future include: Battery Park, Christopher St., E 23rd St., W 69th St., Kent Ave. in Greenpoint and Red Hook, Brooklyn. 212-742-1969 nywatertaxi.com

NY Waterway The areas largest private ferry operator. Free shuttle buses meet ferries at W 38th St. Terminal and run through midtown and there is a Downtown Express Bus. 800-533-3779 nywaterway.com

SeaConn Fast ferry to operate between Manhattan and the Connecticut shore offering trips to LaGuardia, Wall St and high-speed service to Martha's Vineyard. 203-624-7200 seaconn.com ✗

Seastreak One of Europe's largest ferry companies, operates commuter routes and baseball trips from the New Jersey Highlands. 800-262-8743 seastreak.com

Staten Island Ferry Operating since 1905, four ferries make the 5.6 mile, 25-minute trip 104 times daily between St. George and Whitehall. New modernized terminals and boats, based on the Kennedy Class fleet that carry 3500 passengers enter service in 2004. No vehicles are allowed on ferries until further notice due to security concerns. 718-815-2628 ci.nyc.ny.us

Statue of Liberty Ferry Circle Line is the official boat operator for the National Park Service monuments. Boats run from the Battery and Liberty State Park about every 20 minutes to visit both Liberty and Ellis Island. Admission to the monuments is free, passengers pay for ferry only. The pedestal and statue remain closed sine 9/11/01. 212-269-5755 statueoflibertyferry.com

Fishing

❝New York Harbor has almost 1,000 miles of shoreline on rivers, tidal straits, bays, and creeks, and with easy access to the riches of the New York Bight—it's not surprising that fishing is an important local activity. New York Harbor has a great variety of fishes with perhaps as many as 250 species recorded. This diversity is predicated on a mix of offshore, coastal, estuarine, anadromous (freshwater spawning) and, during summer, even tropical fishes. When Henry Hudson sailed into the Harbor and lower Hudson in 1609, his first mate observed "many Salmon and Mullets and Rays very great." Although his species identifications were not always correct, it is clear that fish were highly abundant. Although its fisheries declined during its decades of rampant pollution, today, the harbor once again is home to large numbers of striped bass, bluefish, weakfish, fluke, porgy, and a host of others, and anglers are increasingly taking notice. ❞

John Waldman, Senior Scientist - Hudson River Foundation and author of
Heartbeats in the Muck: The History, Sea Life, and Environment of New York Harbor

Fish

At the New York Aquarium there is an exhibit called Native Sea Life. In it, local fisherman can see the fish that nibble their lines and sometimes are pulled in for sport or the family dinner table. It's just a glimpse of what inhabits the coastline of New York City.

Black fish – tautog *Tautoga onitis* Blackfish are a popular fish with anglers along a jetty or from a party boat. They are easy to catch and are good eating (what could be better?). A member of the wrasse family, this fish

has the buck-toothed incisors that are characteristic of that family. Blackfish feed primarily on mussels, but will eat almost any mollusk (shellfish) or crustacean (shrimp and lobsters). Therefore any scrap of food on a hook will make tempting bait. Blackfish can be almost as long as 36 in. and over 24 pounds, but that would be a monster in New York waters. It does have a minimum size limit of 14 in. in NY.

Bluefish *Pomatomus saltatrix* To imagine a more ferocious predator than the bluefish, one might envision sharks or piranha. But probably only man can be compared, for the bluefish wantonly cuts into schools of prey and kills in excess of what it needs to consume. Bluefish are common to New York waters throughout the summer. They are excellent sport fish, although one needs a steel leader to prevent their sharp teeth from cutting the line. They also are good to eat, especially if brought right to the grill and cooked fresh. "Snappers" are small bluefish and are often a child's first fishing experience since they bite any line and can be caught almost on every cast. Bluefish can weigh over 30 pounds. The maximum length is 51.18 inches. In Florida some reported "shark attacks" may have actually been when swimmers happened into a school of feeding bluefish. A toe could easily be taken by an adult bluefish.

Fluke- Summer flounder

Paralichthys dentatus Fluke is another favorite of New York fishers. It is a flatfish that lives its adult life on its side. As a newly hatched larval fish, it swims upright and looks like any "normal" fish. As it develops, it turns to its side; in this case, to its left side. One eye migrates to the side, so that both eyes are on the left side. Other flounders turn the opposite way to become members of the "right-handed" family. The juvenile fish then goes to the bottom where it lives its life completely sideways. The side facing up develops coloration

Courtesy of South Street Seaport Museum

that matches the surroundings, and the downward side is white. Hold a fluke perpendicular, and you will see a normal fish; dorsal fin up, pectoral fins on the sides, tail fin vertical, vent on the bottom, normal in every way except that both eyes are on one side and the sides are different colors. Fluke are excellent eating, with firm white flesh.

Menhaden *Brevoortia tyrannus*
Schools of menhaden mass like clouds in the surface waters of New York throughout the summer and young menhaden can fill the inlets around the harbor. Like the herds on African plains these "grazers" are massed in great hordes. They are the prey for the predators like stripers and blues. Smaller fish are taken by birds when the predators drive them to the surface. Menhaden feed by straining plankton from the rich waters around New York. On the inner side or their gills are protrusions called "gill rakers". As the fish swim with open mouths, the gill rakers filter the plankton (mostly algae) from the water. They therefore will not take a hook, and are caught only by net or "jigging" where they are so close together that a plain hook or "jig" is likely to catch into the body of one or another. They are excellent bait for stripers. Menhaden are poor quality for human food and are harvested usually for bait or, by the ton, for oil, fishmeal, or fertilizer.

Sand tiger Shark *Carcharias Taurus*
The sand tiger shark is ONE of the common sharks off NYC. Most people would rather not know about the shark populations around the beaches of NYC, but they are out there. Fortunately, most, like the sand tiger are not dangerous to humans. The sand tiger is a popular shark in aquariums because it has a mouthful of sharp teeth and excite the public viewer. These teeth are designed to catch fish. They are thin and sharply pointed. Dangerous sharks usually have flat teeth that are good for biting pieces out of large prey. These sharks rarely come near the beaches of NYC.

Other sharks that are in NY waters are the sand bar shark, that is also a fish eater, and so while it probably patrols the sand bars just off the beaches of Coney Island, bathers will never be aware that a grey, six foot, sharky-looking, shark, swims so near. The Aquarium has also noted small thresher sharks that fishermen have caught in their nets. These young animals must have been born in the area, for the adults are off-shore sharks. They are know for the extraordinarily long tail that they use to herd fish into tight balls when they feed. Local fishermen often land the smooth dogfish that is also called "sand shark". This is a totally harmless shark that feeds on small fish, crustaceans, and mollusks.

Shad *Alosa sapidissima* The shad is another member of the herring family, like the menhaden. It is "anadromous", meaning it runs from the ocean upriver to spawn. Shad have thinner gill rakers than the menhaden, and consume slightly larger plankton, mostly copepods and small shrimp. They are caught in the Hudson as they go upriver to spawn every spring. Shad have a large mouth compared to other herring and will actually take a hook. They provide a good fight if they can be tempted to bite. Shad are flavorful smoked, and are a favorite "planked" around fires at Shad festivals along the Hudson. Adults can average 20 to 23 inches in length and five to six pounds in weight. The maximum size is 29.9 inches and a weight of 12 pounds.

Striped bass *Morone saxatilis* The striped bass is the premiere sport fish in New York waters. It also makes a wonderful meal. This popular fish has been raised in aquaculture and introduced to lakes and into the Pacific along the west coast. Stripers can be huge, although the chance of catching a giant is an unfulfilled dream for most New York anglers. The maximum-recorded length is 78.7 inches. (Bigger than most fishermen) and over 125 pounds! Stripers run along the sandy beaches all along the east coast. They stay close to shore so that they are within range of surf casters or pier fishermen. The State of New York imposes a minimum size limit on striped bass. Only fish over 28 in. can be kept. Smaller fish must be released, but are still fun to catch.

Paul L. Sieswerda, Curator
NY Aquarium and author of *Sharks*

Fishing Season & Catch Limits
Size (inches) & Bag Limit (#)
Updates are available online at decs dec.state.ny.us

American Lobster:	All year, 3-1/4" carapace/6" Permit req.
Blackfish:	Oct - May, 14"/10#
Black Sea Bass:	May - Feb, 12"/25#
Blue Claw Crab:	All year, no size limit/50#
Bluefish:	All year, no size limit/10#
Flounder:	March -June/Sept-Nov, 11"/15#
Fluke:	All year, 17"/ 7#
Horseshoe Crab:	All year, no size limit/5#
Porgy:	All year, 10"/50#
Stripped Bass:	April 15 - Dec 15, 28"/1# or 2# aboard party/charter. Marine waters below GW
Weakfish:	All year, 16"/6#

Saltwater Fishing

The marine waters of New York City offer some of the finest opportunities for saltwater fishing in the world. The Atlantic's second largest stripped bass spawning run passes through the harbor to the Hudson River each spring and fall. Recreational saltwater fishing is available without a license in the marine waters of the city. Shore casting is allowed from sandy beaches only and forbidden from rocky areas, jetties and historic structures. It is prohibited to fish from guarded city beaches May 15 to September 15, between the hours of 8 a.m. and 8 p.m. Smitty's Fishing Station in Broad Channel and The Boat Livery on City Island rent small fishing skiffs for half and full day use.

Fishing Permits

Atlantic HMS Permit Recreational vessel owners who target highly migratory species (HMS), like tuna, swordfish, sharks, etc. in federal waters must obtain a federal fishing permit ($22) and are subject to new regulations that include bag limits. nmfspermits.com

Gateway National Recreation Area Fishing sites include: Barren Island, Canarsie Pier, Fort Tilden, Breezy Point, Miller Field, Fort Wadsworth, and Great Kills Park. Special use permits ($50), which include parking for fishing, off-road vehicle access, and car-top boating. Applicants for fishing parking permit must present driver's license, car registration and a 7-foot-long fishing rod. nps.gov/gate

- Fort Tilden 718-338-4300
- Floyd Bennett Field 718-338-3799
- Fort Wadsworth, SI 718-987-6700

SUNY Maritime College A seasonal permit ($40) for fishing access to the campus, purchase at security gate. 718-409-7200 sunymaritime.com

Freshwater Fishing

Freshwater action in NYS requires a license ($15/day-$19/yr) for anyone over the age of 16. Anglers must have the license in their possession while fishing. Licenses are available for purchase at the office of the county clerk, sporting goods stores and bait and tackle shops. All fishing in City Parks is catch and release, allowed in season only. Barbless hooks must be used and lead weights are not allowed. City Park's freshwater ponds, some stocked with bigmouth bass, include:

- Baisley Park, Queens
- Central Park, Manhattan
- Clove Lakes, Staten Island
- Crotona Park, Bronx
- Meadow & Willow Lakes, Queens
- Kissena Lake, Queens
- Oakland Lake, Queens
- Prospect Park, Brooklyn
- Van Cortland, Bronx
- Wolfe's Pond, Staten Island

NYSDEC, Region 2 Administers licenses and freshwater regulations. 718-482-4900 dec.state.ny.us

Saltwater Fishing Party & Charter Boats

The Sheepshead Bay fishing fleet is moored at ten concrete piers on Emmons Avenue. Vessels range in size from small inshore skiffs to large offshore cabin cruisers and the charge per passenger ranges from $25 to $40. Bait and tackle are furnished. Headboats fish for specific species depending on the season. Half day, full day and night fishing trips are offered. Some boats offer offshore, wreck and Hudson Canyon trips for tuna. The Hudson Canyon is a vast gorge carved by the flow of the Hudson River thousands of years ago. It extends more than 400 miles seaward and drops off near Montauk at the continental shelf.

Manhattan

Fish NY Charters	212-529-1049

Bronx

Daybreak III	718-409-9765
Island Current	917-417-7557
North Star II	718-885-9182
Riptide III	718-885-9182
Skipjack	718-885-9116

Brooklyn

Atlantic Charter	800-664-7402
Big M Express	917-822-6770
Blue Sea V	718-332-9148
Brooklyn VI	718-743-8464
Bullet Charters	718-265-6915
Capt. Dave	718-491-9702
Dorothy B VIII	718-646-4057
Elsie K. Princess	718-444-9391
Explorer	718-680-2207
Flamingo III	718-763-8745
Jet	718-634-4669

Brooklyn (cont.)

Karen Ann	718-634-4669
Jamaica Bay	718-474-4427
Lady L Charters	718-336-8957
Lark III	718-645-6942
Miss Nell	718-891-0337
Mulligan Charters	718-241-7066
Navigator	917-609-7735
Ocean Eagle II	718-258-4126
Pastime Princess	718-252-4398
Sea Queen IV & V	718-332-2423
Stella Maris	718-769-5678
Sunshine	718-945-6931
Super Ranger	718-368-9902
Tampa VII	718-769-5363

Queens

Angler	718-659-8181

Staten Island

Atlantis Princess	718-966-2845
Capt. Paul's	718-966-6990

Fly-Fishing

" Just a 15-minute ride south of Manhattan lays Jamaica Bay, a large estuary with every kind of water, flats, rips, creeks, bays, beachfront and deeps, and most important, all fishable with a fly-rod. A diverse and viable fishery, our area gets the very first fish of the year and ends up with them last. The spring fishing starts in mid-April with the fish in the back bays where the water is warmest and the baits are large and slow. The bass are hungry after wintering in the Hudson and are in general the biggest fish of the year, producing fish in the 20-pound class. Amongst these fish is a rebounding body of weakfish, some weighing in at 10 pounds. As the summer comes on and the water warms the fish spread to the outside areas in the rips and up on the flats, they are joined by the tooth riddled bluefish that come to feed on the abundant sand eels. Then comes the super-fast false albacore and to a lesser extent, bonito and Spanish mackerel. We even get lucky sometimes and get some skipjack and even mahi mahi to chase. The rain bait has hatched by then and all these torpedoes ball them up and blast through them like rockets. With the onset of shorter days and colder nights the bass fishing in the fall is something to witness as the fish, school after school, come right to us on their way to either the Chesapeake or the Hudson. It is possible to catch almost a dozen species in any season, and all on flies. **"**

By Capt. Brendan P. McCarthy, Urban Fly Guides

Fly-Fishing Charters & Guides

Manhattan

Capt. Joe Shastay	captjoeshastay.com	973-239-1988
Rocket Charters	rocketcharters.com	212-529-6910
Urban Fly Guides	mctrout.com	212-727-3166

Brooklyn

One More Cast Charters	islandwebs.com/onemorecast	718-945-2255

Staten Island

Fin Chaser Charters	finchaser.com	718-356-6436
On The Bight Charters	home.att.net/~onthebite	718-967-9095
Rodbender Charters	islandwebs.com/rodbenders.htm	718-356-0553

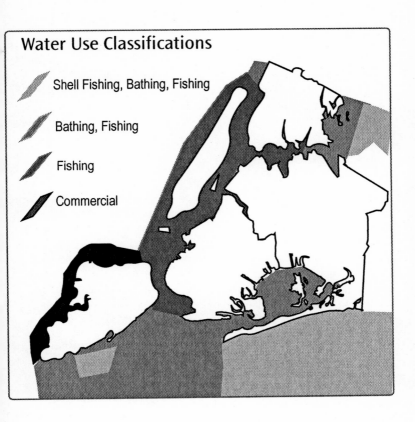

Water Use Classifications

- Shell Fishing, Bathing, Fishing
- Bathing, Fishing
- Fishing
- Commercial

Shellfish Harvesting

Shellfish are filter feeders, meaning they pump water to capture food and in the process clean the water. One oyster can filter 25-40 gallons of water a day. Oysters cluster into reef structures that also provide marine habitat for hundreds of species. Prior to the 1920s, New York Harbor was one of the most productive shellfish grounds in the world. Oysters, clams, mussels and scallops were plentiful and vital to the local economy until overharvesting and pollution shut down the industry. Today, shellfish can be taken only from certified waters, which is limited to the Atlantic Coast from Fort Tilden to East Rockaway, within the 3-mile limit. A permit is not required for recreational shellfish harvesting from state lands. The limit is one bushel per day. Hard clams are commercially harvested under special permit in Raritan Bay and must be transplanted to certified Long Island waters to clean out for 21 days before sale.

Marine Conservation

Excessive commercial fishing has wiped out 90% of the worlds large fish populations. Species in danger include cod, halibut, flounder, marlin, shark swordfish, and tuna.

Catch Limits: Adhere to size and catch limits, seasons and gear restrictions. Participate in the catch and release of saltwater game fish and fish tagging programs.

Oyster Gardening: Volunteers and school classes grow seed oysters at private piers and docks to help re-establish oyster populations. Once mature, the oysters are used in reef restoration projects throughout the NY/NJ Harbor Estuary. 732-291-0176 nynjbaykeeper.org

Recycle Fishing Line: Discarded fishing line lasts over 600 years in the marine environment. Monofilament fishing line can injure swimmers and divers, entangle and poison wildlife, and damage boat motors. There are recycling bins at Ranger Stations at Gateway National Recreation Area. To start a line recycling program contact: Pure Fishing 800-BERKLEY

Artificial Reefs

The flat sandy bottom of New York City's coastal waters provides little natural habitat. Artificial structures enhance underwater habitat and provide new opportunities for anglers and divers. New York State has built over 300 patch reefs, using everything from M1 Army tanks to construction rubble. The only patch reef within city limits is the Rockaway Reef, which is made up of 6,000 tires. It is located 1.6 nautical miles south of Rockaway Beach in 40 feet of water and covers 413 acres. Natural oyster reefs take form on piles of discarded shells dumped at spots in the harbor, one near Liberty Island, by Baykeeper. New York donated over 1,000 decom-missioned "Red Bird" subway cars, in-service since the 1964 World's Fair, to reefs from New Jersey Highlands to the Georgia coast. NY State opted not to participate in the program because of environmental concerns.

Fish Monitoring

Artificial Reef Monitoring Anglers can help monitor fish populations at NYS artificial reefs. dec.state.ny.us

Fish Tagging Program American Littoral Society members participate in the world's largest tag and release program monitoring stripped bass, summer flounder and bluefish. Anyone catching a tagged fish is asked to return the tag. alsnyc.org

Striped Bass Cooperative Anglers Program Fishermen record fishing trips to aid biologists effective fisheries management. NYS Dept. Environmental Conservation 631-444-0488 dec.state.ny.us

Fishing Programs

BPC School Outreach Program
Battery Park City. School groups learn how to fish from local master anglers. 212-267-9700 bpcparks.org

Big City Fishing Hudson River Park. Loaner rod and reel program set up at piers in the park on summer weekends. 212-791-2530 hudsonriverpark.org

Dana Discovery Center Central Park 110th. St. Rod and reel loaner program for catch-and-release fishing from April to October, Tuesday to Sunday 10 a.m. - 4 p.m. 212-860-1370

Fish nKids Inc. Staten Island. Free equipment and fishing instruction for young anglers. 718-442-9089 community.silive.com/cc/fishnkidsinc

Getting Started in Fishing
In-class program and fishing trips that cover aquatic life, fish identification and environmental conservation. 718-482-4022 dec.state.ny.us

Go Fish Battery Park City. Free catch and release fishing events for all ages. 212-267-9700 bpcparks.org

Go Fish Festival Stuyvesant Park. Rod and reel loaner fishing program. 212-427-3956 eastrivercrew.org

Gone Fishing South St. Seaport
Students onboard the *Pioneer* use an otter trawl to catch fish and learn about estuary ecology. 212-748-8600 southstseaport.org

I Fish NY Fishing clinics at State parks. 718-482-4875 dec.state.ny.us

Macy's Fishing Contest Catch & release program at city parks for kids 15 and under. 718-421-2021

Master Anglers Battery Park City. Learn from seasoned experts to become part of a volunteer corps that facilitates free fishing programs. 212-267-9700 bpcparks.org

My First Fish Commemorates very first fish caught with a certificate that tells the type of fish and location caught. dec.state.ny.us

Sportfishing & Aquatic Resources Education Program (SAREP) Cornell University Cooperative program works with youth serving organizations to teach fishing and marine ecology. 212-340-2974 cce.cornell.edu/sarepnyc

Fish Consumption Advisory

New York Harbor is the cleanest it has been in 50 years. In spite of improved water quality, it is not safe to eat local fish because they may contain harmful chemicals, such as PCBs. The NYC Dept. of Health advises anglers to eat no more than one meal per week of fish and shellfish caught in the waters around the city. Women of childbearing age, infants and children under the age of 15 should not eat any local fish. health.state.ny.us/nysdoh/fish/fish.htm

Fishing Clubs & Outfitters

Manhattan

Capital Fishing Tackle Company
218 W 23 St. Fresh, salt and fly tackle shop. 212-929-6123

Coastal Conservation Assn. of NY
Marine conservation organization with chapters in each borough. 877-98-CCANY ccany.org

Juliana Anglers Women's fly fishing club meets 3rd Thurs. at Orvis Store. Clinics, lessons and trips julianasanglers.com

NYC Trout Unlimited Freshwater conservation organization, which has re-introduced book trout to Alley Pond. nyctu.org

Orvis 522 Fifth Ave. Fly clinics, school, fly tackle and retailer. 212-827-0698

Paragon Sports 867 Broadway Salt & fly tackle. 212-255-8036

Theodore Gordon Flyfishers
Catch & release flyfishing and conservation organization. "Trout in the Classroom" program with schools. 718-885-1596 tgf.org

Universal Angler 37 W 43rd St. Flyfishing tackle, clinics, instruction and fly-fishing travel. 212-398-1932

Urban Angler 206 5th Ave. 3rd Flr. Fly shop, custom rods, guides and travel. 212-979-7600 urban-angler.com

World Fishing of Japan
Fly-fishing club, clinics and tournaments. wffj.org

Bronx

Ampere Fishing & Yacht Club
1610 Bayshore Ave. Fishing outings. 718-822-8707

Layton Avenue Fishing Club
505 Edison Ave. Books are currently closed to new members. 718-904-7092

Brooklyn

Bay Ridge Rod & Gun Club
Sportsmen's club founded in 1954. Fishing outings and youth fishing programs. 718-745-1067

Gateway Striper Club Surf fishing club. Fishing outings, clinics and youth fishing programs. 718-768-9794

Helen Keller Fishing Club
Deep sea fishing club for persons with visual or hearing impairments formed in 1948. Volunteer drivers assist club members in exchange for free fishing opportunities. 718-522-2122 x-347

Metropolitan Rod & Gun Club
162 Pacific St. Sportsmen's club has youth fishing program. 718-625-8019

Prospect Park Anglers Freshwater fishing club. AnglersAssociation/index.html.wrightmichael.tripod.com/ProspectPark

Wild Trout University 2251 Knapp St. Fly fishing lessons. 718-646-0583 fly-fishingschool.com

Queens

Bayside Anglers Conducts free saltwater clinics at Gantry State Park. baysideanglers.com

Broad Channel Anglers broadchannelny.com

Phishing Phools 718-479-5042

Rockaway Surf Anglers 718-634-7198

Salty Flyrodders Saltwater fly club with 200 members. Fly-casting clinics and trips. saltyflyrodders.org

Shad Creek Assn. 529 Cross Bay Blvd. 718-474-5476

Striper Surf Club Formed 1948, one of state's oldest surf fishing clubs. stripersurfclub.com

Staten Island

Beachcomber Surf & Gun Club Surf fishing and hunting club founded in 1947. 718-698-2821

SI Federation of Sportsmen's Clubs 50 year old coalition of Staten Island sportsmen's clubs. 718-981-0372

Staten Island Tuna Club At Great Kills Bait & Tackle, 16 Highpoint Rd. 718-667-5141

The Reel Brothers Fisherman's Club Sports fishing club. Party boat outing and trips. 718-448-8479

Zimmer Fish & Game Protective Assn. Sportsmen's club fishing and youth programs. 718-948-9599

Bait & Tackle Shops

Manhattan	Bishop B & T	718 Broadway	212-979-1088
	Capitol Fishing Tackle Co	218 W 23 St	212-929-6132
	Harlem B & T	2303 12 Ave	212-283-8813
	Pacific Aquarium	46 Delancy St	212-995-5895
Bronx	Al's Tackle Shop	86 Lincoln Av, Pelham	914-738-4589
	City Island B & T	632 City Island Ave	718-885-2153
	Franks Sport Shop	430 E Tremont Ave	718-299-9628
	Interboro B & T	3561 E Tremont Ave	718-863-8085
	Jack's B & T	551 City Island Ave	718-885-2042
	The Boat Livery	663 City Island Ave	718-885-1843
Brklyn	Amoco Fishing Station Bait Shop	6201 Av U, Mill Basin 320 Van Brunt St	718-625-0978
	Bernie's B & T	3128 Emmons Ave	718-646-7600

Bait & Tackle Shops

Brooklyn	Bo-Gi's	2125 Knapp St	718-743-2277
	Chris' B & T	58 Bay Ridge Ave	718-836-2003
	Dream Fishing Tackle	673 Manhattan Ave	718-389-9670
	Name-It B & T	2157 Bath Ave	718-373-6233
	One Stop Bait & Fuel	2875 Flatbush Ave	718-258-0086
	Parkway Fishing Center	3 Plumb 3rd St	718-763-9265
	Pop Klee's Fishing Tackle	1443 E 94th St	718-251-1424
	Seaman's B & T	Seaman's Marine	718-525-6430
	16th Street B&T	1602b Mermaid Ave	718-265-9902
	Stella Maris B & T	2702 Emmons Ave	718-646-9754
	Shoreway Marine	Knapp St	718-648-0046
	Tastee Bait Co	3035 Emmons Ave	718-769-1816
	Triangle Sports	182 Flatbush Ave	718-638-5300
Queens	Crossbay B & T	164-26 Crossbay Blvd	718-835-1018
	Crossbay Fishing Station	163-01 Crossbay Blvd	718-843-3800
	First Fishing Supplies	150-46 Northern Blvd	718-886-7322
	Pro-Fishing & Tackle	134-22 Northern Blvd	718-461-9612
	Seaman's Wholesale Bait	25 1st St	718-525-6430
	Seoul Fishing & Tackle	5319 Roosevelt Ave	718-565-2376
	Skippy's B & T	10 Front St	718-599-7297
	Smitty's Fishing Station	224 9th St	718-945-2642
Staten Island	Biggie's	65 Page Ave	718-966-9206
	Fred's Tackle Shop	6276 Amboy Rd	718-984-2828
	Great Kills B & T	4044 Hylan Blvd	718-356-0055
	Michaels' B & T	187 Mansion Ave	718-984-9733
	Scag's B & T	114 Victory Blvd	718-727-7373

Fishing Events

Beachcomber Striped Bass Surf Tournament	718-698-2821
Staten Island Surf waters	October
"Catch & Release" Striped Bass Tournament	ccany.org
Coastal Conservation Assn. of NY	May
"It's a FLUKE" Tournament	718-474-5476
Jamaica Bay Shad Creek Assn.	July
Last Chance Catch & Release Surf Fishing Tournament	ccany.org
Fort Tilden, Queens Coastal Conservation Assn. of NY	November
Macallan Manhattan Cup Striped Bass Derby	ccany.org
Chelsea Piers Coastal Conservation Assn. of NY	May
Macy's Fishing Contest at Prospect Park	Urban Park Rangers
Freshwater Catch & Release for kids 15 years and under.	
New York State Free Fishing Days	
Freshwater fish without a license	June (last weekend)
Old Mill Yacht Club Fluke & Ladies Fluke Contests	718-835-0454
	August/July
RYC Annual Flounder Tournament	718-843-3153
	April
Snapper Derby	baysideanglers.com
Bayside Anglers annual event at Bayside Marina - ages 16 & under	August
Staten Island Fishing Show & Flea Market	scottsbt.com
Rods/Reels/Tackle/Lures /Nautical Antique & Collectibles	April
Tamaqua 2-day Shark Tournament	tamaquamarina.com
Rockaway jetty	July
Tamaqua 48 hr Fishing Marathon (Stripers, Bluefish, Fluke)	tamaquamarina.com
Tamaque Marina, Gerritsen Beach Brooklyn	August
Tamaqua 24 hr Striped Bass Tournament	tamaquamarina.com
Tamaque Marina, Gerritsen Beach Brooklyn	October

Harbor Fortifications

The remains of dozens of military forts stand sentry at the portals of New York Harbor. Built to defend the city from naval assault, the seacoast forts were vital strategic defenses from the time of the Revolution to WWII. The surviving structures represent every technological advancement in fortification engineering from before the Civil War to the guided missile era. There were several distinct periods of seacoast fort construction: First System from 1794 to 1800; Second System from 1804 to 1812; Third System from 1816 to 1867; post-Civil War period from 1870 to 1875; the Endicott and Taft Boards from 1890 to 1917; and the Modernization Program beginning in 1940 to 1950. Many coastal forts were converted to anti-aircraft artillery units following WWII.

Castle Clinton

Battery Park, Manhattan
Built: 1808
Current Use: Nat'l Monument/Museum
Contact: NPS 212-344-7220 nps.gov/cacl

Circular fort made of red sandstone was originally named Southwest Battery when built on rocks 200 feet off the tip of Manhattan. It was built to defend the city in the War of 1812, but never had occasion to fire on the enemy and was renamed for Mayor DeWitt Clinton. It was later joined to the Battery by landfill. Since it was ceded to the city in 1823, it has served as a restaurant, opera house, immigration depot, and first home of the NY Aquarium. The centerpiece of Battery Park, Castle Clinton offers historic exhibits and tours. It is a ferry ticketing office and performance venue. Renovations include adding a roof and second level. 🚇 Subway 1/9 to South Ferry.

Castle Williams

Governors Island, Manhattan
Built: 1807-1811
Current Use: National Monument
Contact: NPS 212-514-8296
governorsislandnationalmonument.org

The sister fort of Castle Clinton sits on a rocky promontory looking out on the harbor channel. It looks like a medieval castle with its high, 8-foot thick sandstone walls. Named for its designer, Lt. Colonel Jonathan Williams, it was the first casement fort built in North America. The fort played a vital role in the city's defense in the War of 1812. Castle Williams served as a POW camp during the Civil War. Access is by public tour, offered seasonally. 🚢 Ferry from the Battery Maritime Building.

Fort Gibson

Ellis Island, Manhattan
Built: 1808
Current Use: Nat'l Monument/Museum
Contact: NPS 212-363-3200

Part of the city's coastal defenses, the site was used as a battery and munitions arsenal for the Union Army during the Civil War. Oyster Island was renamed Ellis Island, and in 1890 it was chosen as the Immigration Station for the port of New York. The archeological remains of Fort Gibson are located at the southeast end of the island. ⛴ Statue of Liberty ferry.

Fort Hamilton

The Narrows, Brooklyn
Built: 1825-1831
Current Use: Active Army Post/Museum
Contact: 718-630-4349

The oldest granite fort in the harbor and one of the oldest Army posts in the country. A small Battery was first used here on July 4, 1776, when General Know fired on the *HMS Asia*

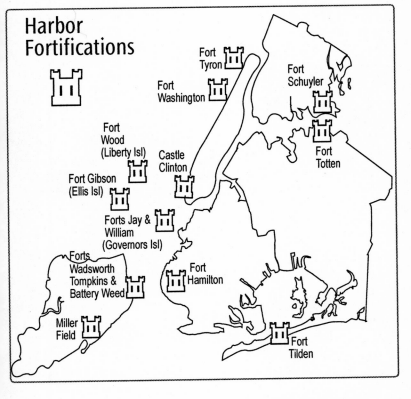

Harbor Fortifications

Fort Tyron

Fort Washington

Fort Schuyler

Fort Wood (Liberty Isl)

Castle Clinton

Fort Gibson (Ellis Isl)

Fort Totten

Forts Jay & William (Governors Isl)

Forts Wadsworth Tompkins & Battery Weed

Fort Hamilton

Miller Field

Fort Tilden

as it approached the harbor. Both Capt. Robert E. Lee and "Stonewall" Jackson served at the fort. It is today home to the Army Recruiting Battalion, Reserve and National Guard units, and the Harbor Defense Museum. 🚇 Subway R to 95th St.

Fort Jay (Fort Columbus)

Governors Island, Manhattan
Built: 1798/rebuilt 1806-1809
Current Use: National Monument
Contact: NPS 212-514-8296
governorsislandnationalmonument.org

The star-shaped fort is located on the highest point of the island and has earthen covered walls and a dry moat. It is named for statesman John Jay, the first Chief Justice of the Supreme Court. Access is by public tour only. 🚇 Ferry at Battery Maritime Bldg.

Fort Lafayette

The Narrows, Brooklyn
Built: 1822
Current Use: Tower of Verrazano Bridge

Originally called Fort Diamond, the Naval Magazine stood off the coast of Fort Hamilton on Hendricks Reef. It was razed in 1960 to construct the Verrazano Bridge across the Narrows.

Fort Schuyler

Throgs Neck, Bronx
Built: 1826-1845
Current Use: Maritime College/Museum
Contact: 212-409-7218

The granite fort built to protect the East River approach to New York Harbor has an irregular pentagon shape, based on French forts. During the Spanish-American War mines were planted in the water between the fort and its counterpoint, Fort Totten. Decommissioned in 1934, the fort has been restored and is now on the grounds of SUNY Maritime College, and is home to the Maritime Industry Museum. National Register of Historic Places. 🚇 Subway 6 to Westchester Sq. then Bx40 Bus.

Fort Tilden

Rockaway Peninsula, Queens
Built: 1917
Current Use: GNRA
Contact: NPS 718-318-4300
geocities.com/fort_tilden

Military post and naval air station on 317 acres of land named for former Governor Samuel J. Tilden. Battery Harris worked together with a battery 6 miles across the harbor in N.J. It was a Nike missile site for much of the cold war, active to 1974. Today, hiking trails pass the buried remains of gun platforms and batteries. Ranger-led tours. 🚇 Subway A to Rockaway Park/Beach 116th St., then transfer to Q35 Green bus.

Fort Totten

Willet's Point, Queens
Built: 1858
Current Use: NYC Park
Contact: Historical Center 718-352-0180

Originally called the Fort at Willet's Point, it guards the "back door" to New York Harbor together with Fort Schuyler. The fort served as a school for the Corps of Engineers and a staging facility for various commands until the Gulf War. The Nike missile defense system was developed there. It contains landmark buildings, such as the 1870 Officer's Club. Tours by appointment. 🚆 LIRR to Bayside.

Fort Washington & Fort Tryon

Hudson River, Manhattan
Built: 1776
Current Use: City Parks

The last stronghold against the British forces on Manhattan. It fell on November 16, 1776. In the battle, Margaret Corbin took up her fallen husband's post and became the first American woman wounded on the battlefield. In 1779, "Capt. Molly," was compensated by Congress for her distinguished bravery. A commemorative plaque marks Fort Tryon near the park's observation platform. 🚇 Subway A to 190th St.

Fort Wadsworth (1900)
Fort Tompkins (1807)
Battery Weed (1860)

The Narrows, Staten Island
Current Use: GNRA
Contact: NPS 718-354-4500

Fort Wadsworth is the oldest continuously manned military installation in the country, first fortified by the Dutch in 1636, active during the Revolutionary War and enlarged for the War of 1812. The entire complex of forts and batteries at the site were consolidated as Fort Wadsworth. Open to the public. Offers guided tours, exhibits and film

about the forts history. 🚢 SI Ferry to Bus S51.

Fort Wood

Liberty (Bedloe) Island, New York Harbor
Built: 1808-1811
Current Use: National Monument
Contact: NPS 212-363-3200 nps.gov/stli

Originally known as Star Fort because of its 11 point star-shaped battery, it was named for Eleazor Wood, a hero of the War of 1812. In 1861 the fort was used as an infirmary for sick Confederate prisoners of war. Some of the old ramparts can be seen at the entrance to the Statue of Liberty, which is through the old fort's 20-foot thick walls and sally port door (little doors to a fort meant to protect defenders). Inside, a stairway leads to a promenade that was a gun platform along the wall of the fort.
🚢 Statue of Liberty ferry.

Miller Field

Atlantic Ocean, Staten Island
Built: 1919
Current Use: GNRA
Contact: NPS 718-351-6970
geocities.com/miller_field

The only Air Service Coast Defense Station on the East Coast at the time it was built. The airbase included seaplane ramps, hangars, a sod runway and Elm Tree Lighthouse. It has served as a Coast Guard Artillery gun site, Nike Missile repair depot, a base for US Army Special Forces and a complex of athletic fields today.
🚢 SI Ferry to Bus S76.

Historic Ships

❝Rescuing an old wooden barge from the bottom of the river has led to my romance with New York Harbor. I adore all the sensations of life at its edge and the camaraderie that develops among people who have shared our shoreline and water highways. New York City's floating historic treasures pioneer paths and fond memories back to our once-bustling waterfront neighborhoods. Seek them out and you too will most certainly delight in the lore, profiles and technologies that have led to our modern maritime achievements. ❞

David Sharps, President
Waterfront Museum (waterfrontmuseum.org)

New York Harbor's historic ships are unique cultural resources that provide insight into the maritime heritage of the city. At sea and ashore, the vessels are historical and educational entities that present an intimate view of life at sea. They chart the growth of the port and trace innovation in maritime technology. Historically significant ships are difficult and costly to restore and maintain. Volunteers, both skilled and apprentice, assist in the preservation of ships and in the process also preserve the maritime trades. The National Maritime Heritage Program of the National Park Service establishes guidelines for ship preservation. To be designated "historic," a ship must be eligible for listing in the National Register of Historic Places, which only accepts U.S. built vessels. Hudson River Park has developed rules for vessels that are granted berths at park piers. The larg-

est fleet of privately maintained historic ships in the country is tied up at South Street Seaport. The collection epitomizes a range of craft that once sailed the harbor in the 19th and early 20th centuries. Hudson River Park has designated piers 25, 54 and 97 to house historic ships. Pier 63 Maritime, actually a Lackawanna Railroad barge, provides fendering for restored and restoring vessels. Many historic ships have training and internship programs that teach maritime trades to school aged youth and volunteers are welcomed aboard to assist in vessel maintenance. All, but a few, of the harbor's historic ships are afloat and open to public tours.

North River Historic Ship Society

Organization of historic ship owners that works to protect, preserve and promote the storied vessels in NY Harbor. nhss.org

Clearwater

Pier 40 Hudson River Park
Built: 1969 South Bristol, Me
Current Use: Environmental School
clearwater.org
A replica modeled after classic sloops that once carried cargo on the Hudson River in the 19th century, called America's Environmental Flagship.

Fire Fighter

FDNY Marine Company 9, Staten Island
Built: 1938 United Shipyards of S.I.
Current Use: Active fireboat
The most famous and decorated fireboat of all time, the 134-foot *Fire Fighter* can do 15 knots and has water guns with output of 20,000 gallons of water per minute. The boat was designed by William Gibbs. It is the only fireboat honored with the "Gallant Ship Award," which it received for rescuing 30 seamen from fire aboard the *Esso Brussels* and *Sea Witch* collision in the harbor in 1972. A National Historic Landmark.

Growler

Pier 86 Intrepid Sea-Air-Space Museum
Built: 1958 Portsmouth Naval Shipyard, NH
Current Use: Floating Exhibit
212-245-0072 intrepidmuseum.org
The only guided missile submarine open to the public, *Growler* was one of three subs designed to carry Regulus cruise missiles. She was dispatched on nuclear deterrent patrol from 1958 to 1964 and was scheduled to become a torpedo target, when the ship was saved by the Intrepid Museum in 1988.

Intrepid

Pier 86 Intrepid Sea-Air-Space Museum
Built: 1943 Newport News
Current Use: Dockside museum
212-245-0072 intrepidmuseum.org
One of 24 Essex Class carriers, *Intrepid* weighs 42,000 tons and is as tall as a 16-story building. She could reach speeds of 30 knots. *Intrepid* has had an active career beginning in WWII, where she joined the fleet at Leyte Gulf, the largest naval engagement in history. She has survived kamikaze hits, seven bomb attacks and a torpedo strike. She served in Korea and Vietnam, and was the prime recovery vessel for NASA, finally retiring in 1974. On National Register of Historic Places and a National Historic Landmark.

John J. Harvey

Pier 63 Maritime
Built: 1931 Todd Shipyards, Brooklyn
Current Use: Retired fireboat
212-874-4771 fireboat.org
The longest serving FDNY fireboat until it retired in 1995. It was the fastest large fireboat in the world, clocking over 17 knots, and once the most powerful with pumping capacity of 18,250 GPM. The vessel was bought at auction in 1999 and today shares its classic water display at harbors events. She returned to active duty 9/11/01 to aid in World Trade Center relief efforts. On the National Register of Historic Places

Lehigh Valley RR Barge No. 79

Pier 45 Red Hook, Brooklyn
Built: 1914 Perth Amboy Dry Dock Co.
Current Use: Dockside museum
718-624-4719 waterfrontmuseum.org
Rescued and restored in 1986, the
vessel is the only surviving wooden-
covered barge of the Lighterage
Era (1860-1960) afloat today.
Educational programs, events and
live performances take place at
the Columbia St. Marine Terminal
mooring. The barge will return to its
Conover St. pier, upon completion of
pier repairs. On the National Register
of Historic Places.

Leilani

Sheepshead Bay, Brooklyn
Built: 1903 Lawley Shipyard, MA
Current Use: Charter yacht
718-332-1727 classicyachtleilani.com
A typical racer, day sailor originally
designed as a gaff-rigged yawl and
modernized to a 50-foot Bermuda
rigged yawl in 1947.

Lettie G. Howard

Pier 16 South Street Seaport Museum
Built: 1893 Essex, MA
Current Use: Museum/Sailing School
212-748-8786 southstseaport.org
The schooner was employed in the
fishing and oystering trades. It sailed
out of Gloucester, off the Yucatan
Peninsula, and Gulf of Mexico until
the 1960s. The vessel is used for
sea education programs. National
Register of Historic Places and a
National Historic Landmark.

Lightship Ambrose LV-87

Pier 16 South Street Seaport Museum
Built: 1908 NY Ship Bldg. Co. Camden, NJ
Current Use: Floating Exhibit
212-748-8725 southstseaport.org
The 488 ton lightship served to aid
navigation at the main entrance
to New York Harbor, 8 miles east
of Rockaway Point. She served the
Ambrose lightship station from when
it was first established in 1908 until
1933, then served as the Scotland
lightship near Sandy Hook until
1963. On the National Register of
Historic Places.

Lightship Frying Pan LV-115

Pier 63 Maritime
Built: 1929 Charleston Drydock, SC
Current Use: Attraction/Event Space
212-989-6363 fryingpan.com
Served from 1930 to 1965 as the
lightship at Frying Pan Shoals, at the
entrance to Cape Fear River in North
Carolina and was recovered from the
bottom of Chesapeake Bay by the
current owner in 1989. One of only 13
lightships surviving from more than
100 built. The exterior is restored,
while the interior retains its sunken
ship appearance. The empty engine
room is used as a dance floor and
exhibit space. On the National Register
of Historic Places.

Lightship Nantucket LV-112

National Lighthouse Museum, S. I.
Built: 1936 Pusey & Jones Wilmington, DE
Current Use: Floating Exhibit
718-556-1681 lighthousemuseum.org

At 150 feet in length she is the largest lightship ever built in the United States. The vessel was paid for by the British as compensation for sinking her predecessor Lightship 117 in a collision with the luxury liner *Olympic* in 1934. *Lightship Nantucket* will berth at Pier 1 at the museum.

Lightship St. John LV-84
Beard Street Pier, Brooklyn
Built: 1907 NY Ship Building Camden, NJ
Current Use: Submerged awaiting salvage
A sister ship to the *Ambrose* that today sits in 20 feet of water in the Erie Basin. Only the masts are visible. *St. John* guided ships entering the St. John River in Florida from 1929 to 1954 and served as a relief ship in New York until 1965, then a floating classroom and a restaurant.

Lilac
Pier 40 Hudson River Park
Built: 1933
Current Use: Floating Exhibit
steamerlilac.com
Recently rescued and towed from Norfolk, VA, the 800-ton, 173-ft. steamship was built for the U.S. Lighthouse Service and later served as a training vessel of the Seafarers' International Union.

Marion M.
Pier 16 South Street Seaport Museum
Built: 1932 Virginia
Current Use: Floating exhibit/Work boat
Contact: 212-748-8725 southstseaport.org
A wooden-hulled chandlery lighter of Standard Boat Co. on Staten Island,

Shipworms

The cleaner water quality in New York Harbor has caused a resurgence in all forms of marine life, including the reappearance of wood boring organisms. Shipworms and wood-eating gribbles destroy wooden ships, barges and pilings. The pests are responsible for destroying the Hudson River piers and threaten many of the historic wooden vessels in the port. Preventive measures include use of toxic-free antifouling treatments and paints.

she provided supplies to ships at anchor in New York Harbor. Prior to that she was a motor freighter and an offshore fishing boat. *Marion M.* is now a work boat that supports the other ships in the museum's fleet.

Noble Houseboat Studio
Noble Maritime Museum, Staten Island
Current Use: Gallery exhibit
718-447-6490 noblemaritime.org
Built by noted maritime artist John Noble, who constructed it from salvaged boats, including a 100-year-old teakwood saloon from an abandoned yacht. The furnished artists studio was dismantled and reassembled at the museum, where it is on permanent display.

Peking
Pier 16 South Street Seaport Museum
Built: 1911 Hamburg, Germany
Current Use: Floating Exhibit

B ard Brothers, Maritime Artists, James (1815-1897) and John (1815-1856). Born in Chelsea in 1815, twin brothers James and John Bard collaborated on their first ship portrait for Cornelius Vanderbilt at the age of twelve. It became the first of many for the brothers, who worked together to create over 350 ship portraits between 1831 and 1849. Masterfully combining elements of both folk and fine art, the self-taught artists were particularly lauded for the detail with which they depicted the steamboats, schooners and sloops navigating the Hudson River and New York Harbor. After John Bard's death in 1856, James continued to work alone until 1890, and at the time of his retirement had reportedly completed over 4,000 paintings.

212-748-8786 southstseaport.org
A four-masted bark built for commercial use to carry cargo on long distance sailing voyages. She later served as a training vessel in England.

Pioneer
Pier 16 South Street Seaport Museum
Built: 1885 Pioneer Ironworks, PA
Current Use: Excursion Boat
212-748-8786 southstseaport.org
The only iron-hulled American sailing schooner still in existence, she was the delivery vehicle of her day. Originally used to carry sand mined near the mouth of the Delaware, she was re-rigged as a schooner in 1895.

Tug Bertha
Pier 63 Maritime
Built: 1925 Newcastle, UK
Current Use: Under restoration
sosny.org
A Canadian lumber tug crafted with a flat bottom and winches to move over land between creeks. She retired in 1980, then served as a beached bar on Dear Lake and was rescued by current owner in 1999.

Tug Helen McAllister
Pier 16 South Street Seaport Museum
Built: 1900 Burlee Dry Dock of S.I.
Current Use: Under restoration
212-748-8786 southstseaport.org
Steel tug 111-foot-long donated to the museum by McAllister Brothers of New York, a 138 year old towing firm.

Tug NY Central No. 13
Pier 63 Maritime, W 23rd St.
Built: 1887 Dialogue Shipbldg. Camden, NJ
Current Use: Under restoration
212-594-4681 tug13.com
One of few surviving iron hulled tugs, the 82-ft. 119 ton vessel pushed barges that carried boxcars across the harbor for the NY Central Railroad. Later named the *Hay-De*, she served the Kosnac Floating Derrick Corp. She was slated to be sunk as an artificial reef when rescued in 2002.

Tug NY Central No. 31 Pilothouse
Pier 16 South Street Seaport Museum
Current Use: Ticketing booth
The wooden pilothouse of a steel-hulled railroad tug sits in the middle

of Pier 16, and is used as ticket office for historic ships tours and excursion boats departing from the piers that surround it.

Tug Pegasus
Pier 62 Chelsea Piers
Built: 1907 Skinner Baltimore, MD
Current Use: Floating Exhibit
tugpegasus.org
One of only four "Battleship Tugs"—named for their size and 650 horsepower steam engines. *Pegasus* worked in New York Harbor for 90 years. The nonprofit created to restore the tug conducts shipboard Marine Adventure Program, in conjunction with the Police Athletic League, teaches kids maritime trades. On the National Register of Historic Places.

Tug W. O. Decker
Pier 16 South Street Seaport Museum
Built: 1930 Russell Shipyard, LIC
Current Use: Museum/Excursion Boat
212-748-8786 southstseaport.org
One of the last steam-powered docking tugs built in the harbor, now re-powered with diesel. The museum operates tours of the working waterfront aboard the little tug. On National Register of Historic Places.

Ventura Cutter
North Cove, Battery Park City.
Built: 1921 Herreshoff Co., RI
Current Use: Excursion/Charter
Atlantic Sail 212-786-1204
Wooden sailing ship with a hull made of solid mahogany and decks made of Indian teak originally launched as a duck hunting yacht by the founder of Citibank. National Historic Landmark.

Wavertree
Pier 16 South Street Seaport Museum
Built: 1885 Southampton, UK
Current Use: Floating Exhibit
212-748-8786 southstseaport.org
The largest sailing ship afloat and one of the last built of wrought iron. A tramp ship, *Wavertree* took on cargo for hire from India to South America. Sold in 1910, she was used as a warehouse in Chile and was later converted to a sand barge before being acquired by the museum in 1968. On the National Register of Historic Places.

Yankee
Pier 25 Hudson River Park
Built: 1907 Neafie & Levy, PA
Current Use: Floating Exhibit/Event Space
212-267-7236 historicferryyankee.com

Propeller-driven steam ferry boat that once transported immigrants from ocean liners to Ellis Island. Requisitioned into service in both WWI and WWII, she has also carried passengers as a tour boat and Statue of Liberty Ferry. On National Register of Historic Places.

Launches

❝ Centuries of development at the water's edge have proved that infrastructure in a "hostile" environment like the waterfront is extremely expensive to build and maintain. The gradual resuscitation of area waters has produced a "catch-22": improved water quality is more hospitable to virtually all forms of aquatic life, including the tiny parasites which feast on wooden structures known as "marine borers."

Many agencies and organizations are beginning to turn to look for alternative materials like recycled plastic or fiber-reinforced composites. To help address this infrastructure crisis, MWA launched a Community Dock Initiative to build small (10x20) floating docks using plastic "lumber" made from recycled plastic milk jugs. This project, funded by the Plastic Lumber Trade Association and the Hudson River Estuary Program of New York State is creating a double benefit for our waterfront. First, we're demonstrating the potential for using recycled plastic materials in recreational waterfront infrastructure. Second, the Community Dock project is helping to support the swelling number of community and small boating efforts springing up in area waters. **❞**

Carter Craft, Metropolitan Waterfront Alliance (waterwire.com)

Canoes, kayaks and rowboats must be hand carried to the water. There is no right to cross private property without the permission of the landowner to gain access to a navigable waterway. Beach launches offer shallow water entry, but there is often glass on the banks of city waterways. Floating docks provide deep water access. Davits with hand winches are used to hoist boats, usually Whitehall Gigs, in and out of the water from piers. The city requires a permit for the use of City Park kayak and canoe launch facilities. A seasonal Launch Permit can be obtained at City Park offices located in each borough at a cost of $15. The season opens May through November and launch sites are open for use one hour after dawn until one hour before dusk. A permit is not necessary at public launches that are not maintained by the city, such as the car-top launch at Floyd Bennett Field and community docks

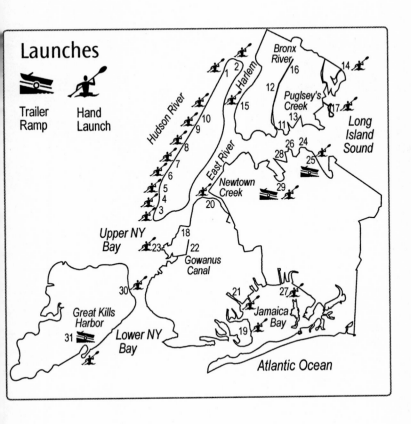

Launches

Trailer Ramp

Hand Launch

Hudson River

Harlem

Bronx River

East River

Puglsey's Creek

Long Island Sound

Newtown Creek

Upper NY Bay

Gowanus Canal

Great Kills Harbor

Lower NY Bay

Jamaica Bay

Atlantic Ocean

in Hudson River Park. Ocean beach launching at Rockaway and Coney Island is permitted only in the off-season. Kayakers can launch from Gateway National Recreation Area beaches—Plumb, Fort Tilden, Breezy Pt.—anytime of year. There are a shortage of places to store non-motorized, hand launched boats and a lack of parking near launch sites for car-top boats. Some larger marinas offer outdoor rack storage, fees range from $70 a year at Sebago Canoe

Club to $250 for 6 months at the 79th St. Boat Basin. A paved "driveway" launch ramp, where a boat on a trailer is backed into the water and allowed to float off, is an amenity found at most area marinas. Marinas charge a user's for launching and parking ($12). Boat owners without access to a marina or yacht club have a limited number of paved day ramps to trailer launch vessels. Bayside, World's Fair and Great Kills offer free, public ramp access.

Launches

			Trailer Ramp	Hand Launch	Floating Dock	Beach	Davit	Storage	Parking

Manhattan

			Trailer Ramp	Hand Launch	Floating Dock	Beach	Davit	Storage	Parking
�ख	**Community Boathouse**	Harlem River E. Dyckman St		H				S	
		NYRA 212-440-4483 nyrowing.org							
1 ✶	**Dyckman Pier**	Hudson River W Dyckman St		H		B			P
		212-360-8133 nycparks.org							
2	**Inwood Hill Park**	Harlem River W 218 St. & Indian Rd		H		B			
		Inwood Nature Center 212-304-2365							
3	**Pier 25**	Hudson River N. Moore St		H	F				
		Manhattan Youth 212-732-7467							
4	**Pier 26**	Hudson River Just below Canal St		H	F			S	
		Downtown Boathouse 646-613-0375							
5	**Pier 40**	Hudson River W Houston St		H	F		D	S	P
		FTA 212-564-5412 floatingtheapple.org							
6	**Pier 63**	Hudson River W 23 St		H	F			S	P
		MKC 212-924-1788 manhattankayak.com							
7	**Pier 66a**	Hudson River W 26 St		H	F				
		Downtown Boathouse 646-613-0375							
8	**Pier 84**	Hudson River W 46 St		H			D		
		FTA 212-564-5412 floatingtheapple.org							
9	**Riverside Park South**	Hudson River W 72 St		H	F				
		Downtown Boathouse 646-613-0375							
10 ✶	**79 St Boat Basin**	Hudson River W 79 St		H	F			S	
		Boat Basin Marina 212-496-2105							

✶City Parks Dept. Launch Permit Required 212-360-8133 nyc.gov/parks

✗To be built; not yet opened.

Launches

#	Launch	Location	Trailer Ramp	Hand Launch	Floating Dock	Beach	Davit	Storage	Parking	Contact
Bronx										
⚒	**Barretto Point Park**	East River Viele Ave		H		B				212-360-8133 nycparks.org
11	**Clason's Point Park**	East River Soundview Ave		H		B				212-360-8133 nycparks.org
⚒	**Cement Plant**	Bronx River Edgewater Rd		H		B				B R A 718-430-1846 bronxriver.org
12	**East 180th Street**	Bronx River E 180 St		H		B				B R A 718-430-1846 bronxriver.org
⚒	**Hunts Point Riverside Park**	Bronx River Lafayette Ave/Edgewater		H	F					The Point CDC 718-542-4139
13 *	**Pugsley Creek Park**	East River Soundview Ave		H		B			P	212-360-8133 nycparks.org
14 *	**Orchard Beach Lagoon**	L. I. Sound Pelham Bay Park		H		B			P	212-360-8133 nycparks.org
15	**Roberto Clemente Park**	Harlem River W Tremont Ave		H	F			S	P	Empire State Rowing 718-894-7486
16	**Shoelace Park**	Bronx River E 219 St		H		B				B R A 718-430-1846 bronxriver.org
17	**Touring Kayak Club**	L. I. Sound 205 Beach St, City Is		H		B		S	P	718-885-3193 tkcny.org
Brooklyn										
18	**Brooklyn Bridge Park**	East River Under Manhattan Brdg		H		B				718-802-0603 bbpc.net
19	**Floyd Bennett Field**	Jamaica Bay Old seaplane ramp		H		B			P	GNRA 718-338-3799 nps.gov/gate

Launches		Trailer Ramp	Hand Launch	Floating Dock	Beach	Davit	Storage	Parking
Brooklyn (cont.)								
20	**Greenpoint M&D Center**	Newtown Creek		H	F			S	P
		1155 Manhattan Ave	Greenpoint Kayak Club 718-389-5277						
21	**Sebago Canoe Club**	Jamaica Bay		H	F	B		S	P
		Paerdegat Rd	718-241-3683 sebagocanoeclub.org						
22	**2nd St Launch**	Gowanus Canal		H	F				
		End of 2 St	Gowanus Canal Dredgers 718-243-0849						
23 ∗	**Valentino Park**	N Y Harbor		H		B			
		Coffey St	212-360-8133 nycparks.org						
Queens								
24	**Fort Totten**	Little Neck Bay		H		B			P
		Totten Ave	212-360-8133 nycparks.org						
25 ∗	**Bayside Marina**	Little Neck Bay	T	H					P
		28 Ave	212-360-8133 nycparks.org						
26	**Francis Lewis Park**	East River		H		B			P
		Parsons Blvd	212-360-8133 nycparks.org						
27	**Jamaica Bay Beach**	Jamaica Bay		H		B			P
		Addabbo Bdg	212-360-8133 nycparks.org						
28	**Powell's Cove Park**	East River		H		B			
		130 S/ 9 Ave	212-360-8133 nycparks.org						
29 ∗	**World's Fair Marina**	Flushing Bay	T	H	F				P
		1 W F Marina	212-360-8133 nycparks.org						
Staten Island								
30	**Buono Beach**	N Y Harbor		H		B			
		Hylan Blvd	212-360-8133 nycparks.org						
31	**Great Kills Park**	Great Kills Harbor	T	H		B			P
		Hylan Blvd	GNRA 718-338-3799 nps.gov/gate						

Lighthouses

❝ New York City, known for its brightly lit streets and skyscrapers, dazzles residents and tourist alike with its luminous skyline. In the background of this busy city, a different kind of light shines out of sight to most busy New Yorkers - The Lighthouses of New York Harbor. The need for permanent aids to navigation to protect cargo and people coming into port was realized by New York businessmen who solicited the NY Assembly to sponsor a lottery for the building of the Sandy Hook Lighthouse (formerly called New York Lighthouse) in 1764. As the importance of New York Harbor expanded the need for additional lighthouses grew over the years to accommodate the increased traffic into the harbor. Below you will find a list of all the NY Harbor Lights with information to help you explore on your own the beauty of these historic maritime treasures. ❞

Jim Crowley, author of *Lighthouses of New York* (nylighthouses.com)

Ambrose Light Tower

Ambrose Channel, New York Harbor
Current Use: Active
Established: 1967
Owner: USCG
👁 Visible by boat

From 1908 to 1967, three lightships served the Ambrose Channel entrance to New York Harbor. Lightships were used where the water was too deep for a standard lighthouse. In 1967, the floating light was replaced by a Texas-style tower, which was later damaged in a collision with an oil tanker. Since 1999, a solar powered tower with fog signal, radio and radar beacons marks the harbor entrance from the Atlantic Ocean to the Lower Bay.

Blackwell Island Lighthouse

East River, Roosevelt Island
Current Use: Historic site
👁 FDR Dr. or 1ˢᵗ St. in Astoria, Queens

Designed by James Renwick Jr. and built by convict labor in 1872 of locally quarried gray gneiss stone, the octagon-shaped tower stands 50 feet tall at the northern tip of Roosevelt Island. Named for the Blackwell family that owned the island from 1685-1823, it served as a private navigational aid for over 70 years. It is no longer used as a navigational aid, but is still lit at night. An esplanade on the island's westside leads to the lighthouse. On the National Register of Historic Places.

Coney Island Lighthouse

Norton's Point, Brooklyn
Current Use: Active
Established: 1896
Owner: USCG

👁 Shore Greenway or Sea Gate beach.

Located in the gated community of Sea Gate, the skeletal light stands 75 feet tall and its red flashing beacon can be seen for 14 miles, covering the Main Channel. The keeper's cottage is home to the last civilian lightkeeper, Frank Schubert, who has been "keeping a good light" since 1960. The original Fresnel lens is on display at South Street Seaport Museum.

Elm Tree Light

Miller Field, Staten Island
Current Use: Inactive
Established: 1852
Owner: National Park Service

The Swash Channel light also served as Front Range Light for the New Dorp Lighthouse. It was replaced by a concrete aviation tower installed in 1939, which had a green light for aviators and white light for mariners.

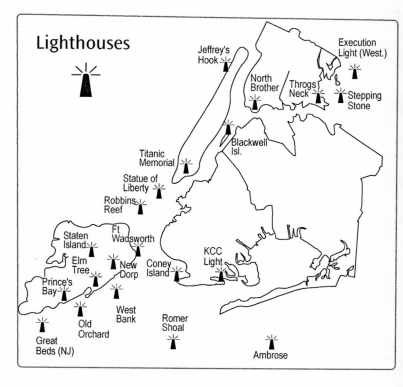

Lighthouses

Jeffrey's Hook
Execution Light (West.)
North Brother
Throgs Neck
Stepping Stone
Blackwell Isl.
Titanic Memorial
Statue of Liberty
Robbins Reef
Staten Island
Ft Wadsworth
Elm Tree
New Dorp
Coney Island
KCC Light
Prince's Bay
West Bank
Romer Shoal
Great Beds (NJ)
Old Orchard
Ambrose

Katherine Walker, Lightkeeper (1848-1931) 4'10" Kate Walker began tending Robbins Reef Lighthouse, located on a tiny reef two miles southwest of the Statue of Liberty, upon the death of her husband John in 1886. His last words were "Mind the light, Kate." Officially given the title of lightkeeper in 1894, Kate was paid $600 a year and is credited with saving as many as 50 people and at least one dog from drowning in the nearby waters. In addition to maintaining the light for 35 years, she raised two children, Jake and Mamie, on Robbins Reef, rowing them one mile each way to Staten Island to attend school. She retired in 1919 at the age of 71, and she moved to the Staten Island shore where she could see the light, now called Kate's Light.

Fort Wadsworth Lighthouse

The Narrows, Staten Island
Current Use: Historic site
Established: 1903
Owner: National Park Service
◉ Fort Thompkins, Staten Island

Active until 1965, when it was rendered obsolete by the Verrazano Bridge. The light atop Battery Weed was visible for 14 miles at sea. It has been restored and efforts are underway for the tower to be re-lit. The park grounds are open to the public daily.

Jeffrey's Hook "Little Red" Lighthouse

Hudson River, Fort Washington Park
Current Use: Private navigation aid
Established: 1921
Owner: NYC Parks
◉ 181st St. Fort Washington Park

The only lighthouse on Manhattan Island, it is located on an outcropping of rocks called Jeffrey's Hook under the George Washington Bridge. It was deactivated in 1947 and slated for demolition. The children's book, "The Little Red Lighthouse and the Great Grey Bridge" by Hildegarde H. Swift, which is about being small in a big world, inspired community action and preservation of the lighthouse. It was relit in 2002 and is open to the public for scheduled tours.

Kingsborough Community College

Sheepshead Bay Channel & Rockaway Inlet
Current Use: Private aid to navigation
Owner: CUNY
◉ KCC campus, Brooklyn

A skeletal tower on top of the Marine Academic Center, the light rises 114 feet above sea level and has a range of 11 miles. It flashes a white light every four seconds.

New Dorp Light

Lower NY Bay, Staten Island
Current Use: Private residence
Established: 1856
◉ Beacon Ave., Staten Island

An inland light, 40 feet high and 192 feet above sea level, active from 1856 to 1964. It served as a rear range light for the Swash Channel with the Elm

Tree tower. On the National Register of Historic Places.

Old Orchard Shoals Light

Gedney Channel, Lower New York Bay
Current Use: Active
Established: 1893
Owner: USCG

Great Kills beach, Staten Island

The white beacon is about three miles off Staten Island's south shore in Raritan Bay. The brown and white tower stands 50.5 feet tall and sits on a caisson foundation. It is a spark plug or "bug light," which is a prefab cast-iron cylinder about 20-feet across that were assembled on-site.

Prince's Bay Light

Mount Loretto Preserve, Staten Island
Current Use: Inactive
Established: 1828
Owner: NYS DEC

Hylan Blvd., Staten Island

A brownstone keeper's house and attached tower. The lighthouse was active from 1828 to 1922, serving the oystermen of Prince's Bay. For many years, Mt. Lorretto orphanage owned the property and a statue of the Virgin Mary once stood in the tower in place of a light. The land is now a State-owned nature preserve and an employee resides in the keeper's house.

Robbins Reef "Kate's" Light

Upper New York Bay
Current Use: Active
Established: 1883 stone; 1933 iron
Owner: USCG

Staten Island Ferry or Battery Park

The 45-foot high lighthouse sits on a small islet in the middle of Upper New York Bay, on the west side of the main channel. Before the light was constructed, this hidden ledge of rocks had caused many wrecks. A spark plug lighthouse known for its lady keeper, Kate Walker.

Romer Shoal Light

Swash Channel, Lower New York Bay
Current Use: Active
Established: 1898
Owner: USCG

Sandy Hook, NJ

A red band marks the 54-foot tall spark plug light fixed with a fourth order Fresnel lens showing a white flashing light. It is approachable by small boat. The lighthouse was originally located at the Lighthouse Service Depot, now the Lighthouse Museum, where it was used to test new oils and lenses. The light may be returned to its original site at the new museum.

Staten Island Light

Ambrose Channel, Staten Island
Current Use: Active
Established: 1912
Owner: USCG

Edinboro Rd., Staten Island

Located on a hilltop in a residential neighborhood, the beacon is visible for a range of 18 miles at sea. The rear channel light works in tandem with the West Bank Lighthouse. It has an octagonal tower and was one

Jeffrey's Hook Lighthouse   © 2002 Jim Crowley

National Lighthouse Museum

One Lighthouse Plaza, Staten Island. 718-556-1681 lighthousemuseum.org.
The museum at the former U.S. Lighthouse Service Depot, which beginning
in 1862 assembled, tested and repaired lighthouses for close to a century. The
museum will be housed in one of the six historic buildings at the old depot. It
will feature a theater, exhibits and a Fresnal lens, which is made of hundreds
of pieces of glass, the range of which is only limited by the curvature of the
earth. The Lightship *Nantucket* will dock onsite at Pier 1. Tours are available
by appointment. 👁 A short walk along the esplanade from St. George Ferry
Terminal. ✗

of the last brick lighthouses built in the country. The keeper's house is a private residence. A NYC Landmark.

Statue of Liberty
Liberty (Bedloe) Island
Current Use: National monument
Established: 1886
Owner: National Park Service
Robert Wagner Park, Circle Line boat

An aid to navigation from 1886 to 1902, *Liberty Enlightening the World* was the first lighthouse to use electricity. An onsite electric plant generated power to the electric torch, which was visible for 24 miles at sea.

Stepping Stone Light
Long Island Sound
Current Use: Active
Established: 1878
Owner: USCG
Beldon's Point, City Island

The red brick lighthouse sits atop a granite foundation, east of the Throgs Neck Bridge. Its green flashing light warns mariners of the mussel encrusted reefs to the south. The keeper's house is no longer in use.

Titanic Memorial Lighthouse
South Street Seaport, Manhattan
Current Use: Memorial
Established: 1915
Fulton & Pearl Sts., Manhattan

A tribute to those lost aboard the *SS Titanic* on April 15, 1912, the 60-foot tall light was originally located on top of the old Seaman's Church Institute at South Street and Coenties Slip. It now marks the entrance to the Seaport district.

The North Brother Light
Bay of Brothers, East River
Current Use: Abandoned
Owner: NYC Parks
Randall's Island

The light served as a guide on the Bay of Brothers from 1869 to 1953, the structure has since been razed. North Brother Island, now a wading bird rookery, was once the forced home to Typhoid Mary and the site where the *General Slocum* was forced to land because of fire.

Throgs Neck Light
East River at Long Island Sound
Current Use: Active
Established: 1827; current tower 1934
Fort Schuyler, Bronx

A skeletal tower houses an automated fixed red light with a range of 11 miles, located under the Throgs Neck Bridge. The first keepers operated a bar at the site.

West Bank Light
Ambrose Channel, Lower New York Bay
Current Use: Active
Established: 1901
Owner: USCG
Coney Island or South Beach

A brown conical tower located 5 miles south of the Verrazano Bridge, at the juncture of the Ambrose Channel. It is the tallest of the offshore lights at 70 feet and shows a fixed white light.

Marinas & Yacht Clubs

Motor boat docks cluster in the sheltered inlets and creeks of Gerritsen Beach, Mill Basin and Howard Beach. Sailboats reign off the coast of City Island and in the protected embayment of Great Kill Harbor. Numerous public and private marinas operate on the city's shores. Most are family-owned facilities. Gateway Marina on Dead Horse Bay is the areas largest full-service facility with 600 slips and moorings. The 79th Street Boat Basin is the city's most well-known marina. For decades, many boats docked at the marina weren't even seaworthy, people lived aboard derelict boats as an alternative to the city's high rents. The rates are still reasonable, but no new year-round permits have been issued since 1990. Today, 70% of the marina's slips are used by seasonal boaters. World's Fair marina has 292 slips and dockage for Mets games and U.S. Open Tennis. The Marine Division of City Parks & Recreation operates three marinas, 79th Street Boat Basin, Bayside and World's Fair, and oversees eight marina concessions. Gateway National Recreation Area has two marinas operated privately under contract with the National Park Service. Each marina employs a dockmaster who oversees the daily operation of the facility.

Yacht clubs provide many marina services; like launch ramps, drydocks and winter storage. Clubs offer racing, cruising and educational activities for both sailors and power boaters. They often have club-owned fleets, club-houses, dining facilities, social activities and junior membership programs. Reciprocal dockage privileges are available to members at hundreds of yacht clubs in the U.S. and abroad. New members must be nominated and approved by current members. Non-sailors are also welcome to join and participate in social programs. Older, well-established clubs, such as the Rockaway Point Yacht Club, have a wait of up to 15 years. Dues vary widely from $25 a year at Deep Creek Yacht Club to $990 annually at the Manhattan Yacht Club. One benefit of membership in Manhattan Yacht Club is access to the clubhouse moored offshore in the inner harbor near Ellis Island. The storied clubs of City Island offer fine dining facilities and private beach rights, and yacht clubs on Sheepshead Bay have waterside swimming pools. Yacht Clubs are headed by an elected commodore. Member boats fly a club burgee, which is a small triangular or swallowtailed flag that enables members to identify club affiliation.

Marinas & Visitor Docks

			Fuel	Repair	Launch	Dock & Dine	Pump-out	Visitor Docks
Manhattan	Dyckman Marina 348 Dyckman St	Hudson River 212-567-5120	F	R	L	D	P	V
	NY Skyport Marina E 23 St	East River 212-686-4546	F					V
	North Cove Marina Battery Park City	Hudson River 212-267-9700				D		V
	Pier 40 Moorings W Houston St	Hudson River 212-791-2530						V
	Surfside 3 Marina Pier 59 W 23 St	Hudson River 212-336-7873				D		V
	79 St Boat Basin Riverside Park	Hudson River 212-496-2105			L	D	P	V
Bronx	Barrons Boat Yard 350 Fordham Pl.	L. I. Sound 718-885-9802		R				V
	Boatmax 2 150 City Island Ave	Eastchester Bay 718-885-2000						V
	Consolidated Yachts 157 Pilot St	Eastchester Bay 718-885-1900		R			P	
	Evers Seaplane 1470 Outlook Ave	Eastchester Bay 718-863-9111						
	Fenton Marine 225 Fordham St	L. I. Sound 718-885-0844		R				
	Gas Dock 673 City Island Ave	Eastchester Bay 718-885-3001	F				P	

Marinas & Visitor Docks

			Fuel	Repair	Launch	Dock & Dine	Pump-out	Visitor-Docks
Bronx	Hammond Cove Marina 140 Reynolds Ave	Locust Point 718-892-3012		R	L	D	P	V
	Kirby St Marina 231 Kirby St	Pelham Bay 718-885-0527						
	Lobster House Docks 691 Bridge St	Eastchester Bay 718-885-1459				D		V
	Metro Marine Sales 1322 Commerce Ave	Westchester Creek 718-823-0300					P	
	Royal Marina 521 City Island Ave	Eastchester Bay 718-885-1800					P	V
	Sailmaker Marina 190 Schofield St	L. I. Sound 718-885-2700					P	V
	Seashore Marina 591 City Island Ave	Eastchester Bay 718-885-0300				D		V
	Stetler Marine 495 City Island Ave	Eastchester Bay 718-885-1300		R				
	The Harbor Restaurant 565 City Island Ave	Eastchester Bay 718-885-1373				D		V
Brooklyn	All Seasons Marina 5300 Kings Plz	Rockaway Inlet 718-253-5434	F	R			P	V
	Bay End Marine 2094 E 68 St	Mill Basin 718-444-7544		R				
	Corvett's Marina 5800 Ave U	Mill Basin 718-252-6726						V

Marinas & Visitor Docks

		Fuel	Repair	Launch	Dock & Dine	Pump-out	Visitor Docks
Dimeglio Marina (NYP) Ave. Y & E 69 St	Mill Basin 718-241-5011						
Futura Marina 2501 Knapp St	Shell Bank Creek 718-743-2800						
Gateway Marina (GNRA) 3260 Flatbush Ave	Jamaica Bay 718-252-8761		R	L		P	V
Marine Basin Marina 1900 Shore Pkwy	Gravesend Bay 718-372-5700	F	R				V
Pkwy Fishing Center 3 Plumb 3 St	Shell Bank Creek 718-763-9265						
Port Sheepshead Marina 10 Webers St	Sheepshead Bay 917-731-8607						V
Riviera Marine 25A Lakon Ct	Shell Bank Creek 718-332-3733		R			P	
Sea Traveler's Marina 2875 Flatbush Ave.	Mill Basin 718-377-0216		R	L		P	
Sheepshead Bay Moorings NYC Parks Dept.	Sheepshead Bay 718-965-8958						V
Tamaqua Marina 84 Ebony Crt	Shell Bank Creek 718-646-9212	F		L			
Venice Marina 3939 Emmons Ave	Plumb Bch Channel 718-646-9283	F	R	L	D	P	V
Woroco Neptune Ave	Coney Island Creek	F					

Marinas & Visitor Docks			Fuel	Repair	Launch	Dock & Dine	Pump-out	Visitor Docks
	Argo Boat Mfg. Co	Jamaica Bay		R				
	251-02 Rockwy Blvd	718-527-9870						
	Bayside Marina	Little Neck Bay			L		P	V
	59-14 Beach Chl Dr	718-229-0097						
	Beach Channel	Jamaica Bay						
	59-14 Beach Chnnl Dr	718-945-4500						
	Capt. Mike's Marina	Shell Bank Basin		R				
	158-35 Cross Bay Blvd	718-641-1659						
	Channel Marine	Jamaica Bay						
	54 W 20 St	718-318-2000						
Queens	Ebb-Tide Marina	Jamaica Bay						
	370 Beach 85 St	718-945-5883						
	L'il Cricket Marina	Shell Bank Basin						
	164-49 Cross Bay Blvd	718-843-6400						
	Lynn Boatyard	Shell Bank Basin		R				
	160-55 Cross Bay Blvd	718-845-9069						
	Pier 92	Atlantic Ocean				D		
	377 Beach 92 St	718-945-2200						
	Seaway Marine Corp	Jamaica Bay	F	R	L	D	P	
	72-46 Thursby Ave	718-474-0443						
	World's Fair (NYP)	Flushing Bay		R	L	D	P	V
	1 World's Fair Marina	718-478-0480						

Marinas & Visitor Docks			Fuel	Repair	Launch	Dock & Dine	Pump-out	Visitor Docks
Atlantis Marina	Great Kills Harbor						P	V
180 Mansion Ave	718-966-9700							
Bliss Marina	Great Kills Harbor							
331 Hillside Ter	718-317-0208							
Captains Marina	Great Kills Harbor							
202 Mansion Ave	718-984-3346							
Lemon Creek (NYP)	Princes Bay							
440 Seguine Ave	718-948-9766							
Mansion Marina	Great Kills Harbor	F						
112 Mansion Ave	718-984-6611							
Nichols (GNRA)	Great Kills Harbor			L		P	V	
Great Kills Park	718-351-8476							
Great Kills Moorings	Great Kills Harbor							V
NYC Parks	718-390-8023							
Port Atlantic Marina	Arthur Kill		R				V	
225 Ellis St	718-948-5677							
Sandy's Marina	Raritan Bay							
500 Bayview Rd	718-317-6557							
SI Boat Sales	Great Kills Harbor	F	R	L			V	
222 Mansion Ave.	718-984-7676							
SI Marina	Kill Van Kull							
1595 Richmond Ter	718-442-8018							
Tottenville Marina	Arthur Kill		R				V	
201 Ellis St	718-948-7520							

Staten Island

Yacht Clubs & Boat Clubs

Manhattan

Manhattan YC	East River	207 Front St	212-619-3656
NY Health & Racket	East River	E 23 St	212-248-1000

Bronx

Ampere YC	L. I. Sound	1610 Bayshore Ave	718-822-8707
Bronxonia YC	Eastchester Bay	518 Ellsworth Ave	718-822-9113
City Island YC	Eastchester Bay	63 Pilot St	718-885-2487
Harlem YC	L. I. Sound	417 Hunter Ave	718-885-3078
Island Boat Club	Eastchester Bay	515 City Island Ave	914-528-5213
Locust Point YC	L. I. Sound	21 Longstreet Ave	718-822-9806
Morris YC	Eastchester Bay	25 City Island Ave	718-885-1596
N. Minneford YC	Eastchester Bay	150 City Island Ave	718-855-2000
NY Athletic Club YC	L. I. Sound	Travers Is, Pelham	914-738-0065
NY Sailing Center	L. I. Sound	560 Minneford Ave	718-885-0335
Riverdale YC	Hudson River	W 254th St	718-543-0792
Sea Anchors YC	Eastchester Bay	1490 Outlook Ave	718-822-8320
S. Minneford YC	L. I. Sound	150 City Island Ave	718-885-3113
Stepping Stone YC		c/o Bronxonia YC	718-822-9113
Stuyvesant YC	Eastchester Bay	10 Centre St	718-885-1023

Brooklyn

Anchor YC	Shell Bank Creek	96 Ebony Ct	718-743-3296
Bergen Beach YC	Mill Basin	2657 E 66 St	718-444-3506
Brooklyn YC	Sheepshead Bay	314 Voorhies Ave	718-646-9420
Canarsie YC	Paerdegat Creek	1310 Paerdegat Ave	718-531-7930
Deep Creek YC	Dead Horse Bay	3260 Flatbush Ave	718-951-6759
Diamond Point YC	Paerdegat Basin	1350 Paerdegat Ave	718-444-7700
Hudson River YC	Paerdegat Basin	Ave U / Bergen Ave	718-338-5256
Midget Squadron YC	Paerdegat Basin	Paerdegat Ave	718-251-9823
Mill Harbor YC	Mill Basin	6097 Strickland Ave	718-241-3900
Miramar YC	Sheepshead Bay	3050 Emmons Ave	718-646-9436

Yacht Clubs & Boat Clubs

Brooklyn (cont.)

Paerdegat Squadron	Paerdegat Basin	1330 Paerdegat Ave. N	718-241-4581
Pilgrim YC	Shell Bank Creek	4 Florence Ave	718-646-9647
Sebago Canoe Club	Paerdegat Creek	Paerdegat Ave	718-434-5787
Sheepshead Bay YC	Sheepshead Bay	3076 Emmons Ave	718-891-0991
Shell Bank YC	Shell Bank Creek	1 Merit Ct	718-769-2112
Varuna Boat Club	Sheepshead Bay	2806 Emmons Ave	718-646-9355

Queens

Anabas Boat Club	Jamaica Bay	1820 Channel Rd	718-474-9167
Arrow YC	Flushing Bay	22-04 119 St	718-359-9229
Belle Harbor YC	Rockaway Inlet	533 Beach 126St	718-945-4445
Bowery Bay Boat Club	Bowery Bay	1750 Steinway St	718-274-0427
College Point YC	East River	304-126 St	718-463-9841
Douglaston YC	Little Neck Bay	600 West Dr	718-229-3900
Howard Beach Club	Hawtree Basin	59 Russell St	718-843-9478
Iroqouis YC	Jamaica Bay	12-00 Church Rd	718-474-9668
North Channel YC	Jamaica Bay	1622 Church Rd	718-318-1312
Old Mill YC	Shell Bank Basin	163-15 Crossbay Blvd	718-835-0454
Riley's YC	Hawtree Basin	99-62 Russell St	718-845-9416
Rockaway Pnt. YC	Rockaway Inlet	Fort Tilden	718-474-9001
Williamsburg YC	Flushing Bay	118-08 29 Ave	718-359-9147

Staten Island

Great Kills YC	Great Kills Harbor	37 Mansion Ave	718-948-9615
Mariners Harbor YC	Kill Van Kull	3387 Richmond Ter	718-442-5843
Princes Bay Boatmen's	Lemon Creek	Seguine Ave	
Richmond Cty YC	Great Kills Harbor	142 Mansion Ave	718-356-4120
Staten Island YC	Great Kills Harbor	147 Mansion Ave	718-948-95 08

Maritime Museums

❝ To really understand New York City, you have to go back to the very beginning, when the Dutch chose Manhattan as the "middelpunt" of their New Netherland colony because of its ice-free harbor and its central location. Then, a mere two decades after its founding, this river town with its vast harbor, founded for the sole purpose of making money, was a vibrant home to immigrants already speaking some 18 different languages. New York, from its very beginnings, has always been what it became: The quintessential American Metropolis, a meeting place for people of all races and cultures. Understanding this vital truth about the city and preserving the heritage of its past is central to the mission of New York's maritime history museums. ❞

Richard Stepler, Director of Publications
& Visiting Exhibitions, South Street Seaport Museum

City Island Nautical Museum
190 Fordham St. Bronx 718-885-0008 cityislandmuseum.org. Housed in one of the areas most interesting buildings PS 17, built in 1897 on one of City Island's highest points. The collection includes paintings, photographs and memorabilia on the role City Island played in the yachting industry, the America's Cup Races and the Hell Gate Pilots. Admission is free. 🚇 Subway 6 to Pelham Bay Park, transfer Bx29 Bus.

Coney Island Museum 1208 Surf Ave. at W 12th St. 718-372-5159 coneyislandusa.com. Shows artifacts of the amusement town's heyday, also a visitor and research center. 🚇 Subway W, F, Q to Stillwell Ave.

Ellis Island Immigration Museum
National Park Service 212-363-3206 ellisisland.com. The Main Building, an ornate French Renaissance Revival structure, houses the museum. Three floors of exhibits chronicle the history of the immigration processing station, where 12 million steerage and third class passengers entered the United States between 1892 and 1954. A family history research center contains ship manifests and passenger lists while the library has a comprehensive oral history collection. The **Statue of Liberty Museum** on Liberty Island is housed in the pedestal of Lady Liberty and displays the original torch. Admission is free. 🚇 Statue of Liberty ferry from Battery Park.

Governors Island New York Harbor 212-514-8296 governorsislandnatio nalmonument.org. Historic island returned to the public after 200 years of restricted military use. The historic district contains landmark forts, Castle William and Fort Jay. The pivotal summit between President Reagan and Mikhail Gorbachev took place on the island. Free walking tours of the historic district. 🚤 Access for scheduled tours. Boats depart Battery Maritime Bldg. Ferry Slip 7. ✗

Greenpoint Monitor Museum greenpointmonitormuseum.org 718-383-2637. The museum was charted in 1996 and is working to establish a home on the Brooklyn waterfront at Bushwick Inlet, which was homeport to the *USS Monitor*. ✗

Hall of Ocean Life American Museum of Natural History 79th St. & CPW 212-769-5100 amnh.org. The iconic 94-foot-long blue whale, first displayed in 1969, dives from the ceiling above the exhibit of marine ecosystems. The museum houses one of the world's largest collections of seashells. 🚇 Subway A, C, B, D to 81st St. or 1, 2, 3, 9 to 79th St.

Harbor Defense Museum Bldg. 230 Fort Hamilton, Brooklyn 718-630-4349. Robert E. Lee served at the Fort in 1840, his house is still there. The museum preserves the heritage of the seacoast defenses in New York Harbor. On the National Register of Historic Places and NYC

Landmark. Admission is free, by reservation. 🚇 Subway R to 95th St.

India House One Hanover Square 212-269-2323 indiahouseclub.org. Founded as a private lunch club by merchant ship owners in 1914, India House preserves a collection of art, which traces the history and expansion of American maritime commerce, and includes the charter for the 1770 Marine Society of the City of New York. Tours by appointment only. 🚇 Subway 4, 5 to Wall St.; A, C to Broadway-Nassau.

Intrepid Sea-Air-Space Museum Pier 86, W 46th St. 212-245-0072 intrepidmuseum.com. A rare look at grand military vessels posed alongside the 900-foot long aircraft carrier *Intrepid* and the guided missile submarine *Growler*, and 25 military aircraft on the ships deck. The floating exhibit also features a Concorde, a 204-foot long supersonic jet retired in 2003. 🚇 Subway A, C, E to 42nd St. Port Authority; M42 Bus to 12th Ave.

Maritime Industry Museum Fort Schuyler, Bronx 212-409-7218 maritimeindustrymuseum.org. One of the largest collections of maritime industry artifacts in the nation located in historic Fort Schuyler on the campus of the SUNY Maritime College. Admission is free. 🚇 Subway 6 to Westchester Square then Bx40 Bus to Fort Schuyler. Or NY Bus Express Bus from Manhattan to Throgs Neck, call for bus schedule 718-994-5500.

John A. Noble, Maritime Artist (1913-1983) Born in Paris, John Noble came to America in 1919. Although he studied to be an artist, Noble made his living as a seaman on schooners and marine salvage vessels from 1928 until 1945. In 1941, on the Kill van Kull, Noble began to build a houseboat studio out of salvaged parts. He retired in 1946 to become a full-time artist. Inspired both by the ships that surrounded him and the men that worked upon them, Noble chronicled New York maritime life as sailing ships disappeared and were replaced by newer vessels. He led the fight to preserve 83-acre Snug Harbor, once a seaman's retirement home, from developers. Now a cultural center, Snug Harbor houses a collection of his work and houseboat studio.

Maritime Collection Museum of the City of New York 1220 5th Ave., Manhattan 212-534-1672 mcny.org. An extensive collection of maritime artifacts, carved figureheads, nautical instruments and prints. The collection also holds about 100 ship's models and paintings by local marine artists. 🚇 Subway 6 to 103rd St.

National Lighthouse Museum One Lighthouse Plz., Staten Island 718-556-1681 lighthousemuseum. org. Located in the storied buildings of the former Lighthouse Depot, the new museum highlights the history and importance of lighthouses. Five of the seven remaining buildings at the 10-acre site are on the National Register of Historic Places. The Administration Building is a New York City Landmark. The museum will feature exhibits on the history of lighthouses, a theater and the *Lightship Nantucket*. A walking tour is available by appointment. 🚢 Staten Island Ferry.

Noble Maritime Collection Snug Harbor Cultural Center, Staten Island 718-441-6490 johnanoble.com. A collection of maritime paintings, drawings and lithographs by artist John A. Noble and other maritime artists. Also on exhibit is Noble's restored houseboat studio. There is a maritime library and over 6,000 historical photographs. 🚢🚌 Staten Island Ferry to Bus S40.

New York Unearthed 17 State St. 212-748-8628. The urban archeological center of South Street Seaport features dioramas and artifacts from the city's archeological digs spanning 6,000 years of history. 🚇 Subway 1, 9 to South Ferry; 4, 5 to Bowling Green; N, R to Whitehall St.

Rockaway Museum 88-08 Rockaway Beach Blvd. 718-474-6760. Memorabilia and archival materials of 350 years on the Rockaways, once home to the world's largest hotel. 🚇 Subway A to Rockaway Park.

Seamen's Church Institute

241 Water St. Manhattan 212-349-9090 seamenschurch.org. A public gallery showing maritime exhibits and a permanent collection of ships models, paintings and artifacts at one of the city's oldest maritime institutions, which was founded in 1834 to minister to merchant seafarers.
📟 Subway A, C to Broadway-Nassau; J, M, Z, 2, 3, 4, 5 to Fulton St.

South Street Seaport Museum

207 Front St, Manhattan 212-748-8600 southstseaport.org. An 11-square-block historic district of 19th century buildings and a fleet of century old vessels at the "Street of Ships" on Pier 16 preserve the heritage of the city's first commercial seaport. The landmark Schermerhorn Row (12 Fulton St.) counting houses, built on landfill in 1812 by ship owner Peter Schermerhorn, are the architectural centerpiece of the seaport. The upper floors of the block-long "Row" and the adjoining A.A. Low Building encompass 24 galleries that house the museum's permanent exhibit "World Port New York," which chronicles the seaports history dating back to the Dutch colonial era. The floors above Heartland Brewery (92-93 South St.) were formerly occupied by the Fulton Ferry Hotel, which inspired writer Joseph Mitchell in *Up in the Old Hotel*. Melville, Walter Lord and Port Life galleries are on Water Street. 📟 Subway A, C to Broadway-Nassau; J, M, Z, 2, 3, 4, 5 to Fulton St.

Snug Harbor Cultural Center

1000 Richmond Terrace, Staten Island 718-448-2500 snug-harbor.org. Established in 1833, Snug Harbor was the nation's first seamen's retirement home and hospital. The sanctuary was created at the bequest of Capt. Robert Randall, who left his fortune to create a home for "aged, decrepit and worn-out sailors." A cultural center since 1976, the 83 acre site is a National Historic Landmark district that contains 26 historic buildings, including 5 Greek Revival structures. 🚢📟 Staten Island Ferry to S40 Bus.

SI Institute of Arts & Sciences

75 Stuyvesant Place, Staten Island 718-727-1135 siiasmuseum.org. Founded in 1881, the collection contains shells, specimens, history archives and a library. 📟 SI Ferry.

Waterfront Museum & Showboat Barge

699 Columbia St. Gowanus Industrial Park in Red Hook, Brooklyn 718-624-4719 waterfrontmuseum. org. The floating museum is housed in a restored 1914 railroad barge. It is the only surviving wooden covered barge of the lighterage era afloat. The barges were used to transport goods. Founded in 1986, the museum has a permanent exhibit of artifacts and serves as a floating classroom to bring maritime history to life for students and visitors. 📟 Subway F, G to Smith-9th St. The barge will return to its mooring at Conover St. once repairs are completed.

Maritime Libraries & Historical Societies

The regional historical societies and libraries help preserve the city's maritime heritage and marine resources through their collections and archives. They offer research assistance, field trips, walking tours and school projects.

American Family Immigration History Center Statue of Liberty-Ellis Island Foundation History Center 292 Madison Ave. Arrival records of more than 22 million immigrants from the Ellis Island Archives. ellisisland.org

Bayside Historical Society Maritime Gallery, Bldg. 208 Fort Totten. Explores Bayside's ties to the sea and features the collection of the Bayside Yacht Club. The society is based at the historic 1870 Officer's Club, a landmark Gothic Revival-Style structure built by the Army Corp of Engineers. On both the State and National Registers of Historic Places. 718-352-1548 baysidehistorical.org

Broad Channel Historical Society Broad Channel Library 16-26 Cross Bay Blvd. Preserves the history of the unique island community. 718-474-1127

Bronx County Historical Society 3309 Bainbrdige Ave. Research library and historical archives of Bronx County. 718-881-8900 bronxhistoricalsociety.org

Brooklyn Historical Society 128 Pierrepont St. The collection highlights Brooklyn's working waterfront. Marcia Reiss wrote numerous historical guides to the borough's waterfront neighborhoods. 718-222-4111 brooklynhistory.org

City Island Historical Society 190 Fordham St. Bronx. The collection and archives cover the island's history in yacht building days. It is housed in the City Island Nautical Museum. 718-885-0008 cityislandmuseum.org

City Island Library 320 City Island Ave. 1,000-volume ship collection, containing material on naval history and warfare, boat construction and maintenance, racing, piracy, and shipwrecks. 718-885-1703

Fort Hamilton Historical Society Brooklyn. Preserves the past of the historic fort. 718-630-4349

Gotham Center of NYC History CUNY Graduate Center 265 Fifth Ave. Promotes the historical assets of NYC and produces the Gotham History Festival. 212-817-8460 gothamcenter.org

Greater Astoria Historical Society 35-20 Broadway, 4th Floor, Long Island City. Dedicated to preserving the past of the Queen's waterfront community. 718-278-0700 astorialic.org

Herman Melville Library & Archives 213 Water St. The archival collection of South Street Seaport Museum, which includes 20,000 books and publications that relate to the history of the Port of New York. The collections also contains photographs, manuscripts, maps, charts and ships' plans.

John Ericsson Society of NY
250 E 63rd St. Organization dedicated to research concerning the life and work of Capt. John Ericsson, the Swedish engineer who designed the groundbreaking *USS Monitor*. 212-980-9655 biderman.net/jesny

Queens Historical Society
143-35 37th Ave. Museum and historical research library and archive located in historic Kingland Homestead farmhouse. 718-939-0647 preserve.org/queens/qhs.htm

City of NY Parks & Recreation
Arsenal, Central Park. A public library devoted to the history of city parks. 212-360-8240

New York City Municipal Archives
31 Chambers St. Over 90,000 cubic feet of records, including the papers of Robert Moses and the original plans for the Brooklyn Bridge. 212-788-8580

New York Correction History Society Chronicles the history of Hart, Welfare and Rikers islands. correctionhistory.org

New York Historical Society
2 W 77th St. The collection documents the history of NYC and includes Audubon prints. 212-873-3400 nyhistory.org

Old York Library CUNY Graduate Center, Seymour B. Durst Reading Room. Unique collection of books, maps, postcards and memorabilia of New York City. oldyorklibrary.org

Roosevelt Island Historical Society
Dedicated to restoring and preserving the island's landmark structures and unique history. 212-688-4836 rooseveltisland.us.rihs

Sandy Ground Historical Society
1538 Woodrow Rd. Staten Island. The museum and library chronicles the oldest community of free slaves in North America, who settled in the area and made a living as oystermen in Raritan Bay. 718-317-5796

Staten Island Historical Society
441 Clarke Ave. Administers Historic Richmond Town and archival records of the history of Richmond County. 718-351-1611 historicrichmondtown.org

Stephen B. Luce Library
SUNY Maritime College, Bronx Archival collection documents maritime history since 1700's, including 80,000 volumes in marine engineering and transportation, naval architecture and oceanography at historic Fort Schuyler. 718-409-7236 sunymaritime.edu

Motor Boating

Over 25,000 pleasure boats are registered in the five boroughs. New York State ranks seventh in the nation for total number of registered vessels, with more than 531,000 in 2002. By federal law, all power-driven vessels, including sailboats with motors, must be registered with the State. Any recreational watercraft operating in State waters for more than 90 days must register with the DMV (Form MV-82B). Registration is valid for three years. Cost depends on the size of the vessel. The registration certificate must be carried at all times when operating the boat. Registration numbers are required to be painted or permanently attached to both the port (left-hand) and starboard (right-hand) side of the bow (front end). The validation sticker displays the month and year of registration. It must be affixed to the hull, within three inches of the registration number. A license is not required to operate a motor boat. Persons under 18 years are required to complete a boating safety course to operate a motor boat alone. As of 2004, anyone operating a "jet ski" or personal watercraft (PWC) must pass a mandatory 8-hour safety course. Federal law requires boaters to motor at a "safe speed." There are no speed limits except "No Wake Zones" and within 100 feet of shore. Pleasure boats must carry a US Coast Guard approved PFD (personal flotation device/life jacket) of the proper size for each person on the vessel. Children under 12 must wear a PFD at all times. Boat owners are responsible for damage caused by the boat's wake. The Good Samaritan law requires every maritime vessel to render assistance to any other vessel that may be in distress at sea.

Recreational Vessel Speed:	5 mph within 100 ft of shore
Currents:	1-2 knots at flood tide; max 6 knots
Knot:	1.06 mph or 1.852 km/hr.
Nautical Mile:	6,076.1 feet or 1,852 meters
League:	3 Nautical Miles
Fathom:	6 Feet

Boating Safety

Safety, noise and crowding are an issue as more pleasure craft ply the waters of NY Harbor. The USCG Auxiliary and US Power Squadron perform free vessel safety inspections and conduct public courses in boating safety and seamanship. The NYS boat handling guide is available at nysparks.com/boats

Coast Guard Auxiliary The volunteer arm of the Coast Guard. 212-668-7990 cgaux.org

Foundation for Safe Boating & Marine Information. Resources to aid boaters. 718-645-1434 boatingandmarineinfo.org

Marine Safety International Maritime simulation center offering training for yacht and commercial mariners at the Marine Air Terminal at LaGuardia Airport. 718-565-4180 marinesafety.com

North River Power Squadron Serving the downtown Manhattan boating community since 1936. 212-217-2900 northriversquadron.org

Sea Scouts BSA Liberty Flotilla Marine branch of the Boy Scouts, teaches safe boating and seamanship. 212-242-1100 seascout.org

US Power Squadron District 4 The world's largest boating organization with chapters in each borough. 800-341-USPS usps-d4.org

Don Riepe

Charles F. "Chap" Chapman, Editor (1881-1976). Founder of the NY Power Squadron, the legendary editor of *Motor Boating & Sailing* from 1912 to 1958 authored "Piloting, Seamanship & Small Boat Handling," the bible of recreational boating. It was originally written as a training manual for the Naval Reserve in WWI. Chapman was founding father of the U.S. Power Squadron and a prime mover in the establishment of motor boat racing as a major sport. He also served as chairman of the American Power Boat Association (APBA) for 25 years.

Navigation

Early mariners relied on "dead reckoning" to figure out their position by charting course, speed, distance and time, as well as using landmarks. Celestial navigators determined geographical position by astronomical observation using a sextant to measure the altitude of the North Star, Polaris. Later sailors used latitude, the distance north or south of the Equator, and longitude, the distance east or west of the Prime Meridian (Greenwich, UK). Nautical miles are used on oceans and coastal waterways. Statute (land) miles are used on inland waterways. Aids to navigation are man-made landmarks, such as buoys, lighthouses and markers that are the road signs of the waterways. Red and green markers indicate the right and left sides of a channel. White markers are state regulatory signs. Nautical charts are maps that graphically depict water, including the water depths, shoreline, currents, shipwrecks, landmarks, bridge clearance and magnetic declination (difference between true north and magnetic north).

New York Harbor Charts

Charts are available on the NOAA website: chartmaker.ncd.noaa.gov. The USCG Local Notice to Mariners weekly chart updates are online at harborops.com and naven.uscg.gov.

12327	New York Harbor
12334	Upper Bay & Narrows
12335	Hudson & East Rivers
12339	East River: Tallman Island to Queensboro Bridge
12363	Western Long Island Sound
12341	Hudson River-Days Pt. to George Washington Bridge
12350	Jamaica Bay/Rockaway Inlet

Nautical Chart Suppliers

Nautical Chart Supply Co.
94 Edgewater, SI 718-876-8200
nauticalchartsupply.com

NY Nautical 40 Broadway
212-962-4522 newyorknautical.com

West Marine 12 W 37th St.
212-594-6065 westmarine.com

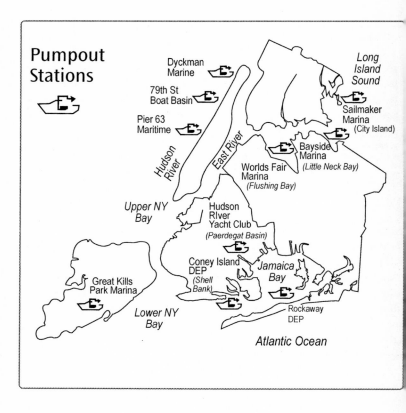

Pumpout Stations

Any boat with a marine head (toilet) should be equipped with a holding tank for wastewater. A pumpout station is a facility that receives waste out of holding tanks. Areas most susceptible to contamination from sewage discharge from boats are sheltered waters with low tidal flushing and shellfish beds. The Hudson River, from the Battery to the Troy Dam, is a NO DISCHARGE ZONE, which makes it illegal to discharge even treated sanitary wastes directly into the water. The NYS Dept. of Environmental Conservation provides grants to help marinas construct and maintain pumpouts. In some areas of the Hudson and Long Island Sound, vessels can hail pumpout boats. Marina and municipal pumpout facilities can be found by calling 800-CALL-FISH. The DEC provides a Pumpout Facilities directory online: cce.cornell.edu/seagrant/pumpouts/pumpouts-search.html.

Robert Fulton, Inventor (1765-1815) Fulton aspired to be an artist and traveled to Europe to pursue painting but soon abandoned art for engineering. After 20 years overseas, Fulton returned to America in 1806 with numerous patents, including a machine for spinning flax and an amphibious boat. Funded by statesman Robert Livingston Jr., Fulton traveled to New York and began construction of what became the first commercially successful power boat, the steamship *Clermont*. For years, Fulton and Livingston had a monopoly on ferry service in the Hudson River. Fulton was also responsible for significant improvements in submarine and torpedo design.

Pumpouts

Manhattan

Dyckman	Hudson	212-567-5120
79 St	Hudson	212-496-2105
Pier 63	Hudson	212-989-9090

Bronx

Sailmaker	LI Sound	718-885-2700

Brooklyn

Coney Island DEP Plant	Shell Bank	311
Hudson YC	Paerdegat	718-338-5256

Queens

Bayside	Little Neck Bay	718-767-7800
Rockaway DEP Plant	Jamaica Bay	311
World's Fair	Flushing Bay	718-478-0480

Staten Island

Great Kills	Great Kills	718-351-8476

New Jersey

Liberty Hrbr	Hudson	201-386-7500
Liberty Ldg	NY Harbor	201-985-8000
Lincoln Hrbr	Hudson	201-319-5100
Newport	Hudson	201-626-5550
Port Imperial	Hudson	201-902-8787

Boater Conservation

It is illegal to dispose of plastic refuse in ocean areas under U.S. control because plastics and polystyrene are deadly to marine life. Dumping garbage within 3 miles of shore is a felony punishable by imprisonment of up to six years and fines up to $250,000.

Boat Discharge: Report boats discharging oil or hazardous substances to USCG. 800-424-8802

Boat Disposal must comply with federal regulations, contact EPA. 212-637-3797 epa.gov/region02/water/oceans/wrecks.htm

Carbon Monoxide Warning: Any boat with the generator exhaust located in the transom and a swim platform can present a lethal hazard, as carbon monoxide gets trapped underneath the swim platform. Carbon Monoxide (CO) is an odorless, colorless, tasteless, and highly toxic gas produced by boat engines, generators, and stoves.

Boat/Jet Ski Rentals

Bayside Marina	28-05 Cross Is Pwy.	Qns	718-229-0097
Boatmax/Ysi-Yacht Scv Intl	150 City Island Ave	Bnx	718-885-3294
Capt. Mike's Marina	158-35 Cross Bay Blvd	Qns	718-641-1659
Jack's Bait & Tackle	551 City Island Ave	Bnx	718-885-2042
Rosenberg's Boat Livery	City Island	Bnx	718-885-1843
Smitty's Fishing Station	224 E. 9 Rd	Qns	718-945-2642
Staten Island Boat Sales	222 Mansion Ave	SI	718-984-7676

Boat Dealers

Argo Boat Mfg	25102 Rockaway Blvd	Qns	718-527-9870
Astro Boat Sales	5300 Kings Plaza	Bkn	718-253-6006
Bliss Marina	331 Hillside Ave	SI	718-317-0208
Boatmax	150 City Island Ave	Bnx	718-885-0250
Bridge Marine Supply	673 City Island Ave	Bnx	718-885-2302
Brooklyn Marine Corp	2835 Flatbush Ave	Bkn	718-531-1616
Captains Marine Mercury	202 Mansion Ave	SI	718-984-3346
Channel Marine Sales	64 W 20 Rd	Qns	718-318-2000
Golden Key Yacht Sales	445 Park Ave., 9th Fl	Man	212-644-1980
Staten Island Boat Sales	222 Mansion Ave	SI	718-984-7676
Surfside 3	Chelsea Piers	Man	212-366-SURF
Ultra Sports Center	City Island	Bnx	718-885-1500

Boat Towing Services

Eastchester Towing Co	Eastchester Bay	718-885-0889
Gateway Marine	Jamaica Bay	718-634-9754
SeaTow	Long Island Sound	718-885-0101
Tow BoatUSA	East River	718-885-3420
Vessel Assist Assn		800-399-1925

Motor & Power Boating Events

NY National Boat Show	discoverboating.com
Jacob Javits Center	Dec-Jan
NY Powerboat Poker Run (NPBA)	nationalpowerboat.com
Hudson River, Liberty Landing Marina	June
NY Super Boat Grand Prix	superboat.com
Hudson River, Battery to 42nd St.	September

Paddling & Rowing

❝I just love it when people ask, "But where do you paddle?" I immediately slip into deadpan mode, give them an ever so slight grin, and shrug: "Well, New York is an island!" Usually it takes a few seconds for the lights to come on, after which they screw up their face and reply: "Oh, that's right! But isn't the water dirty?"

That opens the flood gates and I deluge them with things like: "Well, ecologically speaking, the Hudson was one of the first rivers to go down, but it's also been one of the first rivers to come back up and, currently, the Hudson is alive and vital and home to 206 species of fish." Sometimes I'll go on about the 200 lb. Sturgeon that swim up the Hudson to spawn, or the Sea Horses, or the Blue Crabs that can be found as far north as Albany; but it's usually not necessary, as the ideas have already started to alter their perceptions of the waterway.

So besides the very obvious cardiovascular benefits, the adrenaline rush of wave jumping, and the Zen tranquility of gliding along with the ethereal skyline of New York perched on the horizon, kayaking in New York is a revelation, opening one to a natural world of wonder that's hidden just beyond the concrete and the steel and the glass.❞

Bob Huszar, kayaker & founder of NY Watertrail Assn. (recteck.com)

❝New York is home, and I think it's important to see the beauty where you are. I've learned to enjoy catching a string of small waves here just as much as catching the big ones in the Pacific. It is a beautiful harmony of man and nature: you feel a wave coming up behind you, take a few strokes, and use its energy, and you can go for miles, like the seagulls catch the updrafts of the wind, one after another. Once you push off into the ocean, you don't need to be more than a half mile from shore, and it can be hard to believe you're anywhere near New York City. Some days the water is so flat you can look down to see a perfect mirror image of the birds flying overhead as you paddle along. There are dolphins, sea turtles, porpoises and seals. And all this is within sight of the Manhattan skyline. Eventually you are back in traffic, and eventually someone has cut you off again, but somehow it doesn't matter as much as it did before. And you can't wait to get out there again.❞

Arthur Cholakis, Outrigger - Rockaway Beach, NY

Canoeing

Canoes are great for exploring the shallow creeks that meander through the marshes of Marine Park in Brooklyn, Pelham Bay Park in the Bronx, Alley Creek in Queens and Fresh Kill on Staten Island. The Sebago Canoe Club, established in 1933 on the banks of Paerdegat Basin, is one of the oldest continuously operating paddle clubs and the only club with access to Jamaica Bay. Most clubs have boats available for members to use. Free seasonal canoeing programs are offered by City Parks. Tours of the Bronx River are offered by The Point and Bronx River Alliance and the Gowanus Dredgers provide trips on the Gowanus Canal. Unlike traditional canoes, 45-foot-long, six-person Hawaiian-style outriggers are seafaring boats with a built-in stabilizer. The Liberty World Challenge outrigger canoe race is the largest competitive sporting event on local waters. Nearly 100 international teams participate in the 16-mile race around New York Harbor. Another unique canoe sport, dragon boat racing consists of teams of 20 paddlers who pull to the beat of a drum located at the bow of the 40-foot-long, teak wood canoe. The nation's largest dragon boat festival takes place on Meadow Lake in Flushing Meadows Corona Park and draws crews from around the country.

Liberty World Challenge

© Bridget Gorman

Canoe Clubs

Appalachian Mt. Club of NY/NJ
Canoe & kayak lessons and trips for members, and nonmembers with $15 guest card. Club boats are available for rent. 212-986-1430 amc-ny.org

Bronx River Alliance Monthly canoe trips on the Bronx River and the annual Bronx River Flotilla. 718-430-1846 bronxriver.org

DCH Dragons Competitive dragon boat racing crew based at Pier 1, World's Fair Marina and open to all levels of paddler. dchdragons.com

Gowanus Dredgers Canoe Club
Members pay fee for unlimited use of club canoes. Tours of the Gowanus Canal by reservation. 718-243-0849 waterfrontmuseum.org/dredgers

Metro Athletic Dragons
Dragon boat club based at World's Fair Marina. Youth program for high schoolers. 718-460-8545 madnyc.org

New York Outrigger Club
Pier 63 Maritime. Instruction, team paddling and racing in Hawaiian-style canoes and hosts the Liberty World Challenge. Free introductory paddle. 212-426-8866 newyorkoutrigger.org

NY Wall Street Dragons One of the oldest dragon boat crews in the city, works out at World's Fair Marina and has a juniors program. nywallstreet.org

Outward Bound Groups explore the inlets of Jamaica Bay in 10-person canoes as part of Adventure Program. 718-706-9900 nycoutwardbound.org

Rockaway Beach Outrigger Canoe Club Paddles and stores boats at Riis Park. 917-624-4537

Sebago Canoe Club Access to Jamaica Bay. Club canoes, instruction, storage, canoe fly fishing lessons, trips and youth programs. 718-241-3683 sebagocanoeclub.org

The Point CDC Guided canoe trips on the Bronx River, by appointment. 718-542-4139 thepoint.org

Urban Park Rangers Free guided trips, moonlight paddles and clinics at parks throughout the city. 311 or 866-NYC-HAWK nycparks.org

Women in Canoe Women's dragon boat club out of World's Fair Marina. Formed Breast Cancer Crew for women living with and survivors of breast cancer. 800-454-1909 x1043 womenincanoe.com

Xtreme NY Competitive dragon boat crew. xtremeny.com

Canoeing Sites

- Alley Pond Park
- Bronx River
- Fresh Creek & Richmond Creek
- Gowanus Canal
- Inwood Hill Park, Nature Center
- Jamaica Bay
- Orchard Beach Lagoon
- Marine Park, Salt Marsh Center
- Wm. T. Davis Wild life Refuge
- Wolfe's Pond Park

Kayaking

Kayakers share the water with commercial vessels, excursion boats, ferries and pleasure craft, all of which have right of way in one of the most heavily trafficked waterways in the country. Boats have to be carried to the water's edge and there are few places to launch, and fewer places to store small, hand launched boats. Visibility on the water is crucial and knowledge of local tides and currents is essential. The water is cold, there is chop and the currents are swift, reaching four knots.

Free public kayaking is available at locations along the Hudson River, including Pier 26, Pier 66A & Riverside Park South at 72nd Street. The walk-up program is administered by volunteers of the Downtown Boathouse, which provides sit-on-top kayaks every Saturday and Sunday from May 15th to October 15th. Once paddlers have managed the basics, free guided trips depart weekend mornings to either the Statue of Liberty or the Intrepid. Sebage Canoe Club hosts free kayaking days on Jamaica Bay. Local outfitters provide instruction and guided tours, starting at $40 an hour. For experienced paddlers, the essential kayaking trip is the circumnavigation of Manhattan Island ($200). The 28.5-mile trip takes 7-10 hours and should be timed to take advantage of tides.

Kayaking Clubs & Outfitters

Canarsie Adolescent Recreation Program (C.A.R.P.) Youth paddling on Jamaica Bay. 718-531-7930

Chelsea Piers Sports Center Paddle basics, tours, and private lessons on the Hudson River. 212-336-6068 chelseapiers.com

Columbia Univ. Kayak Club Open to current students and alumni only. columbia.edu/cu/kayak

Downtown Boathouse Pier 26 Hudson River Park. Walk-up kayaking, evening clinics, kayak polo, harbor trips and storage. 646-613-0375 downtownboathouse.org

Eastern Mountain Sports Retailer. 20 W 61st St. 212-397-4860 & 591 Broadway 212-966-8730.

East River Kayak Club 1155 Manhattan Ave. Brooklyn Members build mahogany kayaks and offer a youth kayak-building program. Public launch, dockside storage and new boathouse on Newtown Creek. 718-389-5277 eastriverkayak.org

Greenpoint Canoe & Kayak Brooklyn. Olympic flatwater training and youth programs. 718-349-6410

Hudson River Watertrail Assn. The group is building a "watertrail" on the Hudson River from Albany to NYC with launches every 7 miles. They publishes a detailed guide to the watertrail. hrwa.org

TIDES

Tide:	Vertical movement of a body of water due to gravitational interaction between Sun, Moon and Earth
Tidal Current:	Horizontal movement of a body of water
Tidal Day:	24h:50 min (Lunar Day)
Tidal Cycles:	6h:12.5m (high to low), 6h:12.5m(low to high), 12h:25m (high to high)
Tidal Range:	4 to 6 ft (The difference in height between high and low water)
Ebb Tide:	Outgoing water between high tide and following low tide
Flood Tide:	Incoming water between low tide and following high tide
Neap Tide:	Less than average tide occurring at 1st & 3rd moon quarters
Spring Tide:	Greater than average tide occurring at new and full moons

Inwood Canoe Club PO Box 94, Inwood Sta., NY 10034. Dyckman Marina, Hudson River. Open house each Sun. during summer. Paddling trips and storage. 212-463-7740

Manhattan Kayak Company Pier 63 All level of instruction and unique tours, including full moon paddles, paddle & pub and a popular sushi tour. Public launch & storage. 212-924-1788 manhattankayak.com

Metro Assn. of Sea Kayakers (M.A.S.K.) Instruction and paddling trips. seacanoe.org

NY Adventure Racing Association Hosts cross-training events that include kayaking. nyara.org

NY Kayak Co. Pier 40 HRP. Full service outfitter and folding kayak specialist. Classes and tours for all skill levels, limited storage and retail sales. 212-924-1327 nykayak.com

Sebago Canoe Club Jamaica Bay. Free public kayaking on Saturday mornings and Olympic flatwater sprint racing. Clinics, club boats, instruction, tours and storage. 718-241-3683 sebagocanoeclub.org

Touring Kayak Club of NY Established in 1927, clubhouse is located beachfront on City Island, with view and access to LI Sound. Clinics, storage, races and trips. 718-885-3193 tkcny.org

Urban Kayak Wants to establish free community kayaking at Harlem Piers on the Hudson River. 718-855-8539

Harbo & Samuelson, Rowers. On June 6, 1896 at 5:00 p.m., Norwegian immigrant fishermen, George Harbo (1869-1908) and Frank Samuelson (1865-1946) launched from The Battery and rowed across the Atlantic Ocean to Isles of Scilly in an 18-foot-long boat with a 5-foot beam, they crafted themselves and named *Fox*. The perilous 3,000 mile voyage took 55 days and set a world record that still stands today. They rowed an average distance of 56 miles a day and survived being capsized by a huge wave. The trip was in response to a newspaper challenge to win $10,000, and they had hoped the feat would bring fame and fortune, but had to return to fishing shortly after their success.

Rowing

On December 9, 1824, the first rowing competition in the U.S. took place in New York Harbor, when the New York team rowed the Whitehall *American Star* to victory against a British rowing team before a crowd of 50,000 spectators to win $1000 in prize money. John Magnus was the 14-year-old coxwain who steered the team to victory, and a year later he presented the sleek Brooklyn-built *American Star* as a gift from the city to the Marquis de Lafayette. The boat, still on display in La Grange, France, is the oldest Whitehall in existence. Whitehalls, named for the busy landing at the foot of Whitehall Street, were the workboats and water taxis of the harbor in the 1800s. Classic 25-foot-long, four-oared Whitehall gigs have been revived today in boat building and rowing programs throughout the city. The annual American Star Race commemorates the city's first rowing event and the sturdy Whitehalls of New York Harbor.

Rowing Programs

Brooklyn Sloop Club Youth rowing program. 718-941-9835

East River Apprenticeshop (ERA) Youth rowing program offers free public rows every Thurs. at Pier 26, Hudson River Park. 718-383-4388 erashop.com

East River C.R.E.W. (Community Recreation & Education on the Water) E 90th St. Pier, Harlem. Youth rowing. 212-417-3956 eastrivercrew.org

Team Rowing NYC Public rowing at piers 40 & 84, Red Hook, Brooklyn and Weehawken, NJ. Boat building, coxwain training, youth and adult rowing and races. 212-564-5412 floatingtheapple.org

New York Restoration Project Youth rowing and boat building programs. 212-333-2552 nyrp.org

Rowboat Rentals
- Central Park   212-517-2233
- Clove Lakes   718-390-8031
- Flushing Meadow   718-760-6562
- Prospect Park   718-282-7789

Sculling

The early history of rowing in the U.S. began on the Hudson and Harlem rivers. New York City is the birthplace of both the indoor rowing machine and the sliding seat, invented by John Babcock in 1870. The country's first women's crew launched on the Harlem in 1932. Sculls are the long oars used to propel the shell (boat) through the water. A racing shell is 60-foot-long, 22-inches wide for eight-oarsmen. Columbia's crew has drilled on the 2000 meter, 3-lane Harlem River course since 1872. During the spring race season, shuttles carry spectators from Columbia's Class of 1929 Boathouse to the regatta finish line at Sherman Creek. Races can be viewed from High Bridge Park. College crews also pull on the Orchard Beach Lagoons, which were first dredged in 1964 for Olympic flatwater trials. The first new public rowing boathouse in New York City in nearly 100 years is $10 million Peter J. Sharp Boathouse on the banks of the Harlem River at Swindler's Cove. It is part of an initiative by New York Restoration Project to open access to the waterfront and introduce youth to the Olympic sport of competitive rowing. NY Rowing Association will operate the boathouse and offer an adult learn to row course. A boathouse is also planned at Roberto Clemente State Park, a joint effort of the Empire State Rowing Association and several college crews.

Sculling Clubs & Programs

Empire State Rowing Assn. (ESRA) Roberto Clemente State Park. Boathouse, youth & adult rowing programs, regattas, erg tournaments and clinics. 718-894-7486 empirestaterowing.org

Growing with Rowing (ESRA) Roberto Clemente State Park W Tremont Ave. & Matthewson St. Free rowing indoor and outdoor rowing lessons for adults and children. 718-299-8750

NY Athletic Club Rowing Founded in 1868, the nationally competitive crew has a clubhouse at Travers Island and rows on Orchard Beach Lagoons. 914-738-9803 nyacrowing.net

New York Rowing Association (NYRA) A union of regional rowing groups originally formed in 1866 to promote club rowing. NYRA hosts several regional regattas. Administers 8-week Adult Learn to Row Program. 212-440-4483 nyrowing.org

Peter J. Sharp Boathouse Swindler's Cove, E Dyckman Rd. at 208th St. NYRP floating boathouse, which will be managed by the NYRA. Launch and storage. 212-258-2333 nyrp.org

Row NY Free rowing program for high school girls that combines rowing skills, academic tutoring and self-esteem building. 347-837-2783 rownewyork.org

College Crews

- Columbia University   212-854-CREW   columbia.edu/cu/crew
- Fordham University   718-817-5262   fordhamsoprts.com
- Manhattan College   800-MC2-XCEL   manhattan.edu/clubs/crew
- New York University   212-998-2019   nyu.edu/athletics/clubs/crew
- SUNY Maritime   718-409-7200   sunymaritime.edu/sports

Paddling and Rowing Events

Event	Type	Contact / Date
Achilles Kayak Marathon	**Kayaks**	
Disabled paddlers race around Manhattan Island		October
Aloha Memorial Ceremony	**Outriggers**	ny-aloha-memorial-ceremony.org
Hudson River Hawaiian lei tribute to 9/11		September
American Star Row	**Whitehall Gigs**	floatingtheapple.org 212-564-5412
NY Harbor Commemorates NYC's 1st rowing race		December
Boot Hill Cup Race	**Kayaks**	tkcny.org
Long Island Sound Kayak race around Hart Island		August
Bronx River Flotilla	**Kayaks/Canoes**	bronxriver.org 718-430-4665
Bronx River 7-mile, 3 hr paddle down the river		April
Great Hudson Paddle	**Kayaks/Canoes**	watertrail.hrwa.org
Hudson River 145-mile paddle from Troy to NYC		July
Hong Kong Dragon Boat Fest	**Dragon Boats**	hkdbf-ny.org 718-767-1776
Meadow Lake Flushing Meadows Park, Queens		June
Hook to Hook Row	**Rowboats**	eastrivercrew.org
Harlem/East Rivers Clemente Park to Horn's Hook		July, August
Liberty Int'l Dragon Boat Fest	**Dragon Boats**	libertydragonboat.org
Hudson River 79 St Boat Basin 2-day event		August
Liberty World Challenge	**Outriggers**	newyorkoutrigger.org.
NY Harbor 100 international teams compete		June
Metro Championship	**Sculls**	sunymaritime.edu/sports
Orchard Beach Lagoons NYC college crews compete		November
NYRA Championship Regatta	**Scull/Row**	nyrowing.org
Harlem River 1,000/2,000 meter races Jr. to Masters		June
NYRA Indoor Rowing	**Row/Ergs**	nyrowing.org
Roberto Clemente State Park		February
Sebago's All-Club Invit'l	**Kayaks/Canoes**	sebagocanoeclub.org 718-241-3683
Jamaica Bay International club races		August

Rooms with a View

Only a handful of hotels in the entire city have rooms that offer water views. That may be changing. A Comfort Inn is being built in Sheepshead Bay and there are plans for new hotels in Coney Island and at Brooklyn Bridge Park.

Manhattan

Bentley Hotel 500 E 62nd St. Rates $135-235. Converted steel and glass office building with rooftop eatery offers views of the East River and Queensboro Bridge. 888-66-HOTEL

Best Western Seaport Inn 33 Peck Slip. Rates: $169-$229. Set in a 19th-century building, rooms have terraces looking out on the Brooklyn Bridge, just one block from South Street Seaport. 212-766-6600 bestwestern.com/seaportinn

Embassy Suites NYC 102 North End Ave. Rates: $279. Suites command sweeping views of the Hudson River, Harbor and Statue of Liberty. 212-945-0100 embassynewyork.com

Liberty Inn 51 10th Ave. at 14th St. Rates: $54 for 3 hours. The former Strand Hotel has been a seedy haunt since 1908 with Hudson views from rooms on the west side. 212-741-2333

Ritz Carlton Hotel 2 West St. Battery Park Rates: $199-325. Views of the Statue of Liberty and Upper Harbor. Every harbor view room has a telescope. 800-241-3333

Bronx

Le Refuge Inn 620 City Island Ave. Rates: $96+. A French country inn housed in a restored 19th century sea captain's house. 718-885-2478 lerefugeinn.com

Brooklyn

Windjammer Motor Inn 3206 Emmons Ave. Rates: $95. On Sheepshead Bay. 718-891-6600

Queens

Surfside 3 Motel 164-33 Cross Bay Blvd. Rates: $126. Near transient dockage on Shellbank Basin in Howard Beach. 718-641-8400

Staten Island

Harbor House B&B 1 Hylan Blvd. Rates: $59. Overlooks New York Harbor near Alice Austin House and a kayak launch. 718-876-0056 nyharborhouse.com

Sailing

❝ Plan an urban cruise where the Half Moon once lingered among the canoes of the Lenape and Mohican. Sail and gunkhole in the urban archipelago, instead of just rushing through it. Cruise the Upper Bay and linger in the shallows around the Statue of Liberty and Ellis Islands, away from the commercial shipping. Let the tides sweep your vessel through the Hellgate and along the urban gorge between Roosevelt Island and Manhattan's towers. In the Lower Bay, below the Narrows and the arching Verrazano, drop a hook at Great Kills on Staten Island, or Jamaica Bay, or Sandy Hook. In every direction your gaze will be rewarded by the sights of a thriving port, abundant bird life, and unexpectedly tranquil harbors. **❞**

William Kornblum, author of *At Sea in the City*

The New York Yacht Club's 132 year hold on the America's Cup trophy is the longest winning streak in sporting history. The storied yachting fraternity has successfully defended 25 challenges. The club was founded in 1844 by John C. Stevens and eight friends aboard Steven's yacht *Gimcrack* while sailing in New York Harbor. In 1851, a group of club members won the 100 Guinea Cup defeating 15 British yachts with the schooner yacht *America* in the 53-mile race around Isle of Wight. The win was a triumph of American technological prowess. The syndicate that captured the trophy later assigned the Cup to the New York Yacht Club with a Deed of Gift, under condition that it be preserved as a perpetual Challenge Cup for friendly competition between foreign nations. The trophy was renamed America's Cup. The first challenge race took place in New York Harbor just off Staten Island on August 8, 1870, in which the schooner *Cambria* competed against 23 New York Yacht Club boats, the entire club fleet. The center-board schooner *Magic* won that first contest. In 1893, the series was moved to open seas off the New York coast and in 1930 the race was transferred to Newport, Rhode Island. America's Cup is the oldest trophy in sports and the most coveted award in yachting. The landmark Manhattan clubhouse of NYYC displays the carved eagle escutcheon of the yacht *America*. The next America's Cup contest will take place in 2007.

❝Sailing in the New York Harbor is a gift to be shared with everyone. We have two high and two low tides every day. These tides accentuate and reverse the direction of the Hudson River twice a day with a tidal variance of five knots. We also have major commercial traffic of large cruise ships, freighters, barges, tourist vessels, police boats, fire boats, coast guard boats and ships, numerous commuter vessels, and private owners afloat every day. So, you need to know what you are doing while out and about under sail. The weather is usually very good for afternoon and beautiful evening sails. And if not, because we live on an island, we follow the advice of Mark Twain who said, "If you don't like the weather, wait fifteen minutes. **❞**   T. K. Wallace, Manhattan Yacht Club

Learn to Sail

Basic Keelboat is the introductory course that familiarizes beginners with the sport of sailing. Most schools use standardized certification programs, either the American Sailing Association (ASA) or the U.S. Sailing Training System. Both programs offer basic keelboat and are recognized by national authorities, charter and insurance companies. After learning the basics, club membership is the best way to hone sailing skills and gain access to sailboats. Free youth sailing programs are offered by local

Don Riepe

Morris **"Rosie" Rosenfeld, Maritime Photographer** (1884-1968) One of America's foremost photographers of sailing yachts, began taking photographs in grammar school. In 1910 he opened a photography studio at first specializing in industrial and advertising photography. Rosie began covering the America's Cup race in the 1890s, served as Commodore of the Regatta Circuit Riders and helped found the Press Photographers Association in 1946. Mystic Seaport Museum holds a collection of his black and white prints.

yacht clubs. Experienced sailors have the opportunity to volunteer with community sailing programs and in the process gain free access to boats. Neophytes can learn to sail for free by volunteering aboard the Seaport's historic schooners or the *Clearwater* Hudson River sloop.

Sailing Clubs & Schools

Manhattan

Appalachian Mt. Club NY-NJ, Sailing Committee Sail instruction aboard day sailers and cruisers on the LI Sound. Programs open to non-members with $15 guest card. 212-986-1430 amc-ny.org

Downtown Boathouse Hudson River, Pier 26. Free 6-week sailing course for kids 11 to 13 years old. 212-675-2595 downtownboathouse.org

Columbia U Sailing LI Sound. Sails out of City Island Yacht Club. columbia.edu/cu/sailing

Knickerbocker Sailing Assn. Gay and lesbian sailing club. Fleet, cruising, racing and social activities. 212-613-5868 ksa-nyc.org

Manhattan Sailing Club (MYC) Hudson River at North Cove Yacht Harbor. Dues $990. Started in 1986, the club is credited with reviving the sport of sailing in NY Harbor. Operates a floating clubhouse, designed by Sparkman & Stephens, anchored near Ellis Island. Fleet of J/24s, clubhouse, cruising, regattas, social and youth programs. 212-786-3323 myc.org

   • **Blue Water Society** members of MYC who have completed significant ocean voyages.

Manhattan Sailing School Basic: $540. Sailing school of MYC. 212-786-0400 sailmanhattan.com

New York Yacht Club 37 W 44th St. Sails out of Newport, RI. Fleet, clubhouse, cruising, regattas, and social activities. 212-382-1000 nyyc.org

NYC Community Sailing Assn. Hudson River. Dues: $250. Basic: $325. Club sailing and hosts a frostbite series. Fleet, instruction, cruising and racing. 212-222-1405 sailny.org

NY Harbor Sailing Foundation Promotes amateur sailing in NY

Harbor. Organizes sailing events, regattas and the annual Sailor's Ball. 212-786-1743 nyharborsailing.com

North Cove Sailing School Hudson River at North Cove. Dues: $1000. Basic: $545. Fleet J/24s, charters, instruction, cruising and racing. 201-915-4398 sailnyc.com

Offshore Sailing School Hudson River. Basic: $795. National sailing school offering 3-hour to 3-day courses. 800-221-4326 chelseapiers. com/masailing.htm

Omega Teen Sailing Program North Cove. Free sailing lessons for 8th to 12th graders that reside below Canal Street. nyharborsailing.org

Project City Kids Manhattan Sailing's free youth sailing program administered through existing organizations. 212-945-7676

Sandbaggers A pair of replica sailboats docked at North Cove, the *Bull* and *Bear* were originally used in the 1800s to harvest oysters. They use the weight of sand bags to maintain an even keel. nyharborsailing.org

Sea Scout Ships Marine chapters of the Boy Scouts provide youth instruction and cruising throughout the city. 212-242-1100 seascouts.org

Pier 16 South Street Seaport East River. Free lessons for volunteer crew aboard historic sailing vessels. Also school and group sailing programs. 212-748-8600 southstseaport.org

• **Lettie G. Howard** Sail training and corporate programs aboard a traditional tall ship.

• **Pioneer** Educational sails for school groups includes: knot tying, navigation, and depth measurements. Volunteer opportunities to learn to sail and crew on public sailings.

• **Wavetree** Training in square rig sail handling for volunteers.

Bronx

City Island Yacht Club Eastchester Bay. Club has a long tradition in sail racing on Long Island Sound since 1904. Clubhouse, cruising, launch, marine facilities, non-boater memberships, racing, restaurant and social activities. 718-885-2487 cityislandyc.org

Harlem Yacht Club Eastchester Bay Originated in 1856 as a model yacht club on the Harlem River at 121st St. Dues: $800. Clubhouse, cruising, launching, marine facilities, moorings, racing, restaurant and social activities. 718-885-3078 hyc.org

Morris Yacht & Beach Club Eastchester Bay. Clubhouse on three-acre park and beach. Clubhouse, cruising, marina facilities, moorings, racing and social activities. 718-885-1596

NY Sailing Center & Yacht Club Long Island Sound. Sailing school on the storied waters off City Island for 35 years. Basic: $645, includes 2

half-day practice sails. Club fleet of Pearson 26, instruction, moorings and sailboat rentals. 718-885-0335 startsailing.com

Stuyvesant Yacht Club Eastchester Bay. 1890 club, named for an East River ferryboat, the *Gerard Stuyvesant* that served as their first clubhouse. Clubhouse, fleet, instruction, junior sailing program, launching, marine facilities, moorings, restaurant, social activities and transient moorings ($25/night). 718-885-3422 sailsyc.com

Brooklyn

Deep Creek Yacht Club Jamaica Bay. Dues: $15. Basic: $30. Open to any boater who uses Gateway Marina. Offers beginner sailing program in partnership with the National Park Service. 718-252-8761 deepcreekyachtclub.com

Leilani Charters Sheepshead Bay Private sailing instruction aboard 50-foot 1903 wooden yawl. 718-332-2717 classicyachtleilani.com

Miramar Yacht Club Sheepshead Bay. Clubhouse, club fleet of Ensigns, cruising, launch, marina facilities, racing, social activities and swimming pool. 718-769-3548 miramaryc.com

Sebago Canoe Club Jamaica Bay. Boating club for human-powered boaters has weekly Thurs. evening sails and canoe sailing. Clinics, club facilities, sunfish, cruising and storage. 718-241-3683 sebagocanoeclub.org

Sheepshead Bay Yacht Club Sheepshead Bay. Membership rolls are currently open. Clubhouse, cruising, docks, fleet, launching, racing, restaurant, social activities and swimming pool. 718-891-0991 sheepsheadbayyc.org

Queens

The American Small Craft Assn. (TASCA) Meadow Lake in Flushing Meadow Park. Dues: $40. Basic: $275. Comprehensive course with 7 on water sessions. Free advanced class and use of club boats. Instruction, fleet, cruising, racing and social events. 718-699-1951 sailtasca.org

Outward Bound Student & corporate crews embark on sailing expedition aboard 26-foot-long wooden Monomoy pulling boats to learn seamanship and teamwork. 718-706-9900 nycoutwardbound.org

Rockaway Point Yacht Club Jamaica Bay. Currently a 15-year wait for prospective new members. Beach, clubhouse, cruising, moorings, racing and social activities. 718-474-9001 rockawaypointyachtclub.com

Staten Island

Richmond County Yacht Club Great Kills Harbor. Frostbite race series and youth sail training. Clubhouse, cruising, social activities and youth instruction. 718-356-4120 rcyc.com

George Steers, Shipwright (1819-1856) Steers designed one the most influential yachts in sailing history, the 100-ft. long *America*. At the age of 18, Steers built a boat he named the *John Cox Stevens*. The gesture led Stevens, a wealthy yachtsman, to hire George to build *Gimcrack*, the boat upon which the New York Yacht Club was founded. The new club employed Steers to design a world-class racing yacht under unique conditions of payment. Steers would be paid the sum of $30,000, only if the vessel could beat all competitors in a series of trial races, if not they were to get nothing. It was built at William H. Brown's shipyard in Manhattan on the East River. In the end, Steers received $20,000 of the fee, because *America* was beaten in trials. In 1851, Steers' *America* sailed to victory in the 100 Guinea Cup, winning with an 18-minute lead over contenders, effectively announcing American technological superiority and revolutionizing yacht design.

Sailing Events

Around Long Island Regatta		alir.org
190-mi, Rockaway Pt around Montauk to Manhasset Bay		August
Eastchester Bay Yacht Racing Assn		ebyra..org
Year-round racing		
Lady Liberty Regatta	212-786-1743	nyharborsailing.com
Top women sailors compete in New York Harbor		September
Mayor's Cup Schooner Race		sailmanhattan.com
The oldest continuously held sailing race in the U.S.		September
NY/NJ Sail Expo		sailamerica.com
Sail boat show at Liberty Landing Marina		September
Stonewall Sails	212-613-5868	ksa-nyc.org
Gay-Pride Regatta in New York Harbor		June
World Regatta		nyharborsailing.com
Olympians from 30 countries compete in NY Harbor		June 2004

Scuba Diving

" Diving the waters in and around the New York Bight has always brought misconceptions from some and enjoyment for those willing to explore. I have been diving local waters for over 15 years now and it's my favorite place to dive. The history in this area has brought us many different shipwrecks dating back to the early 1800s to the present and let's not forget, man made reefs and wonderful jetties to dive as well. New York waters on the average offer 10 to 15 feet of visibility inshore. Offshore waters offer 20 to 50 feet of visibility, and we have been known to get 80 feet of visibility when the Gulf Stream visits each year.

Beach 8th St. Far Rockaway is by far one of our best shore dives with depths ranging from 15 feet of water to 50 feet in the deepest parts of the channel. There are over four different jetty systems to explore. The area serves local instructors for introductory Open Water Dives. For the more advanced diver, you can do drift dives to the "Atlantic Beach Bridge" and see the many different species of marine life that abound here. Remember to do drift diving while towing a dive flag. While exploring this site you will see lobster, flounder, fluke, bluefish, and some of the biggest stripped bass I have ever seen and these are just a few of the species that live in the area.

I have logged more than 50 dives on the Black Warrior shipwreck and was part of the recovery of her bow anchor as well as recovering many different artifacts like shoes, old bottles, knives and forks engraved with the ships name, portholes and I have also used her remains to spearfish some very large fish, lobsters also make there homes here. The Black Warrior is visited by many divers, beginner and advanced alike, exploring her for artifacts and to look at the marine life that abounds here. "

Louie Schreiner, NorthEastAquanauts.com

SCUBA: Self-Contained Underwater Breathing Apparatus	
Dive Season:	May - September
Bottom Temperature:	Summer 50F/10C ; Winter 40F/4.4C
Currents:	Variable
Visibility:	Low near shore; offshore up to 60 ft
Equipment:	Thick wetsuit, hood, boots, gloves Twin tanks, knife

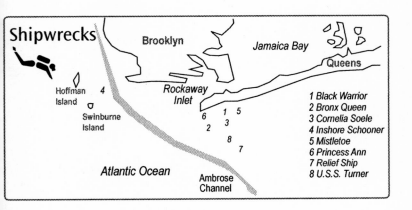

Shipwrecks

Brooklyn

Jamaica Bay

Queens

Hoffman Island 4

Rockaway Inlet

Swinburne Island

6 1 5
2 3

8
7

Atlantic Ocean

Ambrose Channel

1 Black Warrior
2 Bronx Queen
3 Cornelia Soele
4 Inshore Schooner
5 Mistletoe
6 Princess Ann
7 Relief Ship
8 U.S.S. Turner

Wrecks of NY Harbor

There are more wrecks per square mile in the waters surrounding New York Harbor than any place else on the planet. So many that the area is known as "Wreck Valley." About 100 wrecks are explored regularly by divers. Most were sent to the bottom by storms, sandbars and collisions. The wrecks form accidental reefs, which create fascinating underwater scenes and are a great place to catch lobster (aka "bugs"). Divers must be cautious of not to get entangled in fishing line at wreck sites, which are also popular fishing spots.

Wrecks of New York Harbor

Black Warrior

Built:	1852
Sank:	February 20, 1857
Location:	26951.8 43755.3

A 225-foot-long wooden side-wheel steamer that ran aground on the Rockaway sandbar and now sits in 35 feet of water off Jacob Riis Park.

Bronx Queen

Built:	1942
Sank:	December 2, 1989
Location:	26968.8 43735.1

A fishing party boat, converted from a WWII sub chaser, that foundered off Breezy Point where she now rests at a depth of 35 feet.

Cornelia Soule

Built:	unknown
Sank:	April 26, 1902
Location:	26954.7 43759.1

A 3-masted wooden-hulled schooner, wrecked one mile off Rockaway Point that lies in 25 feet.

Inshore Schooner

Built:	unknown
Sank:	circa 1860s
Location:	27030.1 43774.5

Unidentified wooden schooner that
sits in 30 feet of water southwest of
the Verrazano Bridge.

Mistletoe

Built:	1872
Sank:	October 5, 1924
Location:	26933.3 43747.6

A wooden paddle-wheel lighthouse
tender that was converted to a fishing
charter. It burned to the waterline and
sank. She is in 42 feet of water 4 miles
southwest of East Rockaway Inlet.

Princess Ann

Built:	1897
Sank:	February 6, 1920
Location:	26968.3 43758.1

Three-decked passenger liner that ran
aground on the Rockaway shoals and
now sits in 20 feet of water east of
Rockaway Point.

Relief Ship

Built:	1904
Sank:	1960
Location:	26903.5 43695.9

A relief lightship struck by a freighter
while on station. She lies in 100 feet of
water just off Ambrose Light.

USS Turner

Built:	1942
Sank:	January 3, 1944
Location:	26936.4 43725.6

A destroyer that sank in Ambrose
Channel in an explosion, which
resulted in 136 fatalities. The wreck
was dragged from shipping lanes and
is scattered in 50 feet of water 5 miles
off Debs Inlet.

Dive Clubs & Outfitters

The first step to scuba diving is
certification. Dive shops and clubs
conduct Open Water Certification
programs, which prepare the
beginner for dives of up to 60 feet.
Instruction starts with classroom
and pool sessions then progresses
to open water. Costs range from $99
to $299, plus an additional $200 for
the requisite four open water dives.
Only a mask, snorkel and fins are
needed, instructors provide all other
equipment. Certificates are issued by
several agencies, last a lifetime and
are recognized worldwide.

Manhattan

Adventure Scuba 331 E 70th St.
PADI dive center with an onsite pool.
Dive shop, gas fills, instruction, trips
and youth programs. 212-628-8896
adventurescubany.com

Aqua-Lung School of New York
443 W 50th St. Instruction, travel and
underwater photography.
212-582-2800 aqua-trax.com

Leisure Pro 42 W 8th St 3rd Flr.
Retailer. 212-645-1234 leisurepro.com

Mad Dog Expeditions Extreme
dive adventure travel and
technical training. 212-744-6763
maddogexpeditions.com

NYC Sea Gypsies Club of over 100
divers. Local dive trips and vacations.
seagypsies.org

Pan Aqua Diving 460 W 43rd St. Dive shop, gear rentals, gas fills and instruction. 212-736-3483.

Scuba Network 655 6th Ave. 212-243-2988 & 124 E 57th St. 212-750-9160. Retail chain, gear rental, instruction and local trips. scubanetwork.com

Sea Horse Divers 1416 2nd Ave. 212-517-2055 & 40-42 W 72nd St. 212-769-3483. Dive shop, gear rental, instruction, sales, local trips and vacations. seahorse-divers.com

Underwater Frontiers Scuba vacations, such as Yoga/Dive packages. 800-934-8399 underwaterfrontiers.com

Village Divers 125 E 4th St. Dive shop, rental, gas fills, instruction and local trips. 212-780-0879 villagedivers.com

Village Dive Club Gay/lesbian dive group. Instruction, local trips and dive vacations. 646-638-2826 villagediveclub.org

Bronx

Capt. Mike's Diving 530 City Is Ave. Gear rental, gas fills, instruction, night dives, local trips, salvage, vacations and youth programs. 718-885-1588 captainmikesdiving.com

Kips Bay Boys & Girls Club 1930 Randall Ave. Youth instruction. 718-893-8600 kipsbay.org

Brooklyn

Aqua-Trax Dive & Travel Services Dive instruction, scuba vacations, trips and underwater photography. 718-317-1150 aqua-trax.com

Atlantic Divers 501 Kings Hwy. Dive shop, instruction, local dive trips and travel. 718-376-5454 atlanticdiversny.com

Kings County Divers 2417 Ave. U. Club, gas fills, instruction, nitrox training, local dive trips and scuba vacations, social activities and youth programs. 718-648-4232 kcdivers.com

No Limitz 3179 Emmons Ave. Retailer and gas fills. 718-743-0054

Ocean Horizons Scuba 861 71st St. Dive shop, instruction, local trips and dive vacations. 718-833-0366 oceanhorizonscuba.com

Park Slope Scuba (aka Paradise Dive) 328 Flatbush Ave. Dive shop, instruction, local dive trips and scuba vacations. 718-230-0001 parkslopescuba.com

SCUBA Network 290 Atlantic Ave. Retail chain. 718-802-0700

SCUBA Network 200 6th St. Retail chain. Instruction, gear rental and local trips. 718-237-1919 scubanetwork.com

Stingray Divers 762 Grand St. Instruction, gas fills, gear rental, local trips and rebreather and tech training. 718-384-1280 stingraydivers.com

Urban Divers Conducts programs that promote awareness of the underwater environment.

718-802-9874 angelfire.com/ny4/
urbandivers

YMCA Scuba Dive instruction.
ymcascuba.org

Queens

Almost Paradise Dive Center
120 Beach 9th St. Shore dive center
with 200-foot beach off 20' deep
main channel. Parking, restrooms,
showers. 718-471-2400 scubaparadise.
com (Currently closed because the
property was sold to developers. Its
future is uncertain.)

Aquatic Voyagers Scuba Club
(AVSC) National Assn. of Black Scuba
Divers. Instruction, dive trips and
youth programs. avscdivers.org

NE Aquanauts 65-43 Parsons Blvd.
Guided wreck tours, instruction,
local trips salvage and underwater
photography. 718-380-4567
northeastaquanauts.com

Scuba World 35-44 Union St.
Flushing. Dive shop, instruction and
gas fills. 718-888-0245

Tsunami Surf & Dive Shop 192
Beach 92nd St. Gear rentals and youth
programs. 718-945-5223

Staten Island

Down Under Sports 88 Guyon Ave.
Dive shop, instruction and local trips.
718-980-7547 downundersports.com

Dive Boats

Dive boats offer regularly scheduled
wreck diving and packages include
full wet suit and tank, also gas fills,
training, wreck tours and overnight
trips. Charters run $70 for two trips.
Overnight packages (2 days diving &
stay onboard) are about $150.

Eastern Dive Boat Assn. edba.com
Organization of dive boat operators.

Jeanne II Capt. Reddan Pier 5,
Sheepshead Bay, Brooklyn.
718-332-9574 jeanne-ii.com

John Jack Capt. Zero. 718-979-7731
captainzero.com

Karen Tamaqua Marina, Brooklyn.
Capt. Hayes a former commander of
NYPD SCUBA team. 718-421-5547

My Marian Capt. DeMarigny.
Private charters only. 718-241-2218

Sea Hawk Little Neck. Capt. Persico
718-279-1345

Scuba Events

Beneath the Sea	beneaththesea.org
Consumer scuba & dive travel show	March
Underwater Cleanup	projectaware.org
Project AWARE/Almost Paradise & NE Aquanauts	September

Shore Greenways

Greenways are dedicated off-street paths designed for walkers and cyclists that often follow the shoreline or link to the water allowing users to safely enjoy the city seascape without having to travel on heavily trafficked streets. Ocean Parkway Greenway is the country's oldest. Opened in 1895, the roadside path connects Prospect Park and the beaches of Coney Island. It is a National Scenic Landmark that was designed by Frederick Olmstead and Calvert Vaux, the architects of Prospect and Central parks. Robert Moses incorporated greenways and esplanades in the construction of the city's circumferential parkway system over 50 years ago. Many are still in use or undergoing rehabilitation, including the Belt Parkway in Brooklyn and the Bronx River and Hutchinson River Parkway greenways in the Bronx. The Greenway Plan presented by the city in 1993 initiated development of an ambitious urban network of 350 miles of interlocking trails. To date, there are about 90 miles of car-free paths. A 32-mile route circumnavigates Manhattan using both on-street and scenic off-street paths. Greenways criss-cross the five boroughs affording new access to emerging waterfronts. Miles of greenway trace the shoreline of Lower New York Bay, Little Neck Bay, Jamaica Bay and Flushing Bay and boardwalks rim the Atlantic Coast of Brooklyn, Queens and Staten Island. Most of the East River crossings have paths providing links to the other boroughs, and cyclists can board the SI Ferry to pick up the Staten Island trails. Annual bike tours allow riders to travel routes otherwise closed to cyclists. The city's web of paths link to the 150-mile-long Hudson River Greenway that follows the historic river from Troy to Battery Park and connects to the East Coast Greenway, which will extend from Maine to Florida. Off-trail biking is banned in city parks and National Park Service facilities to protect vegetation and habitat. Only Wolfe's Pond Park offers eight miles of multi-use trails open to mountain bikers.

Greenway Groups

Brooklyn Waterfront Greenway
brooklyngreenway.org.

Hudson River Greenway
hudsongreenway.state.ny.us

Old Croton Aqueduct Trail
adk.nyc.org/Trails/

Don Riepe

Cycling & Walking Clubs

Century Road Club Largest racing club in the U.S. 212-222-8062 crca.net

Fast & Fabulous Gay/lesbian cycling club. Weekly rides. 212-567-7160 fastnfab.org

5 Boro Bike Club Day rides, road touring, repair clinics and social events. 212-932-2300 x115 5bbc.org

NYC Mountain Bikers Mountain biking. nycmb.org

NY Cycle Club Rides, road touring, repair clinics and social events. 212-828-5711 nycc.org

Shorewalkers Walking tours along the city's shore. 212-330-7686 shorewalkers.org

Staten Island Bicycle Assn. Meets Sat. 8:30 am at Miller Field. 718-948-2025 sibike.org

Time's Up Critical Mass ride the last Fri. of each month and Blue Tours of city waterfronts. 212-802-8222 times-up.org

Transportation Alternatives Advocacy group for greenways and alternative transportation. TA's website is the best resource to city biking and maps. 212-629-8080 transalt.org

Take a Walk NY Free urban adventure walks. 212-379-8339 walkny.org

Weekday Cyclists Meets every Tues. & Thurs. 10 am at Central Park's Loeb Boathouse. members.aol.com/trudyth

Shore Greenways

#	Greenway	Miles	Water Bodies	Endpoints
Manhattan				
1	**East River Esplanade**	12.5	East River	Wall to 37th St & 60th to 125th St
2	**Harlem River Espl.**	🚲1.5	Harlem River	E 125 St to E 145 St
3	**Harlem R Speedway**	2	Harlem River	E 155 St to Dyckman Rd
4	**Randall's Island Loop**	1	Harlem River	Wards Island Footbridge to Hell Gate Path
5	**Hudson River Gwy**	12	Hudson River	Battery Park to Dyckman Rd
6	**Roosevelt Isl. Loop**	3.5	East River	Perimeter path around island
Bronx				
7	**Bronx River Trailway**	3	Bronx River	E 233 St to Gun Hill Rd. 🚲2.5 Bronx Park to Soundview Park
8	**Hutchinson River**	🚲6	East River	Pelham Bay Park to Ferry Point Park
9	**Mosholu-Pelham**	14	Bronx River	Van Cortlandt to Pelham Bay Park
10	**Putnam RR Trail**	🚲1.5	Harlem River	Van Cortlandt Park to 225th St
11	**Soundview Gwy**	🚲	East Rivers	Soundview Park to Ferry Point Park
Brooklyn				
12	**Brooklyn Waterfront**	🚲18	East River	Newtown Creek to Erie Basin
13	**Coney Island Bdwlk**	3	Atlantic Ocean	Beach Season - Bikes allowed 5a-10a
14	**Ocean Pkwy Gwy**	6	Atlantic Ocean	Prospect Park to Coney Island Bdwlk
15	**Rockaway Gateway**	3	Jamaica Bay	Marine Park to Riis Park (Queens)
16	**Shore Pkwy Gwy**	6	NY Bay	Owl's Head Park to Bensonhurst Park
17	**Shore Pkwy Gwy**	9.5	Jamaica Bay	Sheepshead/Knapp St to Pennsylvania Ave
Queens				
18	**Cross Bay Blvd**	6	Jamaica Bay	Shore Pkwy Gwy to Rockaway Bdwlk
19	**Flushing Bay Promenade**	1.5	Flushing Bay	Harper St to LaGuardia Airport

Prepared with assistance from Transportation Alternatives.

Greenways

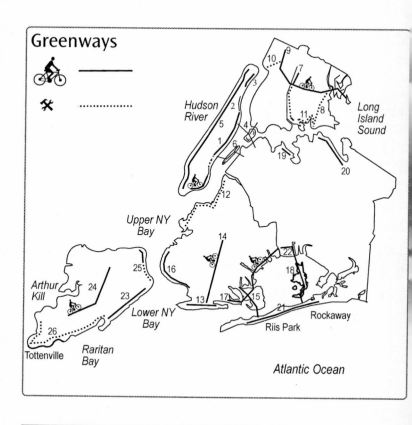

Hudson River

Long Island Sound

Upper NY Bay

Arthur Kill

Lower NY Bay

Tottenville

Raritan Bay

Riis Park

Rockaway

Atlantic Ocean

Bicycles Onboard

🚌 Buses: QBx1 Whitestone Bridge bus has bike rack. Bikes load at two locations Queens: Whitestone Expwy. Service Rd. at 20th Ave. Bronx: Hutchinson River Expwy Service Rd. at Lafayette Ave.

⛴ Ferries: Free or $1 charge.

🚆 Rail: Metro-North/LIRR permit required, $5 for lifetime. 212-532-4900

🚋 Roosevelt Island Tram 24/7

🚇 Subway & PATH trains: 24/7 Avoid rush hour.

Bicycle Racks & Rentals

City Racks Bike parking racks are placed for free by the city upon request. 212-442-7687

Bike Rentals Most local bike shops have hybrids available, rates vary.

River Bikes ($9/hr) Rental kiosks along the Hudson River Park at Piers 26 and 84. 212-967-5444

Cycling Events

Event	Website	Month
Balance Bar Adventure Sprint	balancebaradventure.com	
15-mi bike, 5-mi run, 1-mi kayak race @ Pelham Bay Park		May
Bike New York	bikenewyork.org	
42-mile 5 boro tour on car-free roads		May
Bike Summer NY	bikesummer.org	
Month long celebration of biking, with rides, events & more		June/July
Great Saunter	shorewalkers.org	
Walk around the rim of Manhattan Island		May
Hazon NY Jewish Environmental Bike Ride	hazon.org	
130 mi 2-day ride from E. Hampton to Manhattan		August
MS Bike Tour	msnyc.org	
30, 60 & 100 mi routes. Harlem R, Hudson R, GWB, Lincoln T, Rockland Cty		September
NYC Bicycle Show	nycswim.org	
Bike manufacturers, Equipment Companies and Local Clubs		May
NYC Century Bike Tour	transalt.org	
15, 35, 55,75,100 mi routes thru 5 boros.		September
NYC Cycling Championship	nycbikerace.com	
62.5 mi pro-cycling event.		August
Tour de Bronx	tourdebronx.org	
25, 40 mi routes Free event.		October
Tour de Cure	tour.diabetes.org	
		June

Surfing

"New York City has an intense surf culture brewing in its belly and is home to some of the most hardcore surfers in the world. Where else do surfers have to dodge speeding taxis, maneuver boards on subway cars to weave their way through the hoods of Brooklyn and Queens to finally emerge at Rockaway Beach, trudge through knee deep snow, and finally immerse themselves in 36° F water for a surf session. Rockaway has some of the best and most consistent lefthanders on the East Coast. A dredging super hollow freight train of a left that is very difficult to ride because of the currents and the amount of water it throws over itself. However, the locals here have found a way to tame this beast, and sometimes just being a spectator of the sport has people lined up along the boardwalk gawking as these surfers hurl themselves over the edge only feet away from the rocky outcrop of the jetties."

Alexander Karinsky, Gotham Surf Club

In 1912, the world's most famous surfer and Olympic swim champion, Duke Paoa Kahanamoku, demonstrated surf boarding on Beach 38 in Rockaway. Ever since, surfing has been a year-round tradition in Rockaway Beach. It is the only surfable break within city limits and is accessible by subway. The legal break during the summer season is Beach 88 through Beach 90. The most consistent surf arrives in the fall and winter, when surfers have their pick of beaches. The take-off zone is off the long rock jetty, where surfers sit on their boards waiting their turn at the waves. The jetty creates a hollow take off with left beach-break over wood pilings. The shallow water

causes plunging waves, called dumpers because the waves turn over on themselves. There are about 100 regulars who surf Rockaway Beach. The line-up includes short boarders, long boarders, knee boarders and belly boarders. A few are national competitors. On good days, areas of ridable surf are crowded. First surfer on the wave has right of way. The waves, currents, rocks and riptides make the jetties very dangerous for inexperienced surfers. Wet suits are required most of the year. The best time to surf is at high tide. The average wave size is three to five feet with longshore drift traveling east-west, parallel to the shore. During hurricane season, distant storms send swells exceeding ten feet. Surfing requires lots of practice. Beginners start out on longboards 8 to 10-foot in length, which provide a stable platform and catch waves easier and earlier. Surfers must learn to read wave condition, ocean currents, weather patterns and tides.

Windsurfers rig and launch on Dead Horse Bay at Plumb Beach. The shallow water is flat to moderately choppy, making it a great place for beginners. Kite-boarders also fly there. In 6 to 8 knot winds, a kite surfer can travel 20 mph piloted by a 20-meter foil kite, making up to 30-foot lifts on a 6-foot surfboard. Winds are best in spring and fall, and wind strength better in late afternoon. Sailboarders also launch from the bay side of Breezy Point.

Surf Sites

Breezy Point Surf Beach 219th St. Surfboarding at the remote western end of Rockaway Peninsula, which is part of Gateway National Recreation Area. No facilities. 🚌 Fishing area parking permit from Fort Tilden Ranger Station to access beach.

Plumb Beach (GNRA) nps.gov/gate. The place for kite boarding and windsurfing with beachside parking. 🚇 Subway D, Q to Sheepshead Bay, the parking lot is accessible from the eastbound Belt Pkwy. right after Exit 9 (Knapp St).

Rockaway Beach Beach 88-92 St. Surfboarding and bodyboarding.

Don Riepe

WAVES	Wave Crest:	Highest part of a wave
	Wave Trough:	Lowest part of a wave
	Wave Height:	Vertical distance between trough & crest
	Wavelength:	Horizontal distance between two crests
	Wave Period:	Time required for two wave crests to pass the same point
	Fetch:	Distance over which wind blows in the same direction
	Swell:	Waves that have moved past the wind that generated them

Beach 90 is the official surf, used during lifeguard hours in the summer season. Surfers venture to other beaches off-season. 🚇 Subway A to Far Rockaway, change to S shuttle at Broad Channel, then Beach 90th St.

Surfpark A year-round indoor surfing/bodyboarding facility planned as part of the Randall's Island Aquatic Complex, a 17-acre outdoor/indoor waterpark. Surfpark includes a wave pool that could produce wave face heights of 4 to 8 feet and ride lengths of 100 feet. If the proposed park is approved, it is scheduled to open 2005. surfparks.com ✗

Learn to Surf

Buddy Sammis Rockaway Beach $50/hr. lessons in basic technique, wave etiquette, wave conditions and boarding safety. 718-634-0802, after 8:30 p.m. or call Tsunami Shop.

Kevin McNamee-Adrian Foley Memorial Surf Camp Breezy Point. Surf camp for kids and adults. breezypointsurfcamp.org

Surf Clubs & Shops

Breezy Point Surf Shop 61 Pointe Breeze Ave. Boards and summer apparel. Open by request winter months. 718-634-8830 fortunecity.com/business/bren/509

Gotham Surf Club 139 Beach 97 St. Club competition and surf promo parties. gothamsurfclub.com

Hurricane Hopefuls 139 N 6th St. Williamsburg, Brooklyn. Chowder bar that doubles as a surf shop.

NY Bodyboarding Gallery, store and surf reports. nybodyboarding.com

New York Pipe Dreams 1623 York Ave. Surf board sales and repair. 212-535-7473 newyorkpipedreams.com

New York City Spongers
Bodyboarding club, photos, forum and reports. nycspongers.com

North East Kitesurfers (NEKS)
Online community & listserv. groups.yahoo.com/group/neks

Quiksilver Boardriders Club
109 -111 Spring St. 212-334-4500 & 3 Times Square. 212-840-8111 Surfwear, boards and gear. quiksilver.com

Rockaway Beach Surf Shop
177 Beach 116th St. Board sales, repair and surfwear. 718-474-9345

Surfrider Foundation of NYC
Surf advocacy and conservation organization working to protect the beaches and waves. surfrider.org/nyc

Tsunami Surf & Dive Shop
192 Beach 92 St. Only place in NYC to rent a surf board. Choice of long, short or boogie boards only $25 a day. Boards, gear rental and surfwear. 718-945-5223

Surf Reports

iwindsurf.com Plumb Beach conditions

Newyorksurf.com Local surf news, forecasts and forums. A to Far Rockaway, change to S shuttle at Broad Channel, then Beach 90th St.

Surfing Events

Duke Kahanamoku Surf Tournament	Tsunami Surf Shop	
Rockaway Beach 90 Street	October	
Kevin McNamee-Adrian Foley Memorial Surf Camp	breezypointsurfcamp.org	
Surf Camp in Breezy Point	July	
New York Surf Film Festival	surffilmfest.com	
Annual event to promote surf culture	November	
"NYC Wipeout" Cable Show	nycwipeout@hotmail.com	
TW/Cablevision Manhattan Channel 67 & Queens Public TV	Mon. 11:30p & 3p	

Swimming

❝Though organized swims around Manhattan have been held for years, only now are people beginning to discover the fantastic swimming possibilities for New York City waters. To walk from the skyscrapers to the river for a dip is a fantastic thrill that will revolutionize the way you (and whoever sees you) think about life here. The water is great. There are now various plans for beaches and floating pools (once a fixture of the lower Hudson) along Manhattan and parts of the harbor. Dive in. **❞**

Teddy Jefferson, co-founder of Swim the Apple

New York City hosts the world's longest swim marathon, the Manhattan Island Marathon. Organized in 1982, the demanding race attracts close to 100 swimmers, from world-class marathoners to local relay teams. It is among the top three marathons in the world and a qualifier for the English Channel swim. Swimmers have 9 hours to complete the 28.5 mile counter-clockwise, tide-assisted circuit around Manhattan, going up the East River, through the Harlem River to the northern tip of Manhattan, and down the Hudson River back to the Battery. The record is 5 hours 45 minutes and 25 seconds set in 1995 by Australian Shelly Taylor-Smith, who retired in 1998 following a record fifth victory in the marathon swim. A growing number of competitive open water events allow people to legally swim in the Hudson and East rivers. Otherwise, swimming is permitted only at approved beaches.

Coney Island is home to the famous Polar Bear Club, the country's oldest fraternity of cold water swimmers. The club's New Year's Day plunge into the frigid Atlantic is a 100 year old tradition. The Polar Bears host weekly swims during the winter months and the club is the official registrar of winter swimming nationwide. The average dip lasts about five minutes in water temperatures 40 degrees and below. For the less adventurous, City Parks maintains 53 outdoor pools and 10 indoor pools. The city's first public swimming pools were floating bathhouses anchored in the East and Hudson rivers. Launched in the late 1870s, the pools were closed by 1910 because of water pollution. A few were converted to freshwater pools, the last of these was off Riverside Park and closed in 1935. Today, since the rivers are cleaner there is renewed interest in building floating pools.

Bernarr MacFadden, Physical Trainer & Publisher (1868-1955) An advocate of winter bathing as a tonic for health and vitality, MacFadden founded the Coney Island Polar Bear Club in 1903. He arrived in New York City 9 years earlier with only $50 cash, changed his name from Bernard, set up shop as a personal fitness trainer and was the first person to become a millionaire in the alternative health field. His magazine, Physical Culture remained in publication for over 50 years and his publishing empire survives today under the name Sterling MacFadden. He also discovered Charles Atlas who mythologized the Coney Island beach bully to sell mail-order weight training courses.

Open Water Swimming

It is safe to swim in city waters except following heavy or sustained rains when the outflow from storm drains may carry sewage and advisories recommend waiting 12 hours before swimming.

Coney Island Polar Bear Club
The winterbathers meet Sun, Nov. to April at 1:00 p.m. on the boardwalk at Stillwell Ave. for weekly swims. 718-356-7741 winterbathers.com

Manhattan Island Foundation
Organizes competitive open water swims and raises funds for Learn to Swim program. 212-873-8311 swimnyc.org

Neptune Foundation Formed to build floating pools and has a prototype, which may be located in the East River off Greenpoint, Brooklyn summer 2004. 212-427-3514.

Swim the Apple NY Harbor swimming guerillas advocating access development of riverside beaches, swimming docks and floating pools. 212-721-8502 swimtheapple.org

Learn to Swim

Asphalt Green Swim camp. 212-369-8890 asphaltgreen.org

Learn to Swim Free swimming lessons conducted at Parks Dept. pools. 718-699-4219 nycgovparks.org

Lifeguard School There is a shortage of lifeguards in the city. City Parks is recruiting lifeguards from overseas in order to open beaches and pools. Free lifeguard training is open to anyone over 16 years old and guarantees a summer job. 212-830-7880 or 311 nycgovparks.org

Red Cross Lifeguard and water safety training. 212-787-1000 nyredcross.org

Swim-to-Safety Free city-wide drowning prevention program for kids with little or no swimming ability. 718-792-1800 x251 swim-to-safety.org

YMCA-NY Swim lessons at locations citywide. ymcanyc.org

YWCA-NY Program in adapted swimming for children with disabilities. 212-730-9750 ywcanyc.org

Gertrude Ederle, Swimmer (1906-2003) Known as "Trudy, Queen of the Seas," Gertrude Ederle grew up on the Upper West Side of Manhattan and gained international fame in 1926 by being the first woman to successfully swim across the English Channel. Only 19 years old, Ederle swam 35 miles in 14 hours, 39 minutes, bettering the men's record by nearly two hours. Upon her return to New York, Trudy was greeted with a ticker tape parade attended by two million people. Gertrude Ederle's swimming career began at age 14 when she swam past 51 international athletes to win a 3.5 mile race from Manhattan to Brighton Beach. From 1921 to 1925, Ederle set 29 U.S. and world records for swimming. In 1924, she won three Olympic medals and a year later, swam 21 miles from the Battery to Sandy Hook, NJ in 7 hours 11 minutes, breaking the men's record. Ederle eventually become deaf from her channel swim and in later life devoted herself to teaching aquatics to hearing-impaired children.

Swim Events

Cove to Cove Swim	nycswim.org	
.5 mi Battery Park City, South Cove to North Cove	July	
Great Hudson River Swim	nycswim.org	
2.8 mi 79th St Boat Basin to Pier 62 @ 23 St	August	
Ken Killian NYC Ocean Mile	metroswim.org	
1 mi Open water swim at Jacob Riis Park	July	
Little Red Lighthouse Swim	nycswim.org	
7.8 mi Pier 62 to Fort Washington Park	September	
Manhattan Island Marathon Swim	nycswim.org	
28.5 mi Manhattan circuit swim	June	
National One Hour Postal Championship	swimnem.org	
Timed swim in any 25-yard or longer pool	January	
NYC Triathlon	nyctri.com	
Swim Hudson River/Bike Hudson Park/Run Central Park	August	
Park to Park One Miler	nycswim.org	
1 mi South Cove to Pier 25	August	
Polar Bear New Years Day Swim	winterbathers.com	
Meet Coney Island Boardwalk at Stillwell Ave	January 1 @ 1 p.m.	
Race for the River	nycswim.org	
2.4 mi Pier 62 to North Cove Marina	July	

Underwater Archaeology

❝New York is incredibly rich in archaeological sites which tell us about life in the city's past. Archaeologists have explored how Native Americans lived in the area all the way back to the time people first arrived here 11,000 years ago, after the retreat of the last glacier at the end of the ice ages. Then, sea levels were much lower because so much of the earth's water was tied up in the ice sheets, and the shore was almost a hundred miles to the east of where it is today. They have also learned that when the sea had risen to its modern levels, about 4000 years ago, the area's new coastal location made it extremely rich in resources, first for the Indians who lived here and then for the Europeans and Africans who first arrived in the 1600s. These newcomers gradually turned New York's coast into one of the largest ports in the world. Archaeologists working on the old East River waterfront have discovered the 17th and 18th century technology the Europeans used to construct that port by adding landfill; they have uncovered many of the wharves and the hulls of a couple of ships that early engineers used to hold the fill in place. They have also studied the remains of a vessel that construction workers found in 1916 while they were digging a subway tunnel near the World Trade Center. Some think this was Adrian Block's ship, the *Tijger,* which burned in the Hudson in 1614. This is only one of hundreds of ships and boats that sank in the harbor. Archaeologists fantasize about excavating *HMS Hussar*, the British frigate that sank in 1780 while trying to scoot through Hells Gate from the East River to Long Island Sound to get away from George Washington's troops. The *Hussar* is reputed to have gone down with 50 American prisoners-of-war manacled in its hold as well as $100 million in gold bullion slated to pay the British Army.

But archaeologists are firm proponents of preservation. They would prefer that if a site - even the *Hussar* - is not threatened; it should be preserved and not excavated at all. Sites are like endangered species - once they are destroyed they are gone forever, and excavation is a form of destruction. New York's sites have suffered irrevocably from urban development and the construction of the highways that ring its shores. They also suffer from looters, who destroy them to find artifacts to sell or to add to their own collections. In so doing, the looters destroy the information that the sites contain about the city's past.❞

Diana diZerega Wall, Prof. of Anthropology at City College and co-author of *Unearthing Gotham: The Archaeology of New York City*

Archaeology is about revealing the mysteries of the past by studying the remains people left behind. Unlike sites on land, underwater sites capture a moment in time, because a sinking ship carries everything to the bottom. The Abandoned Shipwreck Act of 1987 transferred ownership of all abandoned shipwrecks found in submerged lands–usually within three nautical miles offshore–to the people of the State. The NYS Education Department is responsible for the protection and management of submerged educational and historical resources. By law, no collecting or excavating may occur on underwater sites without a permit. A Section 233 Permit provides for archeological and paleontological research on State lands. Recognizing the cultural value of shipwrecks, New York State establishes Submerged Heritage Preserves of sunken vessels that are of importance to maritime history. The preserves help protect artifacts for historians and provide public access for recreational scuba divers. Placing a mooring buoy at the site helps divers find the site, and protects it from accidental anchor damage. New York has established three preserves in upstate Lake George. Anyone can propose an underwater preserve site by submitting a letter describing the site in detail with supporting materials to: the Office of General Services, NYS Department of Conservation, NYS Education Department, Office of Parks and Historic Preservation and the NYS Department of State.

Access to and recovery of other shipwrecks within United States waters (except those owned by the military) outside of state territorial limits are still governed by admiralty (maritime) law. UNESCO has adopted an international convention on the protection of underwater cultural heritage sites aimed at protecting historic wrecks and artifacts in international waters from treasure hunters and looters.

Treasure Wreck The 114-foot-long *Hussar* has been the object of search, salvage and speculation since 1780 when it struck Pot Rock and sank in the Hell Gate carrying a purported treasure. The British made several attempts to locate the vessel. Thomas Jefferson financed an early search and Simon Lake, inventor of the submarine, surveyed the site in the 1930s. A current effort claims to have located not only the *Hussar,* but the *HMS Lexington* off the coast of Port Morris in the federal shipping lane. 718-824-9583 hmshussar.com

Water Street Wreck In 1982, during construction of a high-rise at 175 Water St. in Manhattan, the hull of an 18th century merchant ship was discovered in colonial era landfill. It was nicknamed the Ronson Ship after the developer who held up construction while archeologists excavated the wreck. The ship, a British merchant frigate, was too costly to remove and conserve. Only the bow was preserved and it is on display at the Maritime Museum in Newport News, Virginia.

City Archaeology

Archaeology Society of Staten Island Meets monthly at Wagner College. Lectures, research and archaeology tours. assi-aia.com

Brooklyn College Archeological Research Center Students and volunteers excavate NYC sites, including shore locations. depthome.brooklyn.cuny.edu/anthro/dept/digshome.htm

Geoarcheology Research Associates 5912 Spencer Ave. Riverdale, Bronx. Contractor has assessed the archeological potential of buried shorelines flanking the existing navigation channels in New York Harbor. 718-601-3861

Girls Dig It Archaeology program for girls 12-14 years old. 800-374-4475 nyu.edu/classes/mcgee/digit

Institute of Marine Archaeology Dedicated to field research and educational programs of historic and prehistoric sites. One of its goals is to involve the sport diving community with underwater cultural resource management.

NOAA Maritime Archaeology Program Protects and manages shipwrecks and underwater sites within 13 National Marine Sanctuaries. sanctuaries.noaa.gov

Nautical Research Guild International organization of nautical archeologists, historians, maritime artists and ship modelers. naut-res-guild.org

Navy Historical Center Underwater Archaeology Historic preservation of sunken Navy ship and aircraft wrecks. history.navy.mil/branches/nhcorg12.htm

NYS Archaeological Assn. Metro. Chapter Meets at Hunter College Room 710, 2nd Tuesday of the month. home.eznet.net/~spoon/nychap.html

NYS Museum (NYSED) Issues permits for underwater projects of a scientific or educational nature and administers applications for underwater preserves. nysm.nysed.gov

NY Unearthed 17 State St. NY's only museum devoted to archaeology, housing over two million artifacts. Visitors can watch conservators at work, see a 3D cross-section of an archeological site and take a simulated ride to a dig. 212-748-8628 southstreetseaport.org

Submerged Resource Center Unit of National Park Service National Maritime Initiative. Documents the location and condition of shipwrecks within units of the park system and issues permits to academics researching the wrecks. They recently investigated the steam ferryboat *Ellis Island*, which was built in 1904 and sank in its ferry slip at the island in 1968 after having served as transport for the U.S. Immigration Service for 50 years. data2.itc.nps.gov/submerged

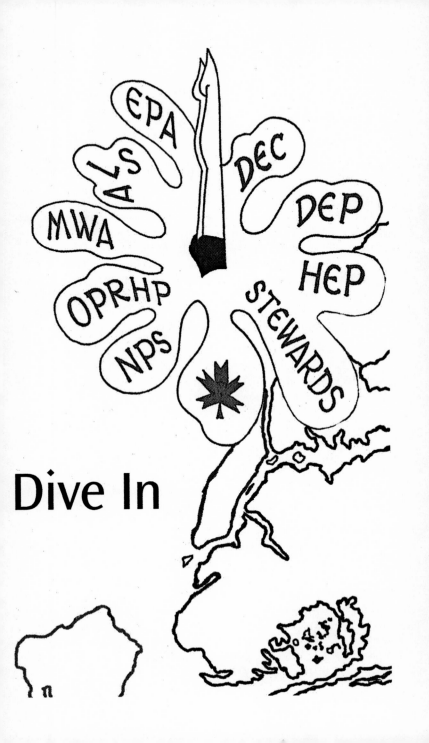

Natural Waterfront

❝New York City has 578 miles of waterfront. Over the past 200 years, almost all of New York City's waterfront has been altered either by fill, bulkhead, rip-rap, seawall, etc. to accommodate housing, shipping and industry. With the decline of the port over the past 50 years or so, many of these derelict sites of rotting piers and eroding bulkheads have been slowly reverting to a somewhat natural state and function as natural habitat. In recent years, federal agencies such as the Army Corps of Engineers have put forth plans to restore natural shorefront areas at several sites within the NYC harbor. They have also provided clean fill from inlet dredging to restore eroded beachfronts and dunes at coastal sites such as Breezy Point, Queens and Plumb Beach in Brooklyn, a popular windsurfing spot.

New York City's natural waterfront contains many great public beaches such as Riis Park and Rockaway Beach in Queens, South Beach in Staten Island, Coney Island and Manhattan Beach in Brooklyn and Orchard Beach in the Bronx. These are primarily natural areas although they are routinely "managed" by sand cleaning machines and visited by thousands of beach-goers during the summer season so that natural dunes are not allowed to develop. An exception is the a 2-mile long stretch of beach in Arverne, Queens which has a nicely developing vegetated primary dune and nesting Least terns and Piping Plovers. Another natural beachfront is the last mile of beach at Breezy Point, Queens which is protected by the National Park Service and has one of the state's largest colony of nesting Common Terns, Piping Plovers and Black Skimmers.

Other natural areas of waterfront include those managed by federal, state and city environmental agencies. The Jamaica Bay Wildlife Refuge, part of Gateway National Recreation Area, contains some of the best saltmarsh habitat in the city where thousands of shorebirds, waterfowl, horseshoe crabs and other intertidal marine life are protected. The New York City Department of Parks and Recreation manages wetland preserves such as Dubos Point in Arverne, Queens and the Saltmarsh Nature Center in Marine Park, Brooklyn. These areas are examples of waterfront sites that have eroded bulkheads and disturbed shorelines where *Spartina* marshes and sandy beaches are once again developing behind remnant pilings. The Alley Pond Environmental Center in Flushing, Queens has some nice trails to marsh overlooks and is actively restoring degraded upland and shoreline habitats. NYC Parks also manages natural area waterfront parks such as Pelham Bay Park in the Bronx and Inwood Park in Manhattan. As New York City is located along the Atlantic and Hudson flyways, these natural areas are important migratory, breeding and wintering sites for over 300 species of birds.

New York City has many islands which provide natural waterfront habitat for large colonies of wading birds such as egrets, herons and ibis. In the 1980's, New York City Audubon initiated a "Harbor Herons Project" whereby these sites have been put into protected status and are monitored each year to determine nesting bird productivity. In the Arthur Kill and Kill Van Kull in Staten Island there are three major sites: Shooter's Island, Prall's Island and Isle of Meadows. Adjacent to Staten Island are two sites managed by the National Park Service: Hoffman and Swinburne Islands. The North and South Brother Islands in the East River provide dense vegetated cover and habitat for nesting cormorants, night herons and other wading birds. Although the shorelines of most islands are either rip-rapped with huge boulders or contain debris fields of old piers, derelict boats, etc. they provide suitable nesting habitat within and are isolated enough for the birds to nest relatively undisturbed. Given a chance nature will heal itself and disturbed sites will slowly revert to functioning as natural habitat.

Much of the city's waterfront also contains miles of accessible parkland with recreational walkways and great views of the harbor, Hudson River and East River. Areas such as Bay Ridge, Battery Park, Riverside Park and Roosevelt Island contain access for people to walk along the water's edge and have a great view of the harbor or Hudson River. While technically not natural, those shorelines that are rip-rapped simulate a rocky coastal shoreline where seaweeds, barnacles and other marine organisms can attach and thrive. There are also some plans (or ideas) for possibly "softening" the seawall effect along the East River by creating a terraced edge that could be planted with seaside vegetation. While they are still much pressure for commercial development along the waterfront, there is a growing grassroots movement to protect and restore natural areas and provide public access to the shoreline. The natural waterfront is one of the great benefits of living in New York City. ❯❯

By Don Riepe, Jamaica Bay Guardian
and Director of the NY Chapter
of the American Littoral Society

NY/NJ Harbor Estuary

The New York – New Jersey Harbor Estuary is one of the city's great natural resources. It is where freshwater from the Hudson River mixes with seawater from the Atlantic Ocean within the sheltered bays of New York Harbor. Here, tidal activity blends a nutrient rich soup that creates one of the most productive environments on earth. The estuary is home to a whole host of fish, shellfish, birds, plant species and other wildlife. The core of the estuary encompasses the waters from the harbor entrance between Rockaway Point and Sandy Hook, NJ, up the Hudson River to the Piermont Marsh near the Tappan Zee Bridge. It covers 770 miles of shore, 534.5 miles within city limits. Only about 25% of the city's original wetlands still exist, scattered in every borough. These are important migratory bird breeding and foraging areas. Wetlands are economically valuable because they absorb stormwater, trap pollutants, and buffer the city from flooding and storms. Deemed an "Estuary of National Significance" in 1988, the EPA created the NY/NJ Harbor Estuary Program to protect and restore the natural resources of the estuarine environment. It is one of 28 such estuary programs nationwide. New Yorker's are rediscovering the estuary thanks to improvements in water quality, which are chiefly due to the federal Clean Water Act enacted in the 1970s with the goal of reducing pollutants from factories and waste treatment plants (point sources). Unfortunately, the effects of past pollution lives on and the health of the estuarine system is threatened by nonpoint sources of pollution that include combined sewer overflow and uncontrolled stormwater runoff. When it rains, the stormwater carries street litter, fertilizer, spilled oil, and other harmful substances to storm drains, it combines with sewage and flows directly into the surrounding waters. Stormwater runoff is the primary cause of pollution of New York waters.

Actions that Help to Keep the Waterways Clean

Don't litter. Keep litter and other debris off streets and out of storm drains.

Use a broom instead of a hose to clean sidewalks so that trash doesn't wind up in storm drains.

Pick up pet waste or it will go into the water and contaminate fish and shellfish.

Never pour chemicals down sinks or toilets. Use non-toxic household products and cleaners.

Recycle used motor oil, antifreeze and car/boat batteries.

Limit use of lawn fertilizers and pesticides.

Get involved in coastal cleanups, water monitoring, restoration and other activities.

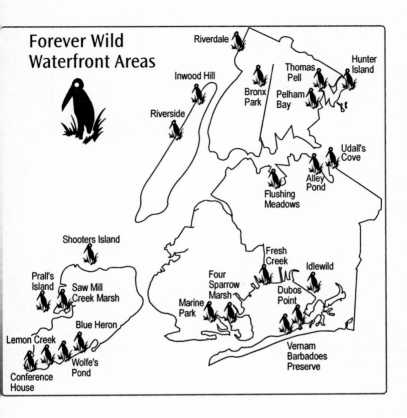

Forever Wild Waterfront Areas

Riverdale
Inwood Hill
Riverside
Thomas Pell
Hunter Island
Bronx Park
Pelham Bay
Udall's Cove
Alley Pond
Flushing Meadows
Shooters Island
Fresh Creek
Idlewild
Prall's Island
Four Sparrow Marsh
Saw Mill Creek Marsh
Dubos Point
Marine Park
Blue Heron
Lemon Creek
Wolfe's Pond
Conference House
Vernam Barbadoes Preserve

Ecologically Sensitive Areas

"Forever Wild" 51 natural preserves have been designated Forever Wild sites within 36 city parks to protect ecologically valuable lands, critical habitats and natural areas from degradation. The sites will be forever kept as wild lands.

Jamaica Bay One of the largest natural ecosystems and the most diverse wetland in the estuary, the bay is losing marshland at a rate of 40 acres a year and scientists warn, unless something is done, it could disappear in 20 years.

Significant Coastal Fish & Wildlife Habitats NYS has designated 15 sites of ecological importance, including: lower Hudson River, North and South Brother islands, Pelham Bay Park wetlands, 5 areas within the Harbor Heron Complex and Lemon Creek on Staten Island, Udall's Cove, Little Neck Bay, Alley Pond Park, and Breezy Point in Queens, and Jamaica Bay straddling Brooklyn and Queens.

Marine Education

Beach Channel High School
Rockaway Park. Marine science
and oceanography. 718-945-6900
beachchannel.net

Coastal Ecosystem Learning Ctr.
New York Aquarium. Program to
protect marine natural resources.
718-265-3400 coastalamerican.gov

Habitat Ecology Learning Program
(HELP) Bronx Zoo. Teacher training
for grades 4-6 that explores wildlife
habitats. 718-220-5131 bronxzoo.com

Junior Oceanographer Program
NY Aquarium. Learn about marine
animals while exploring the beach.
718-265-3448

The Natural Classroom Urban Park
Rangers. Ecology programs, including
aquatic ecosystems, offered at City
Parks in each borough. 212-360-2774
nycparks.org

NY/NJ Harbor Estuary Program
(HEP) Free comprehensive guide,
"Exploring Estuary Education: A
Teachers' Guide to Lessons and Field
Trips in the Harbor Estuary Region."
212-637-3816 harborestuary.org

Sea Partners Campaign USCG
Outreach program that focuses on
maritime pollution issues. uscg.mil/
hq/g-m/nmc/introsp.htm#what

**Sportfishing & Aquatic Resources
Education Program (SAREP)**
Cornell Coop Extension. Aquatic
ecology and conservation education
program in partnership with youth-
serving organizations. 718-328-4800
cce.cornell.edu/sarepnyc

Trout in the Classroom Theodore
Gordon Flyfishers. Conservation,
stewardship and science through the
rearing of Brown Trout. tgf.org

**Urban Waters Environmental
Education Program** South St
Seaport Museum. Youth program
covering the impacts of pollution
on the harbor. 212-748-8600
southstseaport.org

WET in the City Educational
program centered on water resources
and environmental stewardship.
wetcity.org

Time Required for Waste to Dissolve at Sea

Paper:	2-4 week
Cotton Cloth:	1-5 month
Painted Wood:	13 years
Tin Can:	100 years
Aluminium Can:	200-500 years
Plastic bottle:	450 years
Monofiliment Fishing Line:	600 years

Shore Nature Centers

Explore the city's natural shores, riparian habitats and marine ecology at waterside centers located in city, state and national parks located in every borough. Nature and environmental centers offer marine science programs for the general public, individuals, schools and groups.

Manhattan

Inwood Hill Park Urban Ecology Center Hudson& Harlem Rivers W 218th St. & Seaman Ave. 212-304-2365. Located on the last 12 acres of salt marsh in Manhattan. Environmental education, field trips, school programs and urban park ranger activities. 🚍 Subway A to 207th St; 1 to 215th St.

Stuyvesant Cove Environmental Learning Center East River E 22nd St. 718-784-1444 cecenter.org/stuycove.php. A "green" building that employs solar and geothermal energy and will be heated and cooled by river water. Environmental education, exhibits, river ecology and school programs. 🚍 Subway 6 to 23rd St. ✗

The River Project Hudson River Pier 26, 212-233-3030 riverproject.org. Marine biology field station offering hands-on study of the Hudson ecosystem. Exhibits, river ecology and school programs. 🚍 Subway 1, 9 to Franklin St. west to river.

Bronx

Orchard Beach Nature Center Pelham Bay Park 718-885-3466. Teaches about life on the beach. Environmental education, exhibits, field trips and urban park ranger activities. 🚍 Subway 6 to Pelham Bay Park.

Pelham Bay Nature Center Pelham Bay Park Wilkinson Ave. and Bruckner Blvd. 718-885-3467. 660 acres of saltwater marsh, 13 miles of shoreline and acres of forest. Environmental education, exhibits, field trips, school programs and urban park ranger activities. 🚍 Subway 6 to Pelham Bay Park.

Brooklyn

Dead Horse Bay Ecology Village GNRA Floyd Bennett Field, Bldg. 70 718-338-4306 nps.gov/gate. Trails along Rockaway Inlet through the inter-tidal area contain many different species of marine and plant life. Camping is limited to school and scout groups on a reservation basis. Camping, environmental education, field trips and school programs. 🚍 Subway 2, 5 to Nostrand & Flatbush Ave. to Q35 Green Bus to Floyd Bennett Field.

Gateway Environmental Study Center GNRA Bldg. 272, Floyd Bennett Field 718-252-7307. Outdoor classroom operated by the NYC Board of Education. Camping, environmental education, field trips

and teacher leadership programs.
📷 Subway 2, 5 to Nostrand and
Flatbush Ave. then Q35 Green Bus
Line to Floyd Bennett Field.

Salt Marsh Nature Center
Gerritsen Creek 2880 Flatbush Ave.
718-421-2021. 5 miles of shoreline,
restored upland meadows and tidal
flats. Arts & cultural programs,
environmental education, exhibits,
field trips, nature tours, school
programs and urban park ranger
activities. 📷 Subway 2, 5 to Flatbush
Ave. (last stop) transfer to B3
westbound to E 33rd & Ave. U.

Queens

Alley Pond Nature Center
Alley Creek 228-06 Northern Blvd.
718-217-6034 alleypond.com. A
natural habitat of woodlands,
meadows and salt marshes. Camping,
environmental education, field trips,
nature tours, school programs and
urban park ranger activities.
📷 Subway 7 to Main St. transfer to
Q12 Bus.

Jamaica Bay Institute GNRA
Floyd Bennett Field, Bldg. 69
718-482-0122. Research and
education on the natural and
cultural heritage of Jamaica Bay.
📷 Subway 2, 5 to Nostrand &
Flatbush Ave. to Q35 Green Bus to
Floyd Bennett Field. ✖

Jamaica Bay Wildlife Refuge GNRA
Jamaica Bay Crossbay Blvd. Broad
Channel. 718-318-4340. One of the

northeast's largest bird sanctuaries,
containing trails around 9,000 acres
of waterways and two freshwater
ponds. Environmental educational,
programs, exhibits, field trips and
school programs.
📷 Subway A, S to Broadchannel.

Staten Island

Blue Heron Park & Nature Center
222 Poillon Ave.. 718-967-3542
preserve2.org/blueheron. Houses
a nature library and handicap
accessible trails that surround
wetland ponds, swamps and streams
that drain into the Raritan Bay.
Environmental education, field trips,
nature tours, school programs and
urban ranger activities. 📷 SI Ferry;
S78 Bus to Poillon Ave.

Clay Pits Pond Interpretive Center
83 Nielson Ave. 718-967-
1976. Trails pass spring-fed streams,
bogs and ponds. Environmental
education, field trips, nature tours,
school programs and urban ranger
activities. 📷 SI Ferry; Bus S74 to
Sharrots Rd.

Greenbelt Environmental Center
High Rock Park, 200 Nevada Ave.
718-667-7475 sigreenbelt.org. Hiking
trails through the 2,800 acre Staten
Island Greenbelt, containing glacial
ponds, wetlands, forests, meadows
and streams. Environmental
education, field trips, nature tours,
school programs and urban ranger
activities. 📷 SI Ferry; Bus S74 to
Rockland Ave. & Richmond Rd.

Public Waterfront

The waterfront is public land. Everyone has the right to walk on the beach, fish from the shore and navigate the waters. The entitlement to access the coast is known as the Public Trust Doctrine. It has its roots in Roman civil law codified by Emperor Justinian in 530 AD, which states that running water, the sea, and the shores of the sea are common to all mankind. The concept that no individual can own the waters and submerged lands came to be recognized as property held by the State in trust for the people. The doctrine applies to all water influenced by the ocean's tide and includes the beaches up to the mean high water mark. Historically, the waterfront benefits held in trust were those crucial for commerce and navigation. New York's working waterfront often cut communities off from the water. The westward shift in port geography, the migration of manufacturing industry from the water's edge and improvements in water quality over the past half century have sparked new public use priorities. Plans are underway to restore wetland habitat in abandoned waterside lots and improve physical access to coastal recreation, as well as open sightlines from which to view the shore. Piers and warehouses that fell into disrepair after WWII are being transformed to shorefront parks that will link to a city-wide network of greenways. Local citizens are taking responsibility for the city's limited coastal resources in the form of community-minded stewardship. Strategies for future development of the waterfront envision balancing the need for port expansion, opening public access and protecting natural resources by engaging citizen stakeholders in the planning process.

New York City Shoreline
534.5 actual miles of shoreline
146 miles of navigable waters
Every resident lives within 5 miles of the waterfront
40% of the city shoreline is publicly owned
10,000 acres of waterfront parks
3,000 acres of waterfront land are vacant

Stewards

The public nature of coastal resources is the underlying principle of stewardship of its use. The word stems from the medieval steward who managed the property of others. Private stewardship activities protect and preserve the coastal environment, promote a healthy estuary and help to rescue neglected and ecologically sensitive lands.

Citywide

American Conservation Assn.	212-649-5822	
Appalachian Mountain Club	212-986-1430	amc-ny.org
City Parks Foundation	212-360-2744	cityparksfoundation.org
Coalition for the Bight	212-431-9676	
Coalition on Environment & Jewish Life	212-684-6950	coejl.org
Coastal Conservation Assn of NY		ccany.org
Council on the Environment of NYC	212-788-7932	cenyc.org
Environmental Action Coalition	212-825-3367	eacnyc.org
Environ Education Advisory Council		eeac-ny.org
Environmental Defense	212-505-2100	
Friends of Clearwater	212-228-1850	clearwater.org
Friends of Fishes	212-289-3605	friendsoffishes.org
Going Coastal, Inc.	718-243-9056	goingcoastal.org
Green Eagle Isstitute		greeneagle.org
Green Map System	212-674-1631	greenmap.org
Municipal Art Society	212-935-3960	mas.org
Metropolitan Waterfront Alliance	800-364-9943	waterwire.net
Nature Conservancy	212-997-1880	tnc.org
Natural Resources Defense Council	800-200-8858	nrdc.org
Neighborhood Open Space Coalition	212-352-9330	treebranch.com/nosc
NYC Environ Justice Alliance	212-239-8882	nyceja.org
NYC OASIS	212-264-8000	oasisnyc.net
New Yorkers for Parks	212-838-9410	parkscouncil.org
NY League of Conservation Voters	212-361-6350	nylcv.org
NY-NJ Baykeeper	732-291-0176	nynjbaykeeper.org
NY Water Environment Assn		nywea.org

Stewards

Partnership for Parks	212-360-1310	itsmypark.org
Project for Public Spaces	212-620-5660	pps.org
Regional Planning Assn	212-980-8530	rpa.org
Trust for Public Land	212-674-1631	tpl.org
Transportation Alternatives	212-629-8080	transalt.org

Manhattan

Alliance for Downtown NY	212-566-6700	downtownny.com
Battery Park City Authority*	212-417-2000	batteryparkcity.org
Battery Park City Parks Conservancy	212-267-9700	bpcparks.org
Carl Shurz Park Assn	212-570-4751	
Chelsea Waterside Park Assn	212-924-5433	
Conservancy for Battery Park	212-344-3491	thebattery.org
East River C.R.E.W	212-427-3956	eastrivercrew.org
East River Environmental Coalition	212-606-4040	
Federation to Preserve G.V. Waterfront		villagewaterfront.org
Floating the Apple	212-564-5412	floatingtheapple.org
Friends of Fort Tryon Park	212-408-0230	hhoc.org/ffc
Friends of Harlem River Spwy Espl	212-942-6910	
Friends of Highbridge Park	212-645-0576	
Friends of Hudson River Park	212-489-7474	fohrp.org
Friends of Inwood Hill Park	212-298-9149	
Friends of Pier 84	212-757-1600	hellskitchen.net
Friends of Statue of Liberty & Ellis Island.	212-968-1886	
Gracie Mansion Conservancy	212-570-0985	ci.nyc.ny.us
Governors Island Alliance	212-253-2727	rpa.org
Harlem Environmental Impact Project	212-749-5298	
Harlem River Conservancy	914-636-2360	
Hudson River Foundation	212 924-8290	hudsonriver.org
Hudson River Park Trust*	212-791-2530	hudsonriverpark.org

Stewards

Liberty-Ellis Island Foundation	212-561-4517	ellisisland.org
Lower East Side Ecology Center	212-420-0621	
NYC Audubon Society	212-691-7483	nycas.org
NY Restoration Project	212-333-2552	nyrp.org
North River Cmty Environ. Review Brd	212-491-3590	
Randall's Island Sports Foundation*	212-830-7722	risf.org
The River Project	212-431-5787	riverproject.org
Riverside Park Fund	212-870-3070	riversideparkfund.org
Roosevelt Island Operating Corp.*	212-832-4540	rioc.com
Seaport Community Coalition	212-267-5316	
79th St Boat Basin Flora & Fauna Society		nysite.com/nature/index.htm
Shorewalkers	212-663-2167	shorewalkers.org
Sierra Club of NY	212-473-7841	
Stuyvesant Cove Park Assn	212-673-7507	stuyvesantcove.org
Times Up!	212-802-8222	times-up.org
Trout Unlimited (NYC Chapter)	212-677-7171	nyctu.org
Turtle Bay Association	212-253-2727	turtlebay-nyc.org
Urban Trail Club	718-274-0407	nynjtc.org/clubpages
West Harlem Environmental Action	212-961-1000	weact.org
Working Waterfront Assn	212-505-0694	workingwaterfront.org
Van Alen Institute	212-924-7000	vanalen.org
YouthCan	212-769-5039	youthcanworld.org

Bronx

Bronx Council for Environ Quality	718-885-3074	bceq.com
Bronx Green Up	718-817-8026	nybg.org/bgu
Bronx Environmental Action Coalition		eacnyc.org
Bronx River Alliance	718-430-4665	bronxriver.org
Cherry Tree Assn	718-741-2522	
City Island Sound Sloop Club	718-885-1503	Lengerl@aol.com
Friends of Pelham Bay Park	718-885-2390	nrdc.org
Friends of Spuyten Duyvil	718-548-5479	SpuytenDuy@aol.com
Gaia Institute	718-885-1906	gaia-inst.org
Riverdale Nature Preservancy	718-884-5903	

Stewards

Rocking the Boat	718-466-5799	rockingtheboat.org
Sustainable South Bronx	718-617-4668	wajoracarter@SSBx.org
The Point CDC	718-542-4139	the point.org
Wave Hill	718-549-3200	wavehill.com
Wildlife Conservation Society	718-220-5100	wcs.org
Youth Ministries for Peace & Justice	718.328.5622	riverteam@ympj.org

Brooklyn

Bay Improvement Group	718-646-9206	members.aol.com/bayimpgrp
Brighton Beach Neighborhood Assn	718-891-0800	brightonbeach.com
Brooklyn Bridge Park Coalition*	718-802-0603	bbpc.net
Brooklyn Sloop Club	718-941-9835	
Brooklyn Ctr for the Urban Environ	718-788-8500	bcue.org
Brkyln Waterfront Greenway Task Force	718-842-1420	brooklyngreenway.org
Comm to Preserve Brighton/Man Beach	718-332-6749	
Dyker Park Alliance	718-621-1534	dykerheights.com
East River Apprenticeshop	718-383-4388	erashop.com
El Puente	718-452-0404	
Floyd Bennett Field Task Force		floydbennett.org
Friends of the Boardwalk		fobconeyisland.com
Friends Owl's Head Park	718-745-4218	bdh528@aol.com
Friends of Gateway		treebranch.com/ fog/ friends_of_gateway.htm
Friends of Marine Park & GC	917-761-4316	FOMC@aol.com
Gerritsen Beach Cares	718-648-3745	gerritsenbeachcares.org
Gerritsen Creek Assn	718-965-6551	
Gowanus Canal CDC	718-858-0557	gowanus.org
Gowanus Canal Dredgers	718-443-0849	waterfrontmuseum.org/dredgers
Greenpoint Waterfront Assn	718-383-1278	gwapp.org
Greenpt/Williamsburg Watchperson	718-384-3339	fotlah@aol.com
Neighbors United for Columbia Waterfrt	718-852-2876	
Newtown Creek Monitoring Com	718-349-0150	

Stewards

Prospect Park Alliance	718-965-8951	prospectpark.org
Red Hook Civic Assn	718-788-8075	
Red Hook Navy		rhnavy@treebranch.com
South Brooklyn LDC	718-625-8624	redhook-brooklyn.org
SaLt Marsh Alliance	718-421-2021	saltmarshalliance.org
Sheepshead Bay Waterfront Council	718-680-9555	
Sunset Park Restoration Committee	718-871-8340	
Sunset Red Hook LDC	718-499-1249	sunsetparkredhookldc.org
Urban Divers	718-802-9874	urbandivers.org
Watchperson Project	718-384-3339	

Queens

American Littoral Society	718-634-6467	alsnyc.org
Astoria Restoration Assn	718-726-0034	
Beachside Bungalow Preservation Assn		preserve.org
Broad Channel Civic Assn	718-318-4340	
Community Environmental Center	718-784-1444	cecenter.org
Concerned Citizens for Poppenhusen Inst	718-358-0067	
Concerned Citizens for Riis Beach	718-337-9629	
Douglas Manor Environmental Assn	718-225-0386	
Friends of Gantry State Park		queenswest.com/ gantrypark
Friends of Gateway		gateway.treebranch.com
Friends of Queensbridge Park	718-786-0807	
Friends of Rockaway	718-474-4193	pages.prodigy.net/ rockaway/friends.htm
Hunters Point Coalition	718-472-4260	
Jamaica Bay Task Force		treebranch.com/ jamaicabay
Jamaica Bay Guardian	718-634-6467	
Little Neck Pines Assn		littleneckpines.org
Malba Civic Assn		malba.org
Neponsit Property Owners Assn	718 318-8580	
Rockaway Action Committee	718-474-2760	
Rockaway Beach Civic Assn	718-318-1973	

Stewards

Rockaway Park Assn	718-945-0846	
Rockaway Pt & Revitalization Corp	718-471-6040	
Southern Queens Park Assn	718-276-4630	sqany.org
Udalls Cove Preservation Commitee	718-428-5586	

Staten Island

Bloomfield Conservancy	718-568-3615	
Citizens for Last Chance Pond	718-979-6398	community.silive.com
Coalition for the S Beach Pond Park	718-815-7173	
Coalition for Great Kills Harbor Park	718-967-3969	GKHarborPark@aol.com
Coastal Conservation Assn of N Y	718-351-2185	ccany.org
Conference House-Raritan Bay Conservancy	718-356-6368	
Friends of Alice Austen House/Buono Beach	718-816-4506	
Friends of Blue Heron Park	718-317-1732	preserve2.org/blueheron
Friends of Clay Pit Pond Preserve	718-967-1976	njcola@earthlink.net
Greenbelt Conservancy	718-667-5175	sigreenbelt.org
Mariners Marsh Conservancy	718-447-6374	tutti.si.rr.com
Midland Beach Civic Assn		MidbeachCivic@aol.com
Mud Lane Society for Stapleton		preserve2.org/mudlane
Natural Resources Protective Assn	718-987-6037	nrpa.com
New Dorp Central Civic Assn	718-979-6011	ndcca.com
Northern Great Kills Civic Assn	718-227-5676	
N Shore Waterfront Conservancy		nswci@yahoo.com
Preservation League of S. I.		preservesi.org/plsi.htm
Protectors of Pine Oak Woods	718-761-7496	siprotectors.org
SI Friends of Clearwater	718-273-9093	
Staten Island Park Alliance	718-474-2760	community.silive.com
Sweetbay Magnolia Bio-Reserve Conservy	718-273-3740	
Turnaround Friends Seaside Nature Park	718-967-5729	turnaroundfriends.org
Urban Trail Club	718-274-0407	nynjtc.org

* Indicates city-state entities created to develop parcels of public land for public, residential and commercial use, such as Battery Park City, Hudson River Park, Brooklyn Bridge Park and Roosevelt Island Development Corp.

Stakeholders

City

FDNY Marine Division Fireboats have protected the city's waterfront since 1840. Units: Marine Company 1 Manhattan, Marine Co. 6 Brooklyn, Marine Co. 9 Staten Island. nyfd.com/marine/marine.html or fireboat.org/history/fleetlist.asp

NYC Dept. of City Planning (DCP) 22 Reade St. Oversees land use regulation and zoning, and supervises NYC Coastal Mgmt. 212-720-3300 nyc.gov/html/dcp

• **The Waterfront Inventory Act** Inventory of city-owned and leased waterfront properties available online at nylcv.org/Programs/WPC/Waterfront_Properties_NYC.xls

• **Waterfront Revitalization Program (WRP)** Citywide coastal zoning framework for waterfront redevelopment, water dependent industries, public access, water quality, historical and cultural resources and habitat restoration.

NYC Dept. of Environmental Protection (DEP) 59-17 Junction Blvd. Flushing. Delivery of drinking water and treatment of wastewater, administration of pumpouts and enforcement of air, noise and hazardous material rules. Public access permits to fish reservoirs and hike watershed lands. 718-595-6601 ci.nyc.ny.us/html/dep/home.html

NYC Dept. of Health (DOH) Beach water sampling, issues beach swimming advisories, beach closings and fish consumption advisories. 212-442-9666 nyc.gov/html/doh/home.html

NYC Dept. of Parks & Recreation (DPR) 830 5th Ave. Responsible for 28,000 acres of parkland, 14 miles of beach, 3 stadia, 68 pools, 30 rec centers, 20 historic house museums, all city trees, natural preserves and "Forever Wild" sites, and marinas on park property. 800-201-PARK or 311 nycgovparks.org

• **Natural Resource Group** Acquisition, protection, restoration, and management of natural areas.

NYC Dept. of Transportation Oversight of greenways, bike maps and bike rack placement, heliports, Staten Island ferry and free bridges. 311 ci.nyc.ny.us/html/dot/home.html

• **Economic Development Corp.** Port and waterfront redevelopment. 212-312-3600 nycedc.com

NYC Soil & Water Conservation District 290 Broadway, 24th Flr. Water and soil resources preservation and promotes watershed and water monitoring and environmental education. 212-637-3877 nycswcd.net

NYPD Harbor Unit Pier One, 140 58th St. Brooklyn. Monitors: VHF Channel 17. Founded in 1858 to combat piracy, unit patrols city waterways and the waterfront. 718-765-4142 bentwheelclub.org

Wastewater Pollution Control Plants

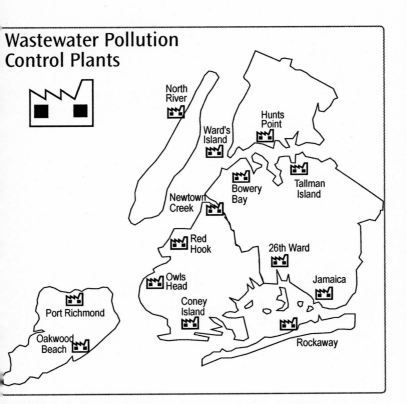

Wastewater Pollution Control Plants

The NYC DEP oversees 6,000 miles of sewers and 14 wastewater treatment plants that process about 1.3 billion gallons of sewage each day. Coney Island is one of the world's largest and oldest plants. Prior to the 20th century, untreated sewage went directly into waterways. Waste treatment plants do what wetlands do naturally, filter and re-oxygenate water. The treated wastewater, called effluent, is released into the water. About 80% of the city's sewers are combined, where the system collects all sewage from toilets, sink drains and storm drains then conveys it to wastewater plants for treatment. During heavy rainstorms, the system capacity is exceeded and sewage and street litter overflow into the marine environment. There are more than 494 overflow discharge points or outfalls. The solution is for runoff discharge to be contained at storage facilities until treatment is possible.

Robert Moses, Urban Planner (1888-1981) Public works inaugurated by Moses transformed the urban landscape and waterfront of New York City. A graduate of Yale, Oxford and Columbia universities, Moses launched his career in public service in 1919 and retired in 1968, at age 80. At one time he held 12 different city and state jobs, including both state and city parks departments simultaneously and was chairman of the Triborough Bridge Authority. He drafted the laws that created most of the jobs he held. Under Moses leadership two million acres of parkland, a dozen bridges, miles of scenic parkways, and long stretches of public beach were built. Moses' portfolio of city projects includes: Harlem River Drive, East River Drive, Randall's Island Park, Orchard Beach, Shore Parkway Greenway and Jacob Riis Park. He established Jamaica Bay as a protected wildlife refuge, redeveloped the dump at Flushing Meadow into the World's Fair grounds, and had a hand in building Shea Stadium, United Nations, Lincoln Center and New York Coliseum.

• **Scuba Unit** Formed in 1967 to perform search, rescue and recovery.
• **Harbor Unit Auxiliary** Volunteer group that assists with harbor patrol. harbor.netfirm

State

NYS Dept. of Environmental Conservation, Region 2 (DEC) One Hunters Point Plz, 47-40 21st St. Long Island City. Stormwater discharge and wetland construction permits. Information on boat launches, fishing licenses, catch limits, and pumpout facilities. Publishes a free guide to freshwater fishing in NYC. Manages Mount Loretto Preserve. 718-482-4900 dec.state.ny.us

• **Bureau of Marine Resources** Management of finfish, crustaceans and shellfish, and marine habitat protection. dec.state.ny.us/website/dfwmr/marine/aboutbmr.htm

• **Natural Heritage Program** Documents and protects the State's rare animals, plants, and significant natural communities—forests, fresh and saltwater wetlands and grasslands. dec.state.ny.us/website/dfwmr/heritage/about.htm

NYS Dept. of Motor Vehicles (DMV) Administers recreational boat registration with form MV-82B. Registration is valid for 3 years. Vessels less than 16' pay $9; from 16' to 26' fee is $18; 26' and over pay $30. 800-CALL-DMV

NYS Dept. of State (DOS), Division of Coastal Resources Helps communities revitalize the waterfront and improve access. 212-417-5801 dos.state.ny.us

• **Coastal Management Program** Establishes state policy for coastal natural resources, public access

and coastal revitalization.
dos.state.ny.us/cstl/cstlwww.html

NYS Dept. of Transportation (DOT) 1 Hunters Point Plz, Long Island City. Responsible for ports, waterways, and transportation. 718-482-4526 dot.state.ny.us

Office of General Services (OGS) Land management division issues permits to build on land under water. ogs.state.ny.us

Office of NYS Parks, Recreation & Historic Preservation (OPRHP) 163 W 125th St. Manages 7 state parks within city limits. Sponsors boating safety courses and recommends properties for the State and National Register of Historic Places. 212-866-2777 nysparks.com

• **Bureau of Marine & Recreational Vehicles** Bureau issues permits for in water regattas and licenses commercial vessels in state waters. Publishes *NYS Boater's Guide.* nysparks.com/boats

Northeast Queens Nature & Historical Preserve Commission Conservation of wetlands on Queens north shore. 718-229-8805

Regional

Clean Ocean & Shore Trust (COAST) A bi-state legislative committee established to provide for the enhancement, enjoyment and conservation of the marine resources of the Hudson-Raritan Estuary and the New York Bight. 212-854-2910 nynjcoast.org

Cornell Cooperative Extension 16 E 34th St. NYC office was established in 1948, programs cover aquaculture, hydrophonic gardening and fishing (SAREP), and other agricultural, nutrition, environmental and related topics. 212-340-2900 cce.cornell.edu/nyc/NewYorkCity.html

Interstate Environmental Commission Regulates, enforces and monitors effluent water quality standards in the interstate marine waters of New York, New Jersey and Connecticut. iec-nynjct.org

Hudson Raritan Estuary Ecosystem Restoration (HRE) Study to identify problems and opportunities for ecological restoration throughout

New York State Shoreline
NYS Marine Coastal District: Atlantic Ocean 3 nautical miles from shore, Long Island Sound, and the Hudson River to the Tappan Zee Bridge
3,200 miles of coastline
70% of the state's population lives within coastal counties
41% of the state shoreline is publicly owned

the estuary region. 212-264-5560
hudsonraritanrestoration.org

**NY-NJ Harbor Estuary Program
(HEP)** 290 Broadway, 24th Floor. A
combined federal, state and municipal
and community endeavor created
by the EPA to preserve, protect
and restore the estuary through
advocacy, education, monitoring,
research, restoration and stewardship
programs. One of 28 such programs
established nationwide. 212-637-3816
harborestuary.org

**NY-NJ Harbor Operations
Safety & Navigation Committee**
Safety forum for commercial and
recreational users of the port. The
Harbor Ops website provides USCG
Local Notice to Mariners and other
up-to-date information on harbor
activity. harborops.com

NY Sea Grant (NOAA) Cooperative
program of SUNY and Cornell
University, which is part of a nationwide network of university-based
research and outreach programs
that promote better understanding,
conservation, and use of America's
coastal resources. 212-637-3816
seagrant.sunysb.edu

**Port Authority of New York/
New Jersey** 225 Park Ave. South.
Founded in 1921, to handle bi-state
conflicts, which had heightened to
a point when NYC and NJ police
exchanged gunfire across the Hudson
River. Oversees all aspects relating
to harbor use and port facilities in
New York and New Jersey, including
interstate tunnels, bridges, marine
terminals and major airports.
212-435-7000 panynj.gov

Federal

Army Corps of Engineers NY Fort
Hamilton, Brooklyn. Since 1890,the
Corps has regulated activities in
U.S. waters, including navigation
channels, dredging projects, beach
nourishment, flood control and issues
permits for wetlands development. It
is one of the largest users of contract
commercial diving services in the
world and a leading provider of
water-based recreation nationwide.
718-491-8715 nan.usace.army.mil

Coastal America Partnership of
federal agencies working to preserve,
protect and restore America's
coastal heritage. 202-401-9928
coastalamerica.gov

United States Shoreline

95,000 miles of national coastline
The U.S. Economic Zone extends 200 miles seaward from the coast
Half of the U.S. population lives within 50 miles of a coast

Frederick Law Olmstead, Landscape Architect (1822-1903) The founder of American landscape architecture, Olmstead created many of the country's first public parks. At age 18, Olmstead moved to New York City to pursue a career in scientific farming. He never attended college and worked as a merchant seamen, newspaper correspondent and a columnist for the New Yorker. He championed conservation and believed that open space should be accessible to all. He was an advocate of the City Beautiful Movement, which held that aesthetically pleasing urban parks had a civilizing effect on cities. He designed the nation's first greenway on Ocean Parkway and Central Park and Prospect Park in collaboration with Calvert Vaux and drafted the blueprints for Riverside Park and Drive. Olmstead succumbed to dementia and spent his final days in an asylum surrounded by grounds he designed. His partner Vaux mysteriously drowned in Gravesend Bay.

Fish & Wildlife Service (Dept. of Interior) Conservation of habitat for birds, fish, wildlife, plant species and endangered species. National fish hatcheries, National Wildlife Refuges and reviews permits for filling in wetlands, construction in navigable waters, dredging and beachfill. 800-344-WILD fws.gov

National Park Service (Dept. of Interior) Administers Gateway National Recreation Area (GNRA), Liberty and Ellis Islands, Castle Clinton and Governors Island historic district. GNRA was conveyed to the federal government in 1972 in an attempt to improve management of the valuable shoreline areas. nps.gov/gate

National Oceanic & Atmospheric Agency (NOAA) (Dept. of Commerce) Surveys coastline and navigable waters, monitors climate activity, fisheries, oceans and marine sanctuaries, and creates marine navigation and charts. noaa.gov

Natural Resources Conservation Service (NRCS) (Dept of Agriculture) Assists private land owners with conservation of water and natural resources, including wetlands restoration. nrcs.usda.gov

U.S. Coast Guard Activities NY (Homeland Security Dept.) 212 Coast Guard Dr., Staten Island. Operates Vessel Traffic Control, regulates ships and shipping, licenses masters and pilots, posts local notice to mariners, and is responsible for port security, marine safety, search & rescue, lighthouses and moveable bridges over navigable waters. 718-354-4197 uscg.mil/1/unit/actny

• **Marine Event Permits** Any event that effects navigable waters, such as regattas, fire works, etc. must submit an application to USCG.

U.S. Commission on Ocean Policy
Formed to develop a long-term national ocean policy that balances environmental and economic issues affecting oceans and coastlines. oceancommission.gov

U.S. Dept. of the Interior
Manages one out of every five acres of land in the country. doi.gov

• U.S. Geological Survey Water resources and coastal and marine geology programs. usgs.gov

U.S. Environmental Protection Agency, (EPA) Region 2 Safeguards public health and the environment. Administers Superfund and federal laws protecting water resources. 212-637-3000 epa.gov/Region2

Waterfront Parks at a Glance

Waterfront Parks Key				
NYC	City Park	🏛		Historic Site
NYS	State Park	🐎		Horseback Riding
NPS	Federal Park	⛳		Golf
🏖	Beach	⚓		Marina
🚴	Bikeway/Greenway	🎪		Picnic Area
🔭	Birding	🎠		Playground
〰	Boardwalk/Esplanade	👫		Ranger Station
⛺	Camping (by permit)	🍴		Refreshments
🐕	Dog Run	🚻		Restrooms
📚	Educational Programs	⛵		Sailing School
🚤	Ferry Landing	🤿		Scuba
🎣	Fishing	🏊		Swimming
🚣	Hand Boat Launch	🛥		Trailer Ramp
🥾	Hiking	👁		Vista
✖	Not yet completed			

Manhattan

Park	Agency	Amenities
Battery Park	NYC	(icons)
Battery Park City	NYS	(icons)
Carl Schurz Park	NYC	(icons)
Detmold Park	NYC	(icons)
Dyckman Fields	NYC	(icons)
Glick Park	NYC	(icons)
East River Park	NYC	(icons)
Ecology (Octagon) Park,	NYC	(icons)
Ellis Island	NPS	(icons)
Fort Tryon	NYC	(icons)
Fort Washington	NYC	(icons)
Governor's Island	NPS	(icons)
Harlem River Esplanade	NYC	(icons)
High Bridge Park	NYC	(icons)
✗ Hudson River Park	C/S	(icons)
Inwood Hill Park	NYC	(icons)
Lighthouse Park, RI	NYC	(icons)
MacArthur Park	NYC	(icons)
Randalls & Wards Island	NYC	(icons)
Riverbank State Park	NYS	(icons)
Riverside Park	NYC	(icons)
Riverside South	NYC	(icons)
Statue of Liberty Park	NPS	(icons)
South Point Park	NYC	(icons)
South Street Seaport		(icons)
Stuyvesant Cove Park	NYC	(icons)
✗ Swindler Cove Park	NYC	(icons)
U.N. Plaza		(icons)
Waterside Plaza		(icons)

Bronx

Park		Features
✕ Barretto Park	NYC	🚣 ♨ 🐟 👁
Bridge Park	NYC	♨ 👁
Bronx River Park	NYC	🔭 ♨ 🛶 🏃 🏛 🎿 🏕 🚻 👁
✕ Castle Hill Park	NYC	🐟
City Island Wetlands	NYC	🔭 👁
Clason's Point Park	NYC	🛶 👁
Co-op City Ballfields		🏕 🚻
East 180 Street	NYC	🛶 🏕 👁
✕ Ferry Point Park	NYC	🚣 🔭 ♨ 🐟 🏃 🦮 🏕 👁
Henry Hudson Park	NYC	🔭 🏃 🏛 🏕 🎿 👁
High Bridge Park	NYC	🏛 🏕 👁
✕ Hunt's Point Park	NYC	🛶 🏕 👁
Pelham Bay Park	NYC	🐟 🚣 🔭 🐾 🐕 🐟 ♨ 🛶 🏃 🐎 🦮 🏕 🎿 🚻 🏊
Pugsleys Creek Park	NYC	🔭 🛶
✕ Regatta Park	NYC	🚣 🐟 👁
Riverdale Park	NYC	🔭 🏃 🏛 👁
Roberto Clemente Park	NYS	🚣 ♨ 🛶 🏕 🎿 🚻 👁
Shoelace Park	NYC	🚣 🔭 🐟 🛶 🏃 🏕 🎿
Soundview Park	NYC	🚣 🔭 ♨ 🐟 👁
Spuyten Duyvil Park	NYC	🔭 🐟 👁
SUNY Maritime College		🚣 ♨ 🐟 🏛 🏕 👁
Tiffany St. Pier	NYC	🐟 🏕 👁
Veteran's Park	NYC	🚣 👁
Wave Hill		🔭 🦮 🏛 🖥 🚻 👁
✕ Yankee Village	NYC	♨ 🎿 👁

Brooklyn

Park		Features
Barge Park	NYC	🎿 👁
Beard St. Piers		♨ 🛶 🏛 🚻 👁
Bensonhurst Park	NYC	🚣 ♨ 🐟 🏕 👁

Brooklyn (cont.)

Name	Agency	Amenities
Bergen Beach	NYC	
Brighton Beach	NYC	
Brooklyn Promenade	DOT	
✗ Brooklyn Bridge Park	C/S	
Canarsie Beach Park	NPS	
Columbia St Esplanade	NYC	
Coney Island Beach	NYC	
Coney Island Creek Park	NYC	
Dreier-Offerman Park	NYC	
Dyker Beach Park	NYC	
✗ East River Park	NYS	
Empire-Fulton Park	NYS	
Floyd Bennett Field	NPS	
Fulton Ferry Landing	NYC	
Grand Ferry Park	NYC	
Kaiser Park	NYC	
Louis Valentino Pier	NYC	
Manhattan Beach	NYC	
Marine Park	NYC	
McGuire Park	NYC	
Owl's Head Park	NYC	
Plumb Beach	NPS	
Red Hook Park	NYC	
Shore Pkwy Greenway	NYC	
69th Street Pier	NYC	

Queens

Park	Agency	Amenities
Alley Pond Park	NYC	(icons)
Astoria Park	NYC	(icons)
Bayswater Pt State Park	NYS	(icons)
Beach Channel Park	NYC	(icons)
✗ Bergen Basin Trail	NYC	(icons)
Brant Point Sanctuary	NYC	(icons)
Breezy Point	NPS	(icons)
Broad Chnl Cmty Park	NYC	(icons)
Broad Channel Park	NYC	(icons)
Crocheron Park	NYC	(icons)
Flushing Bay Promenade	NYC	(icons)
Flushing-Meadows Park	NYC	(icons)
Fort Tilden	NPS	(icons)
Fort Totten	NPS	(icons)
Frank Charles Park	NPS	(icons)
Francis Lewis Park	NYC	(icons)
Gantry Plaza Park	NYS	(icons)
Hamilton Beach Park	NPS	(icons)
Hermon MacNeil Park	NYC	(icons)
Idlewild Park	NYC	(icons)
Jacob Riis Park	NPS	(icons)
Jamaica Bay Park	NYC	(icons)
Jamaica Bay Refuge	NPS	(icons)
John Golden Park	NYC	(icons)
Little Bay Park	NYC	(icons)
Michaelis-Bayswater Park	NYC	(icons)
O'Donohue Park	NYC	(icons)
Powell's Cove Park	NYC	(icons)

Queens (cont.)

Queensbridge Park	NYC	
Rainey Park	NYC	
Ralph DeMarco Park	NYC	
Rockaway Beach	NYC	
Rockaway Park	NYC	
Socrates Sculpture Park	NYC	
Tallman Island	DEP	
Udall's Park Preserve	NYC	

Staten Island

Alice Austin Park	NYC	
Blue Heron Park	NYC	
Clay Pit Pond Park	NYS	
Conference House	NYC	
Faber Park	NYC	
Fort Wadsworth	NPS	
Great Kills Park	NPS	
Lemon Creek Park	NYC	
Mariner's Marsh Park	NYC	
Miller Field	NPS	
Mt. Loretto Preserve	DEC	
Seaside Nature Park	NYC	
Snug Harbor Center	NYC	
South & Midland Beaches	NYC	
Stadium Esplanade Park	NYC	
Tottenville Beach	NYC	
Von Briesen Park	NYC	
William T. Davis Refuge	NYC	
Wolfe's Pond Park	NYC	

Working Waterfront

❝State of the art cruise liners, 35 foot draft container ships, oil tankers, barges carrying sand for construction, tugboats that pull the barges, and police and fireboats are all part of the fleet that serves New York's daily life and finds safe haven and ports of call at docks along its shores. Runners and strollers may see these as they follow the pedestrian paths that have been built over the past decade to open New York City's waterfront for recreational use. Views of tall cranes at work unloading cargo in Staten Island and Brooklyn, cement mixers fed by sand floated in from Long Island to Manhattan's West Side, garbage and refined sewage dumped into scows at terminals in all five boroughs, or a floating Police Station under the Triborough Bridge are less accessible to the public, despite the story they tell of how this island city works. This story is generally hidden from the public using the waterfront for recreation by high, chain link fences, which say "keep out" for security and safety reasons. Next time you are out on a promenade or in a boat see how many elements of the city's working waterfront you can find.**❞**

Ann L. Buttenwieser, Ph.D. is a waterfront planner and author of *Manhattan Water-Bound. Manhattan's Waterfront from the 17th Century to the Present.*

New York City became a global city because it was a great seaport. It is the largest port on the East Coast, the third largest in North America and one of the top 15 ports in the world. New York is the nation's largest coffee, petroleum and auto port. It connects to an extensive intermodal network (affecting more than one mode of transportation) and serves the world's largest and richest consumer market. The port district encompasses 1,500 square miles within a 25-mile radius of the Statue of Liberty. The busiest port in the world throughout most of the 19th and 20th centuries, it fell into decline after WWII. Traffic shifted to the N.J. side of the harbor with the advent of containerized shipping. Thanks to the growth of China trade through the Suez Canal in the past decade, cargo volumes are at record highs and maritime industry is one the largest sectors of the local economy. Seaborne commerce is expected to double over the next 10 years and quadruple by the year 2020.

Port of New York

New York Harbor is a vast, protected natural harbor divided into Lower New York Bay and Upper New York Bay by the Narrows passage. The entrance to the Lower Bay is marked by Rockaway Point on the north and Sandy Hook, NJ on the south. The principal entrance for ocean shipping is Ambrose Channel, which is 2,000 feet wide, 45 feet deep (soon to be dredged to 50') and stretches 17 miles from the Atlantic Ocean to the Upper Bay. 240 miles of federal channels interlace the port district. More than 5,000 commercial vessels call at the port each year. With the exception of bulk commodities like oil and grain, most cargo arrives in standardized containers measured in 20-foot equivalent units, which can be handled by ship, rail and truck. Containerships are the largest vehicles in the world. Faster, cheaper and safer than old freighters, they cruise at 26 knots, displace 100,000 tons when loaded and can turn around in their own length.

The movement of vessels in the harbor is monitored by Vessel Traffic Services operated by the U.S. Coast Guard Activities at Fort Wadsworth surveying the harbor from above the Narrows. All captains must file a sailing plan with Vessel Traffic Services prior to entering port. Within the harbor, pilotage by a licensed harbor pilot is compulsory. Sandy Hook Pilots board every ocean-going vessel entering the harbor to steer it into port. At the docks, docking pilot and tugs take over to maneuver ships thousands of times their weight to a berth. Deep water anchorages accommodate vessels awaiting berthing and favorable tides. Anchorages are located at Gravesend, Bay Ridge, Red Hook, Stapleton and Liberty Island. Once in the Upper Bay, most ships make a sharp left turn at the Statue of Liberty and navigate the narrow Kill van Kull waterway to reach the port's fastest growing terminal at Howland Hook and the big New Jersey facilities at Port Elizabeth and Port Newark.

Port of New York & New Jersey

General Cargo:	21.6 million tons
20' Equivalent Units (TEUs):	3.7 million
Jobs:	230,000 ($10 billion in wages)
Economic Activity:	$25 billion
Top Trading Partners:	China, Italy & Germany
Leading Imports:	Alcoholic beverages, vehicles & furniture
Leading Exports:	Wood pulp, plastics & machinery

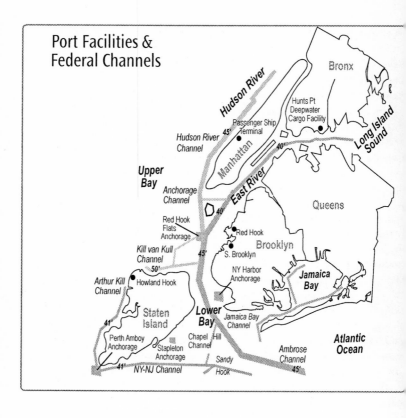

Port Facilities & Federal Channels

Labels within map:

Bronx
Hudson River
Hunts Pt Deepwater Cargo Facility
Long Island Sound
Passenger Ship Terminal
Hudson River Channel 45'
Manhattan
40'
East River
Upper Bay
Anchorage Channel
40'
Queens
Red Hook Flats Anchorage
Red Hook
Brooklyn
Kill van Kull Channel 45'
S. Brooklyn
50'
NY Harbor Anchorage
Jamaica Bay
Arthur Kill Channel
Howland Hook
Staten Island
41
Lower Bay
Jamaica Bay Channel
Perth Amboy Anchorage
Stapleton Anchorage
Chapel Hill Channel
Ambrose Channel
Atlantic Ocean
Sandy Hook
41 NY-NJ Channel
45'

Port Facilities

New York Harbor is one of the world's largest commercial port areas. The biggest maritime construction project since the building of the Erie Canal is occurring over the next five years to modernize infrastructure and ready the port for the new generation of containerships and higher cargo volume. The natural depth of the harbor is 20 feet. Major channels and terminal berthing spaces are being deepened to 50 feet by 2009.

The Kill van Kull will reach 50-foot depth by end of 2004. Terminals are being enlarged to optimize capacity and improvements to intermodal transportation connections will enhance landside access. There are about 200 active marine terminals in the port district. The Port Authority operates 7 public terminals that include: Port Newark, Port Elizabeth, Global Marine Terminal and Auto Marine Terminal in N.J. and Red Hook, South Brooklyn and Howland Hook in the City of New York.

Brooklyn Marine Terminal

Buttermilk Channel

Berths: 6 berths/300-1091 feet
Depth: 32 feet
Cargo: Bulk, container warehouses
Operator: American Warehousing
          90 Columbia St. Brooklyn
          718-330-2950

Built in the 1950s, piers 1 to 6 are to become part of Brooklyn Bridge Park. The future of Piers 7 through 12 is currently under review.

Erie Basin Barge Port

Gowanus Bay

Berths: 4,000 feet
Depth: 35 feet
Cargo: Bulk - oil, gravel
Operator: Hughes Marine 718-237-0875
          hughesmarine.com

The former Fishport is largest private marine facility in the northeast, originally built to rival Fulton Fish Market, and is now homeport to 200 tugboats, barges and other commercial vessels.

Howland Hook Container Terminal

Arthur Kill

Berths: 3 berths/3,000 feet
Depth: 42 feet (50')
Cargo: Container/General Cargo
Operator: HH Container Terminal Inc.
          718-273-7000 hhook.com

Handles about 20% of the ports total cargo. Expansion of the 187 acre site includes: enlarging capacity, dredging to 50 feet and adding on-dock rail service linked to the national rail freight network in N.J. by 2005.

Passenger Ship Terminal

Hudson River

Berths: 5 berths/1,000 feet
Depth: 28-32 feet
Cargo: Ocean liners
Operator: P&O Ports at Piers 88, 90 & 92
          212-246-5450 npst.com

Handles the world's largest ocean liners, including the *Queen Mary II* arriving April 2004.

Red Hook Marine Terminal

Buttermilk Channel

Berths: 3 berths/2.080 feet
Depth: 40 feet

Cargo: Container/General Cargo
Operator: American Stevedoring
          70 Hamilton Ave. 718-875-0777

Red Hook is nations's leading bulk cocoa port. It operates cross-harbor barge service to New Jersey, where it links with the interstate rail network.

South Brooklyn Marine Terminal

Gowanus Bay

Berths: 8 berths/6,135 feet
Depths: 40 feet
Cargo: General Cargo
Operator: American Warehousing
          39th St. Sunset Park
          718-797-4278

The shortest sailing time in and out of the harbor, the terminal is slated to be reactivated to handle autos and containers. It comprises Bush and Brooklyn Army terminals, 65th St. Float Terminal, 1st Ave Float Bridge and Cross Harbor Rail Yards, barging rail cars to Jersey City using vintage 1940's diesel-electric engines. The Cross-Harbor Rail Freight Tunnel is a proposed tunnel under the harbor between Brooklyn and Jersey City linking to the Bay Ridge branch of LIRR. crossharborstudy.org ✂

Port Industry

Harbor Pilots Sandy Hook Pilots 201 Edgewater St. Staten Island. Pilots have been guiding ships in New York Harbor since 1694. Sandy Hook Pilots board incoming vessels at Ambrose Lighthouse to steer them through the sea lanes, shoals and reefs in the harbor. Dispatchers rotate calls among 65 pilots. It takes 7.5 years apprenticeship and a total of 20 years to become a master pilot. 718-448-3900 sandyhookpilots.com

Ship Registry A ship must possess a national identity to enjoy protection under international law. In 2002, U.S. flagged ships carried less than 4% of the cargo entering and leaving U.S. ports. Panama is the world's largest ship register. Flag-of-convenience ships, such as those registered in the Marshall Islands or Liberia, are free to flout U.S. labor, taxation, safety and environmental laws.

Shipyards Caddell Drydock, on Staten Island since 1903, is the largest ship repair facility operating in the harbor. NY Shipyard has repaired ships in an enclosed compound in Red Hook, Brooklyn since 1933. Brooklyn Naval Shipyard has the city's oldest graving dock, built in 1840. Drydocks are large docks from

Deep Green Harbor

Ocean shipping is the most economical and environmentally sound method of moving cargo.

Comprehensive Port Improvement Plan (CPIP) A master plan for expanding the port in an environmentally sound manner that applies "green port" planning principles to limit environmental impacts and protect the harbor's aquatic resources. For example, any dredging that disturbs the harbor environment is accompanied by mitigation measures, such as marsh restoration. cpiponline.org

MARPOL Formed by the first three letters of "marine" and "pollution," MARPOL is an international treaty for the prevention of pollution from ships, including oil, chemicals, garbage and sewage. It mandates proper disposal and/or discharge. 161 nations have implemented MARPOL, including the U.S.

Port Inland Distribution Network (PIDN) A network of regional ports and distribution centers linked by barge and rail. Hubs include the Port of Albany and Bridgeport. New York is the only city in the world where the majority of freight comes in and out by truck. Each barge transporting goods replaces 15,000 trucks a day.

John Wolfe Ambrose, Engineer (1838–1899) The Irish-American builder is responsible for the deep sea channel stretching from the Narrows to the ocean, which bears his name. Ambrose attended New York and Princeton universities and presided over the Brooklyn Wharf and Dry Dock Company. He successfully lobbied Congress for funds to build a channel 2,000 feet wide and 40 feet deep, which could accommodate large ships and open Brooklyn's shores to new commerce. The construction of the straight channel improved the viability of the port. A bust honoring Ambrose looks out over the port from Battery Park.

which water can be pumped out in order to build or repair ships below the waterline.

Significant Maritime and Industrial Areas NYS has designated sites on the city's waterfront where land use will support working waterfront uses: Kill van Kull-Howland Hook to Snug Harbor; Sunset Park, Brooklyn-Erie Basin to Owls Head; Red Hook-Pier 6 to Red Hook Containerport; Brooklyn Navy Yard; Newtown Creek and The Bronx-Port Morris and Hunts Point.

Tugs The tugboat was invented in New York Harbor in 1828. Tugs tow barges and maneuver giant ships through narrow shipping lanes and confined docks. There are over 100 tugs with horsepower ranging up to 10,000 working in the port today. Moran, the largest towing firm on the East Coast, and its rival McAllister started in New York in the 1860s. Towing companies are centered on Staten Island's north shore.

Academic Programs

Center for Maritime Education Merchant marine training offering USCG approved courses. 212-349-9090 seamanschurch.org

Harbor School Bushwick, Brooklyn. Alternative high school for the study of maritime culture in NY Harbor. 718-381-7100

Kingsborough Community College Brooklyn. Maritime Technology 2-year degree program. School operates a training vessel and has a 32-slip marina. 718-368-5525 kbcc.cuny.edu

SUNY Maritime College Bronx. Beginning in 1864 on a ship in the East River, it is the oldest institution of its kind in the U.S. and occupies historic Fort Schuyler since 1938, the school prepares students for careers in the maritime industry. Training vessel 565-foot *Empire State VI*. 718-409-7200 sunymaritime.edu

Stevens Institute of Technology Hoboken, NJ. Center for Maritime Systems. stevens.edu

Port Agencies & Organizations

American Merchant Marine Veterans Edwin J. O'Hara Chapter. Active and retired merchant seamen and others interested in the Maritime. usmm.org

AMVER Automated Mutual Assistance Vessel Rescue System. A voluntary global ship reporting system for search and rescue, operated by USCG. 40% of the world's merchant fleet participate. 212-668-7764 amver.com

Harbor Operations Safety & Navigation Committee Forum for commercial and recreational users of the port. harborops.com

Federal Maritime Commission Regulates shipping in the foreign trades of the U.S. Licenses ocean transportation intermediaries. 718-553-2228 fmc.gov

International Longshoremen's Assn. (ILA) Atlantic Coast District 17 Battery Pl. Union for longshore-men who work for stevedoring companies in the port. 212-425-1200 ilaunion.org

Marine Society of the City of NY 17 Battery Place. Formally chartered by King George III in 1770, it is comprised of former captains and officers of U.S. merchant vessels. 212-425-0448 marinesocietyny.org

Maritime Administration (MARAD) (Dept of Transportation) marad.dot.gov. Responsible for promoting strong Merchant Marine, adequate shipbuilding and repair services, efficient ports, and effective intermodal transportation systems.

Maritime Assn. of the Port of NY/NJ 17 Battery Pl, Ste 913. Formed in 1873, reports ship traffic information. Publishes "Port of NY/NJ Handbook" 212-425-5704 nymaritime.org

NationsPort Coalition of 500 industry, labor and community leaders supporting deep green harbor initiatives to reduce environmental impact of port improvements. 888-656-9566 nationsport.org

New York Shipping Association Represents port employer and ocean carrier interests in the port. 732-452-7824 nysanet.org

Partnership for Sustainable Port 54 Remsen St. Brooklyn. A consulting firm working to promote an environmentally and economically productive port. 718-935-0860 sustainableports.com

Port Authority of NY/NJ Self-supported, bi-state agency formed to promote trade and commerce, and oversee operation of the port. panynj.org

Society of Marine Port Engineers of NY Promotes and protects the

William P. Powell, Seaman and Social Activist (1791-1867). Powell was a black seaman who sailed regularly from the Port of New York. In 1839, Powell founded the Colored Seaman's Home, the largest home for black seafarers in New York City. He ran the home himself for the next 25 years. A supporter of the Underground Railroad, Powell also fought for the rights of black sailors, who were often severely discriminated against, particularly while traveling in the South. His efforts resulted in the foundation of the American Seaman's Protective Union in 1863, the first such organization for black sailors.

interests of the American Merchant Marine. smpe.org

Society of Naval Architects & Marine Engineers (SNAME) Advances the art, science and practice of naval architecture, shipbuilding and engineering. 800-798-2188 sname.org

Traffic Club of New York Group of maritime and intermodal logistics professionals. Established in 1906 to enhance liaison between shippers and carriers. clubnytc.com

U.S. Customs One Penn Plz. Enforces import and export regulations in the port, collects duties and inspects cargo and containers. customs.gov

U.S. Merchant Marine Fleet of privately owned, U.S. registered merchant ships. Once one of the largest fleets in the world. tenford.com

Waterfront Commission Created in 1953, to combat criminal activity and influence in the port. 212-742-9280 waterfrontcommission.org

Seafarer Services

Seafaring is one of the world's most hazardous occupations. Seafarers work at sea for three to four months and are then off duty for an equally long period. Today, there are numerous organizations serving the needs of seafarers. More than 250 ships anchor in the Port of New York each year. The ministries protect seafarer interests and provide outreach programs that include ship visits, counseling and internet access to assist homesick seaman.

Manhattan

Adopt-a-Sailor Volunteer host families for visiting seamen during NYC Fleet Week. 718-273-9626 adopt-a-sailor.org

American Seamen's Friend Society Sailors' Home & Institute 505-507 West St. at Jane St. Designated a NYC Landmark in 2000, the transient hotel originally operated as a home for indigent sailors. Surviving crew of *Titanic* received care there.

Robert Richard Randall, Merchant Seaman (1740-1801). On the advice of his lawyer Alexander Hamilton, Randall's will bequeath property and $10,000 cash for the founding of Sailor's Snug Harbor "for the purpose of maintaining aged, decrepit, and worn-out sailors." It is one of the oldest charitable institutions in the country. Opened in 1833, eight dormatories housed as many as 1,000 men. Capt. Randall's remains were interred at the Staten Island site overlooking the Kill van Kull, and a bronze statue by Augustus St. Gaudens honors him. The sailors home relocated to North Carolina and in the 1970s Snug Harbor became a cultural center.

Apostleship of the Sea Sacred Heart Parish, 457 W 51st St. Port ministry of the Catholic Church. 212-265-5020 aoa-usa.org

Close Knit Club Noble Maritime Collection. Workshop to hand knit scarves for merchant seamen as part of the Christmas-at-Sea program. 718-447-6490 noblemaritime.org

Danish Seamen's Church
102 Willow St, Brooklyn. Founded in 1878, offers support to the sailors aboard Danish ships that anchor in NY Harbor each year. 718-875-0042

Norwegian Seamen's Church
317 E 52nd St. Serving Norwegian sailors and travelers in the harbor for 125 years. 212-319-0370 kjerka.com

Seafarer's House Prospect Park YMCA, Brooklyn. Safe Haven residence for retired seafarers, opened in the 1920s, and featured in the documentary "Sea Stories." Coordinates an Adopt-a-Ship program in partnership with local schools. 718-768-7100 seafarerswelfare.org

Seafarers & International House
123 E 15th St. Affordable guest house for seafarer's and travelers. 212-677-4800 cwdim.com/seafarer

Seamen's Church Institute
241 Water St. Founded 1844 as a floating chapel in the East River, services include a Center of Seafarers Rights, Maritime Training and Christmas-at-Sea program. 212-349-9090 seasmenschurch.org

Soldiers, Sailors, Marines, Airman's Club 283 Lexington Ave. 212-683-4353 ssmaclub.org

Stella Maris Seamen's Center
45 DeGraw St. Red Hook Terminal. Part of the global Apostleship of the Sea. 718-834-1234

Working Waterfront Events

Christmas at Sea	seamenschurch.org
More than 3500 knitters from all 50 States make over 17,000 hand-knitted gifts for mariners in the Christmas-at-Sea program, a tradition started during the Spanish American War of sending holiday care packages to seamen.	December
Fleet Week	fleetweek.navy.mil
Parade of Ships & free public tours of international fleet	May
National Maritime Day	
Begun in 1933, to commemorate the first trans-atlantic steam ship voyage, the day honors shipping & merchant mariners.	May 22
Soldiers, Sailors, Airmen & Marines Club Block Party	212-683-4660
283 Lexington Ave. Club opened in 1919	
Port Industry Day	harborops.com
Conference regarding the business of the port	October
Water Week	dec.state.ny.us
DEC event highlights water preservation & watershed protection	May

Maritime Timelines

1524   Italian explorer, Giovanni Da Verrazano discovers New York Harbor.

1525   Estéban Gomez, a black Portuguese navigator, charts the Lower Hudson River.

1609   Henry Hudson explores the Hudson River.

1611   Adrian Block establishes trading posts on the Battery.

1624   The first settlers arrive in New Amsterdam from Netherlands.

1626   Dutch Gov. Peter Minuet purportedly pays the Indians $24 for Manhattan.

1640   Ferry service begins between Manhattan & Fulton Street, Brooklyn.

1647   The first pier is constructed on the East River at Pearl and Broad Street.

1664   British take control of the city without firing a shot and rename it New York.

1676   "Great Dock" is built at Whitehall. It is the city's main anchorage until 1750.

1686   City government begins to landfill Lower Manhattan shoreline.

1693   The city's first bridge, Kings Bridge is built between Manhattan and The Bronx.

1695   Colonial Governor hires Capt. William Kidd to help stop piracy in the region.

1774   NY Harbor holds its own "Tea Party."

1776   The Battle of Long Island.

1784   *Empress of China* inaugurates America's trade with China.

1800   The federal government takes control of Governors Island.

1801   New York (Brooklyn) Navy Yard opens on Wallabout Bay.

1807   Fulton's steamship *Clermont* makes its historic voyage up the Hudson River.

1811   Cornelius Vanderbilt starts ferry service between Manhattan and Staten Island.

1817   Packet ship, *James Monroe* inaugurates the first scheduled sailings to Liverpool.

1822   Fulton Fish Market opens on the East River.

1824   The country's first dry dock is built on the East River at E 10th Street.

1825   The Erie Canal opens linking New York Harbor to the hinterlands in the west.

1830   New York becomes America's leading port.

1840   The tugboat, *John Fuller* becomes the first fireboat in NY Harbor.

1844   The New York Yacht Club is founded aboard a sailboat in NY Harbor.

1845   The first extreme Clipper, the *Rainbow,* is built at the Smith & Dimon Shipyard.

1846   Hudson River Railroad is built along the westside riverbanks.

1850   Salt marsh that stretches from the Brooklyn Bridge to Bay Ridge are drained.

1851   Hell Gate's obstructions are blasted improving passage to Long Island Sound.

1851   *America* wins England 100 Pound Guinea Cup, later renamed America's Cup.

1853   There are 55 piers on the Hudson River and 57 piers on the East River.

1855   Castle Clinton is joined to the Battery by landfill.

1862   The ironclad *USS Monitor* is launched at Greenpoint, Brooklyn.

1862   City Island's first commercial shipyard opens.

1864   Erie Basin opens in Red Hook, Brooklyn.

1869   Body of a 24 year-old woman is first one buried in Potter's Field, Hart Island.

1870   Floating pools offer free summer recreation in the waters around Manhattan.

1870   Port industry shifts from the East River to the Hudson River & Brooklyn piers.

1873   The first Floating Hospital, *Emma Abbott* is launched by the NY Times.

1880   Coney Island's Iron Pier is built for steamship traffic from Manhattan.

1882	South Street Seaport is the country's first neighborhood with electricity.
1883	Brooklyn Bridge opens.
1885	Pier A is constructed at the Battery.
1886	The Statue of Liberty is dedicated on Bedloe Island.
1888	Pelham Bay Park opens.
1890	City's first sewage treatment plant opens on Coney Island.
1892	Ellis Island welcomes its first immigrant, 15 yr old Annie Moore of Ireland.
1893	The world's fastest yacht, *Feiseen*, is built on City Island by Augustus B. Wood.
1894	Riverside Park extends to the edge of the Hudson River.
1895	The Harlem River Ship Channel opens.
1897	Harbo & Samuelson set record rowing across the Atlantic from The Battery.
1898	The five boroughs are consolidated into Greater New York City.
1903	Williamsburg Bridge opens. Founding of the Coney Island Polar Bear Club.
1907	Chelsea Piers opens to accommodate large ocean liners.
1909	Opening of the Queensboro & Manhattan bridges.
1912	NYC becomes the world's largest port, a position it holds for the next 50 years.
1914	Dredging of Ambrose Channel is completed.
1916	Oyster beds in city waters are closed due to an outbreak of typhoid fever
1917	Croton Aqueduct begins delivering water from the Catskills to the city.
1921	Port Authority of NY/NJ is established.
1927	Holland Tunnel opens for traffic. Cyclone rollercoaster opens on Coney Island.
1930	Statue of Liberty opens to the public.
1931	George Washington Bridge opens. Floyd Bennett Field becomes city's first airport.
1934	East River (FDR) Drive completed along the East River.
1936	Triborough Bridge opens.
1938	Belt Pkwy. and shore greenway constructed on the Brooklyn-Queens waterfront.
1940	New York Yacht Club admits women to membership.
1951	The United Nations headquarters are built on the East River.
1954	Ellis Island Immigration Depot closes. Jamaica Bay designated a wildlife refuge.
1956	World's first container ship sails from Port of New York (Newark) to Houston.
1957	New York Aquarium opens on Coney Island.
1964	Verrazano-Narrows Bridge opens. Steeplechase Park closes.
1966	Brooklyn Navy Yard closes.
1970	Shipping moves from Manhattan to Elizabeth, New Jersey.
1972	The Clean Water Act. GNRA is created. South Street Seaport restoration begins.
1973	World Trade Center Twin Towers are completed.
1979	Empire-Fulton Ferry State Park opens.
1983	Battery Park City esplanade opens on landfill from WTC excavation.
1991	Hudson River Park construction begins.
1993	Riverbank State Park opens.
1995	USCG leaves Governors Island. Chelsea Pier Sports Complex opens.
1999	Gowanus Canal flushing tunnel is repaired.
2001	Twin Towers of the World Trade Center are destroyed by terrorists.
2003	Governors Island is sold to the State of New York for $1.

Glossary

Andromous Marine fishes that leave the ocean and ascend streams to spawn (salmon or shad).

Benthos Wildlife and plants that live on or in the bottom of the sea.

Bight A natural curve in the coastline.

Brownfield EPA classified sites that may be contaminated from former industrial use.

Buffer the Bay Program The acquisition of land surrounding Jamaica Bay that provides a buffer zone between the estuary and upland development.

Catadromous Freshwater fishes that travel to the sea to spawn (eels).

Estuary A partially enclosed coastal body of water, where water from the open sea meets and mixes with freshwater.

Forever Wild Area A special designation that adds protection to city, state or federal parkland from development of any kind.

Freshwater Water that contains less than 1000mg/l of dissolved solids.

Habitat An area where plants and animals live and grow under natural conditions.

Moraine An accumulation of rocky materials transported by glacial ice.

Nonpoint Pollution Source of water pollution that originates from a broad area, such as stormwater runoff.

Point Source Pollution Pollution that originates from a single source or outlet discharging into a natural body of water.

Riparian Zone Located on the bank of a natural waterbody.

Runoff Water that flows over the land surface into a body of water.

Salinity The total quantity of dissolved salt in water.

Salt Marsh A grassy habitat that is covered part of the time by tidal waters.

Sludge Semi-solid materials that settle out of wastewater in sewage treatment.

Superfund Site Federally classified sites that require environmental remedial action.

Tidal Flat Marshy, sandy or muddy areas that are exposed at low tide.

Tributary A creek or river that flows into a larger stream or river.

Watershed All the land and water area that drains into the same body of water.

Wetlands Land areas that are saturated at the rise of the tide, between the terrestrial and aquatic ecosystems.

Going Coastal Reading

Go Coastal

Natural History of New York City John Kiernan, Fordham University Press 1982

At Sea in the City William Kornblum, Algonquin Books 2002

Battery Park City: Politics and Planning on the New York City Waterfront David L.A. Gordon, Rutledge 1997

Beyond the Edge: New York's New Waterfront Raymond W. Gastil, Princeton Architectural Press 2002

Bronx Accent: A Literary & Pictorial History of the Borough Lloyd Ultan & Barbara Unger, Rutgers Press 2000

Bronx Ecology Allen Hershkowitz & Maya Ying Lin, Island Press 2002

Brooklyn's Gold Coast: The Sheepshead Bay Communities Brian Merlis & I. Stephen Miller, Sheepshead Bay Historical Society 1997

Brooklyn Then and Now Marcia Reiss, Advanced Global Distribution 2002

Brooklyn's Waterfront Railways Jay Bendersky, Weekend Chief Publishing 1988

Coney Island Lost and Found Charles Denson, Ten Speed Press 2002

Coney Island Walking Tour Charles Denson, Dreamland Press 1998

Crossing Highbridge: A Memoir of Irish America Maureen Waters, Syracuse Univ. Press 2001

Delirious New York Rem Koolhaas, The Monacelli Press 1994

Discovering Queens Stephen Reichstein, The Stephen Press 2000

Heartbeats in the Muck: The History, Sea Life, and Environment of New York Harbor John Waldman, Lyons Press 1999

Manhattan Seascape: Waterside Views Around New York, Robert Gumbee Hastings House 1975

Manhattan Water-Bound: Planning and Developing Manhattan's Waterfront from the 17th Century to the Present Ann I. Buttenwieser, New York Univ. Press 1999

Maritime Mile: The Story of the Greenwich Village Waterfront Stuart Waldman & Zack Winestine, Mikaya Press 2002

Memories of Clason Point Kelly Sonnenfeld, Dutton Books 1998

Old Rockaway Vincent Seyfried & William Asadorian, Dover 2000

Ship Ablaze: The Tragedy of the Steamboat General Slocum Edward T. O'Donnell, Boadway Books 2003

Secret Places of Staten Island Bruce Kershner, Kendall/Hunt Publishing Co. 1998

Staten Island Margaret Lundrigan & Tova Novarra, Arcadia Tempus Publishing 1999

Staten Island: Gateway to New York Dorothy Smith, Chilton Book Co 1970

The Other Islands of New York City Sharon Seitz & Stuart Miller, Countryman Pr 2002

Throgs Neck, Pelham Bay Bill Twomey, Arcadia Pub. 1998

Walking Around in South Street Ellen Fletcher, South Street Seaport & Leet's Island Books 199

Waterfront: A Journey Around Manhattan Philip Lopate, Crown 2004

Get Wet

All This and Sailing, Too: An Autobiography Olin J. Stephens, Mystic Seaport Museum Pub. 2000

Around Manhattan Island and Other Maritime Tales of New York Brian J. Cudahy, Fordham U. Press 1997

Beachcombing the Atlantic Coast Peggy Kochanoff, Mountain Press 1997

Between Ocean and City Lawrence & Carol Kaplan, Columbia Univ. Press 2003

Bridges of New York City Cara Sutherland, Friedman/Fairfax Publishing 2003

Daring the Sea: The True Story of the First Men to Row Across the Atlantic Ocean David W. Shaw, Birch Lane 1998

Diving into History: A Manual of Underwater Archeology for Divers in New York State Paul Scudiere, New York State Museum 1969

Good Fishing Close to New York City Jim Capossela, Northeast Sportsmen's Press 1985

How We Got to Coney Island: The Development of Mass Transportation in Brooklyn and Queens Brian J. Cudahy, Fordham Univ. Press 2000

Hudson River Water Trail Guide Ian H. Giddy & Hudson River Watertrail Assn. 2003

Identifying and Harvesting Edible and Medicinal Plants in Wild (and Not-So-Wild) Places "Wildman" Steve Brill, William Morrow 1994

International Register of Historic Ships Norman J. Brouwer, A. Nelson 1993

Lighthouses of New York Jim Crowley, Hope Farm Press 2001

Lines: A Half-Century of Yacht Designs by Sparkman & Stephens, 1930-1980 Olin J. Stephens, J. Carter Brown & A. Knight Coolidge, David R. Godine 2003

New York City Audubon Society Guide to Finding Birds in the Metropolitan Area Marcia Fowle & David Kerlinger, Cornell Univ. Press 2001

New York's 50 Best Places to Go Birding in and Around the Big Apple John Thaxton & Allan Messer, City & Company 1998

New York's Forts in the Revolution Robert B. Roberts, Associated Univ. Press 1980

Over and Back: The History of Ferryboats in New York Harbor Brian J. Cudahy, Fordham University Press 1990

Picture History of the Cunard Line 1840-1990 Frank Osborn Braynard & William H. Miller, Dover 1991

Six Bridges: The Legacy of Othmar H. Amman Darl Rastofer, Yale University Press 2000

Shipwrecks of New York Gary Gentile, Gary Gentile Productions 1996

Staten Island Ferry Theodore W. Scull, Quadrant Press 1982

The Bridges of New York Sharon Reier, Dover 2000

The Bridge: The Building of the Verrazano-Narrows Bridge Gay Talese, Walker & Co. 2002

The Cruise Ship Phenomenon in North America Brian Cudahy, Cornell Maritime Press 2001

The Great Bridge David G. McCullough, Simon & Schuster 1982

The Wild Vegetarian Cookbook "Wildman" Steve Brill, Harvard Common Press 2002

Unearthing Gotham: The Archaeology of New York City Anne-Marie Cantwell & Diana diZerega Wall, Yale Univ. Press 2001

Walking Manhattan's Rim: The Great Saunter Cy Adler, Green Eagle Press 2003

Wreck Valley: A Record of Shipwrecks off Long Island's South Shore and New Jersey Daniel Berg, Aqua Explorers 1990

Dive In

Maritime History of New York WPA Writers' Project, Doubleday 1941

A Teacher's Guide to Water Education Resources in the NY-NJ Harbor Estuary 2004 (Free from harborestuary.org)

Maritime New York in Nineteenth-Century Photographs Harry Johnson & Frederick S. Lightfoot, Dover 1980

Naval Shipbuilders of the World: From the Age of Sail to the Present Day, Robert J. Winklareth Naval Institute Press 2000

The Forests and Wetlands of New York City Elizabeth Barlow, Little Brown & Co 1971

The New York Harbor Book Francis J. Duffy, TBW Books 1986

The New York Waterfront Evolution and Building Culture of the Port and Harbor Kevin Bone, The Monacelli Press 1997

Waterfront Blueprint Waterfront Park Coalition (nylcv.org)

Wild New York: A Guide to the Wildlife, Wild Places, & Natural Phenomena of New York City Margaret Mittelbach, Crown Publishers 1997

Children

A Picnic in October Eve Bunting & Nancy Carpenter, Harcourt 1999

America's Champion Swimmer: Gertrude Ederle David A. Adler's, Gulliver Books 2000

Dreaming of America Ellis Island Story Eve Bunting & Ed Stahl, Troll Assoc. 2000

Fireboat: The Heroic Adventures of the John J. Harvey Maira Kalman, G.P. Putnam & Sons 2002

Gowanus Dogs Vernon H. Jensen, Cornell Univ. Press 1974

Riding the Ferry With Captain Cruz Alice K. Flanagan, Children's Press 1997

The Little Red Lighthouse and The Great Gray Bridge Hildegarde H. Swift & Lynd Ward, Harcourt Inc. 1970

Printed in the United States
31665LVS00001B/54